Experiencing
Choral Music

TEACHER WRAPAROUND EDITION
PROFICIENT

MIXED

Developed by

HAL•LEONARD®
CORPORATION

Mc Graw Hill **Glencoe**

New York, New York   Columbus, Ohio   Chicago, Illinois   Peoria, Illinois   Woodland Hills, California

The portions of the National Standards for Music Education included here are reprinted from *National Standards for Arts Education* with permission from MENC—The National Association for Music Education. All rights reserved. Copyright © 1994 by MENC. The complete National Standards and additional materials relating to the Standards are available from MENC, 1806 Robert Fulton Drive, Reston, VA 20191 (telephone 800-336-3768).

A portion of the sales of this material goes to support music education programs through programs of MENC—The National Association for Music Education.

 **Glencoe**

The **McGraw·Hill** Companies

Printed in the United States of America.

Send all inquiries to:
Glencoe/McGraw-Hill
21600 Oxnard Street, Suite 500
Woodland Hills, CA 91367

ISBN 0-07-861119-9 (Student Edition)
ISBN 0-07-861120-2 (Teacher Wraparound Edition)

4 5 6 7 8 9 045 09 08 07

Table of Contents

SECTION		National Standards								
Selection	Concepts and Skills	1	2	3	4	5	6	7	8	9
LESSONS										
Adoramus Te	Appropriate performance techniques; describe music representing the Renaissance period; Picardy third.	a, b, c					b	b, c	a	a, e
Spotlight On Posture & Breath Management	Proper singing posture.	b								
The Little Beggarman	Compare Mixolydian/major scales read rhythmic patterns in simple meter; Irish folk music.	a, b, c, f		b		a	a, b, c	a, b	a, c	a, d
Spotlight On The Physiology Of The Voice	Relationship between science and music; describe how the knowledge of vocal physiology is important to musical vocal performance.	b							a, b	
The Earth Adorned	Breath support; identify melody and harmony; define *homophony*.	a, b		a		a, b	a, b	b		
Spotlight On Diction	Proper diction.	b							b	
God's Gonna Set This World On Fire	Perform African American spirituals; tonic, dominant and subdominant chords.	a, b, c				a	a, c	b		b
Spotlight On Gospel Music	Classify aurally presented music.	a, b, c						a, b		
Cantate Domino	Describe *homophony* and *polyphony*; melismas; classify music of the late Renaissance period.	a, b, c, f					b	a, b		a
Erev Shel Shoshanim	Staggered breathing; visual art and music; music of the Israeli culture.	a, b, c						b	c	a
Spotlight On Vowels	Proper use of vowels.	b								
Sicut Locutus Est	Fugue; describe music of the Baroque period.	a, b, c, d, e					a, c			a, d
Spotlight On The Physiology Of Singing	Sing individually; relationship between other subjects and music.	b							b	
Ya Viene La Vieja	Perform music representing Spanish culture; compound meter.	a, c			a		e			a, d
Esto Les Digo	Suspensions and dissonance; Sing phrases expressively; music-related vocations.	a, c					b, c	a, b		c
Spotlight On Careers In Music	Describe music-related career opportunities; relationship of other subjects and those of music.								b	c
Sanctus	Sing in Latin; perform music of the Classical period.	a, b, c				a, b, c		b		a
Spotlight On Vocal Health	Healthy vocal production.	b								
Der Tanz	Perform music of the Romantic period; 6/8 meter; relate music to poetry.	a, c				a		a	a, c	
Laudate	Read and perform in mixed meter; ABA form; describe and perform music from the Contemporary period.	a, b, c, f				a	b	b	a, b, c	
Spotlight On Concert Etiquette	Exhibit informed concert etiquette in a variety of settings.							a, b		

SECTION		National Standards								
Selection	Concepts and Skills	1	2	3	4	5	6	7	8	9
MUSIC & HISTORY										
Renaissance, Baroque, Classical, Romantic and Contemporary periods	Describe, listen to and analyze music from the five main historical periods.						a, b, c, d, e, f		a, b, c, d, e	a, c, d, e
Spotlight On Musical Theater	Relate music to history; identify the relationships between the other fine arts and music; describe music-related career options including performance; evaluate a musical performance.							b	b	c
CHORAL LIBRARY										
Fiddler Man	Analyze form; rhythmic patterns in simple meter; change timbre of voice to imitate sounds of musical instruments.	a, b, c			a	a	b, c	a, b		c
Spotlight On Arranging	Create and arrange music within specified guidelines.				b					
Finale from The Gondoliers	Articulation; perform music representing the Victorian operetta.	a, b, c				a	b	a, b	a, b, c	a
Spotlight On Vocal Jazz	Repertoire representing diverse styles; classify music by style.	a, b, c								
Holy, Holy, Holy	Syncopation; gospel style.	a, b, c, d				a, b	b, c	a		a
In Flanders Fields	Musical phrasing; suspension; relate music to poetry.	a, b, c, d				a, b	b, c	a	c	a
Jabula Jesu	Perform ostinato and polyrhythmic patterns; creative movement; perform music of the Zulu culture.	a, b, c, d			b	a, b	b, c		b	a
New York State Of Mind	Music in close harmony; scat singing; music representing vocal jazz style.	a, b				b	b	a	a	
O My Luve's Like A Red, Red Rose	Expressive phrasing; dissonance and consonance; relate music to history and culture.	a, b	b		a	a	b	a	a, b	
Plaisir d'amour	Sing in a legato style; modulations; perform music representing the Classical period.	a, c				b	b	a		
Salmo 150	Compound meter; minor tonality; perform music representing the Brazilian culture.	a, c			a	a		a	b	
Seasons Of Love	Read and perform melismatic passages; improvisation.	a, c	c	c	a	b	a	a		
Spotlight On Improvisation	Create rhythmic phrases; improvise musical melodies.	a, b, c		a, b, c						
The Star-Spangled Banner	Accidentals; dotted rhythms; American patriotic music.	a, b				b	b	a		a
Tunggare	Sing intervals in tune; in mixed meter; sing with artistic expression.	a, c			a	a, b	b	a		a
Spotlight On Melismas	Perform melismas accurately.	b								

National Standards High School Grades 9–12

The National Standards for Music Education were developed by the Music Educators National Conference. Reprinted by permission.

MUSIC

The study of music contributes in important ways to the quality of every student's life. Every musical work is a product of its time and place, although some works transcend their original settings and continue to appeal to humans through their timeless and universal attraction. Through singing, playing instruments and composing, students can express themselves creatively, while a knowledge of notation and performance traditions enables them to learn new music independently throughout their lives. Skills in analysis, evaluation and synthesis are important because they enable students to recognize and pursue excellence in the musical experiences and to understand and enrich their environment. Because music is an integral part of human history, the ability to listen with understanding is essential if students are to gain a broad cultural and historical perspective. The adult life of every student is enriched by the skills, knowledge and habits acquired in the study of music.

Every course in music, including performance courses, should provide instruction in creating, performing, listening to and analyzing music, in addition to focusing on its specific subject matter.

1. **Content Standard:** Singing, alone and with others, a varied repertoire of music
   Achievement Standard, Proficient:
   Students
   a. sing with *expression and *technical accuracy a large and varied repertoire of vocal literature with a *level of difficulty of 4, on a scale of 1 to 6, including some songs performed from memory.
   b. sing music written in four parts, with and without accompaniment.
   c. demonstrate well-developed ensemble skills.

   Achievement Standard, Advanced:
   Students
   d. sing with expression and technical accuracy a large and varied repertoire of vocal literature with a level of difficulty of 5, on a scale of 1 to 6.
   e. sing music written in more than four parts.
   f. sing in small ensembles with one student on a part.

2. **Content Standard:** Performing on instruments, alone and with others, a varied repertoire of music
   Achievement Standard, Proficient:
   Students
   a. perform with expression and technical accuracy a large and varied repertoire of instrumental literature with a level of difficulty of 4, on a scale of 1 to 6.
   b. perform an appropriate part in an ensemble, demonstrating well-developed ensemble skills.
   c. perform in small ensembles with one student on a part.

Achievement Standard, Advanced:
Students
   d. perform with expression and technical accuracy a large and varied repertoire of instrumental literature with a level of difficulty of 5, on a scale of 1 to 6.

3. **Content Standard:** Improvising melodies, variations and accompaniments
   Achievement Standard, Proficient:
   Students
   a. improvise stylistically appropriate harmonizing parts.
   b. improvise rhythmic and melodic variations on given pentatonic melodies and melodies in major and minor keys.
   c. improvise original melodies over given chord progressions, each in a consistent *style, *meter and *tonality.
   Achievement Standard, Advanced:
   Students
   d. improvise stylistically appropriate harmonizing parts in a variety of styles.
   e. improvise original melodies in a variety of styles, over given chord progressions, each in a consistent style, meter and tonality.

4. **Content Standard:** Composing and arranging music within specified guidelines
   Achievement Standard, Proficient:
   Students
   a. compose music in several distinct styles, demonstrating creativity in using the *elements of music for expressive effect.
   b. arrange pieces for voices or instruments other than those for which the pieces were written in ways that preserve or enhance the expressive effect of the music.
   c. compose and arrange music for voices and various acoustic and electronic instruments, demonstrating knowledge of the ranges and traditional usages of the sound sources.
   Achievement Standard, Advanced:
   Students
   d. compose music, demonstrating imagination and technical skill in applying the principles of composition.

5. **Content Standard:** Reading and notating music
   Achievement Standard, Proficient:
   Students
   a. demonstrate the ability to read an instrumental or vocal score of up to four *staves by describing how the elements of music are used.
   Students who participate in a choral or instrumental ensemble or class
   b. sight-read, accurately and expressively, music with a level of difficulty of 3, on a scale of 1 to 6.

Achievement Standard, Advanced:
Students

   c. demonstrate the ability to read a full instrumental or vocal score by describing how the elements of music are used and explaining all transpositions and clefs.

   d. interpret nonstandard notation symbols used by some 20th-century [sic] composers.

Students who participate in a choral or instrumental ensemble or class

   e. sight-read, accurately and expressively, music with a level of difficulty of 4, on a scale of 1 to 6.

6. **Content Standard:** Listening to, analyzing and describing music

   Achievement Standard, Proficient:
Students

   a. analyze aural examples of a varied repertoire of music, representing diverse *genres and cultures, by describing the uses of elements of music and expressive devices.

   b. demonstrate extensive knowledge of the technical vocabulary of music.

   c. identify and explain compositional devices and techniques used to provide unity and variety and tension and release in a musical work and give examples of other works that make similar uses of these devices and techniques.

   Achievement Standard, Advanced:
Students

   d. demonstrate the ability to perceive and remember music events by describing in detail significant events[1] occurring in a given aural example.

   e. compare ways in which musical materials are used in a given example relative to ways in which they are used in other works of the same genre or style.

   f. analyze and describe uses of the elements of music in a given work that make it unique, interesting and expressive.

7. **Content Standard:** Evaluating music and music performances

   Achievement Standard, Proficient:
Students

   a. evolve specific criteria for making informed, critical evaluations of the quality and effectiveness of performances, compositions, arrangements and improvisations and apply the criteria in their personal participation in music.

   b. evaluate a performance, composition, arrangement or improvisation by comparing it to similar or exemplary models.

   Achievement Standard, Advanced:
Students

   c. evaluate a given musical work in terms of its aesthetic qualities and explain the musical means it uses to evoke feelings and emotions.

8. **Content Standard:** Understanding relationships between music, the other arts, and disciplines outside the arts

   Achievement Standard, Proficient:
Students

   a. explain how elements, artistic processes (such as imagination or craftsmanship), and organizational principles (such as unity and variety or repetition and contrast) are used in similar and distinctive ways in the various arts and cite examples.

   b. compare characteristics of two or more arts within a particular historical period or style and cite examples from various cultures.

   c. explain ways in which the principles and subject matter of various disciplines outside the arts are interrelated with those of music.[2]

   Achievement Standard, Advanced:
Students

   d. compare the uses of characteristic elements, artistic processes and organizational principles among the arts in different historical periods and different cultures.

   e. explain how the roles of creators, performers, and others involved in the production and presentation of the arts are similar to and different from one another in the various arts.[3]

9. **Content Standard:** Understanding music in relation to history and culture

   Achievement Standard, Proficient:
Students

   a. classify by genre or style and by historical period or culture unfamiliar but representative aural examples of music and explain the reasoning behind their classifications.

   b. identify sources of American music genres[4], trace the evolution of those genres, and cite well-known musicians associated with them.

   c. identify various roles[5] that musicians perform, cite representative individuals who have functioned in each role, and describe their activities and achievements.

   Achievement Standard, Advanced:
Students

   d. identify and explain the stylistic features of a given musical work that serve to define its aesthetic tradition and its historical or cultural context.

   e. identify and describe music genres or styles that show the influence of two or more cultural traditions, identify the cultural source of each influence, and trace the historical conditions that produced the synthesis of influences.

Terms identified by an asterisk (*) are explained further in the glossary of National Standards for Arts Education, published by Music Educators National Conference, © 1994.

1. E.g., fugal entrances, chromatic modulations, developmental devices
2. E.g., language arts: compare the ability of music and literature to convey images, feeling and meanings; physics: describe the physical basis of tone production in string, wind, percussion and electronic instruments and the human voice and of the transmission and perception of sound
3. E.g., creators: painters, composers, choreographers, playwrights; performers: instrumentalists, singers, dancers, actors; others: conductors, costumers, directors, lighting designers
4. E.g., swing, Broadway musical, blues
5. E.g., entertainer, teacher, transmitter of cultural tradition

INTRODUCTION

Experiencing Choral Music is a four-level series designed to build music literacy and promote vocal development for all students and voice categories in grades 6–12. The series is a multitextbook program supported with print materials and audio listening components that enable students to develop music skills and conceptual understanding, and provides teachers with a flexible, integrated program.

Experiencing Choral Music presents beginning, intermediate, proficient and advanced literature for various voice groupings: unison, 2-part/3-part, mixed, treble, and tenor/bass. All selections in *Experiencing Choral Music* are recorded three ways: full performance with voices, accompaniment only, and individual part-dominant recordings. The program also includes companion *Sight-Singing* textbooks that present a sequential approach to musical literacy and is directly correlated to the literature books. This comprehensive choral music program includes student texts, teacher wraparound editions, teacher resource binders, and rehearsal and performance audio recordings designed to enhance student learning while reducing teacher preparation time.

Experiencing Choral Music is a curriculum that provides your students with a meaningful, motivating choral music experience, and will help you and your students build choral music knowledge and skills. For example:

Experiencing Choral Music connects to . . .
the National Standards

The National Standards are correlated to each lesson for quick-and-easy identification and reference. The performance standards related to singing and reading notations are explicit in each lesson, and by using the extension activities, teachers can connect the musical elements through improvisation and composition. Analysis and evaluation are active and consistent components of lessons throughout the series. Additional student activities connect the lessons to the other arts, as well as provide a consistent historical and cultural context.

Experiencing Choral Music connects to . . .
Skill Development

Through the Links to Learning exercises, students build vocal, theory and artistic expression skills necessary to perform each piece. Rhythmic, melodic and articulation skills are developed as needed for expressive interpretation. Students are encouraged to develop listening skills and use their perceptions to improve individual and group performance.

Experiencing Choral Music connects to . . .
Creative Expression/Performance

Student performance provides opportunities for young musicians to demonstrate musical growth, to gain personal satisfaction from achievement, and to experience the joy of music making. To help develop skills, *Experiencing Choral Music* provides vocal, theory and artistic expression exercises, which help prepare students to successfully sing each piece. Conceptual understanding is built throughout the teaching/learning sequence, as the performance is prepared.

Experiencing Choral Music connects to . . .
Historical and Cultural Heritage

Experiencing Choral Music provides a vehicle to help students gain knowledge and understanding of historical and cultural contexts across the curriculum. These concepts are presented in the Getting Started section of each lesson. Also, historical connections through art, history, time lines, performance practices and listening examples are made in Music & History.

Experiencing Choral Music connects to . . .
the Arts and Other Curriculum Areas

Choral music provides a rich opportunity to connect the musical experience to other art disciplines (dance, visual arts, theater), and to enhance the learning in other subject areas.

PROGRAM PHILOSOPHY

Responding to New Trends in Choral Music Education

Experiencing Choral Music is consistent with current educational philosophy that suggests:

- Performance is a product that should be the end result of a sound educational process, building conceptual understanding and skills as the performance is prepared.
- Students are motivated through materials and concepts that are connected to their own lives and interests, and should be exposed to high-quality, challenging musical literature.
- Students learn best when they are active participants in their learning, and when they clearly understand and help set the goals and objectives of the learning outcome.
- Students understand concepts better when they have background information and skills that allow them to place their learning into a larger context.
- Students need to actively manipulate musical concepts and skills through improvisation and/or composition in order to fully assimilate and understand them.

- Students improve when they receive fair, honest and meaningful feedback on their success and failures.
- Students should be encouraged to assess themselves individually and as a group, learning to receive and process constructive criticism, leading to independent self-correction and decision making.

Scope and Depth of Music Literature

Most students are capable of performing more difficult material than they can sight-read. Therefore, the literature in *Experiencing Choral Music* is drawn from many periods and styles of music. The wide range of composers and publishers ensures variety, and allows for various skills and concepts to be developed as each new piece is encountered. The high standards set in *Experiencing Choral Music* provide selections that are inherently powerful and exciting for students. The *Sight-Singing* textbooks provide additional literature for sight-singing purposes. Written in a sequential manner, this component will present students with a developmental process for learning to read music.

Addressing the National Standards

The National Standards for Arts Education, published in 1994, launched a national effort to bring a new vision to arts education for all students. The National Standards provide a framework for achievement in music, with outcomes suggested for grades 4, 8, and 12. *Experiencing Choral Music* addresses the National Standards in several ways.

The most obvious and predominant National Standards addressed in choral ensemble are: (1) singing and (5) reading and notation. However, good performance requires musical understanding that only occurs when all aspects of musical experience are incorporated. The preparation of vocal performance is enriched and deepened by involvement in all nine of the National Standards.

As you teach with *Experiencing Choral Music*, there will be frequent opportunities to deepen or extend student learning through: (2) playing through creating accompaniments, (3) improvisation, (4) composition and arranging, (6) analyzing, (7) assessing, (8) linking with other arts and other academic disciplines, and (9) understanding historical and cultural contexts. The National Standards identified for each lesson and the Extension activities provided in the Teacher Wraparound Edition help you become aware of the National Standards, and the depth of learning that will occur as you implement this choral music program.

Promoting Music Literacy

Experiencing Choral Music promotes music literacy throughout the lessons. Literacy includes oral and aural aspects of music communication—reading, writing, singing and listening. Each lesson begins with Getting Started that (1)

connects the song to the student, and (2) frames the historical and cultural aspect of the music to be performed. From there the students are directed to the Links to Learning that is divided into three categories: Vocal, Theory and Artistic Expression. These exercises emphasize reading development and artistic expression. These may be rhythmic, melodic, harmonic or a combination thereof; and are directly related to the objectives of the lesson. The exercises lead directly into the musical selection. Students are encouraged to sight-sing in every lesson. Sight-singing is approached as a challenge and a means to musical independence for the student.

Literacy goes beyond simply reading pitch and rhythm, extending to the expressive elements of music and appropriate interpretation. Through Artistic Expression, students will be asked to explore interpretive aspects of music making, and are encouraged to suggest their own ideas for phrasing, dynamics, and so on. Through careful listening and constructive critique of their own work, they will gradually become more discriminating about the quality of performance and the impact of that performance on the audience.

Including Authentic Student Assessment

The assessment in *Experiencing Choral Music* is systematic, objective and authentic. There is ongoing informal assessment by teacher observation throughout the lessons. The text is written as a series of action steps for the student, so there are many opportunities for the director to hear and see the level of accomplishment.

Students will find objectives at the beginning of each lesson, and evaluation activities at the end. The Evaluation questions and activities are always related directly to the lesson objectives, and allow students to demonstrate their understanding. By answering the questions, and demonstrating as suggested, students are involved in *self-assessment*. Many times students are involved in their own assessment, constructing rubrics or critiquing their performance to determine what level of success has been achieved, and identifying the next challenge.

The *Teacher Wraparound Edition* includes lesson objectives, and each lesson is taught so the concepts and skills are experienced, labeled, practiced and reinforced, then measured through *formal assessment*. These assessment tasks match the lesson objectives, allowing students to demonstrate understanding of concepts and skills through performance, composition, or writing. Students are frequently required to produce audio- or videotapes. This authentic assessment keeps testing of rote learning to a minimum, and allows measurement of higher-level application of knowledge and skills. A portfolio can be constructed for individual students, groups, or the whole ensemble, demonstrating growth over time.

Connecting the Arts and Other Curriculum Areas

Lessons in *Experiencing Choral Music* integrate many appropriate aspects of musical endeavor into the preparation of a piece. Students compose, improvise, conduct, read, write, sing, play, listen/analyze and assess on an ongoing basis that builds understanding, as well as high standards. In this way, the many aspects of music are integrated for deeper learning.

As one of the arts, music can be linked to other arts through similarities and differences. Throughout the text, and particularly in the historical section, music is compared and contrasted with other arts to determine aspects of confluence and the unique features of each art.

As one way of knowing about the world, music can be compared with concepts and skills from other disciplines as seemingly different as science or mathematics. The integrations between music and other disciplines are kept at the conceptual level, to maintain the integrity of both music and the other subjects. For example, mathematical sets of 2, 3, 4, 5 and 6 might be explored as a link to pieces with changing meter; or the text of a piece might become a starting point for exploration of tone painting. In Music & History, a time line connects music to social studies, and a list of authors for each period provides a link to language and literature.

Providing a Variety of Student Activities

Experiencing Choral Music begins with the choral experience, and builds understanding through active participation in a range of activities including singing, playing, improvising, composing, arranging, moving, writing, listening, analyzing, assessing and connecting to cultures, periods or disciplines. Lessons are written with the heading "Direct students to . . ." so there is always an emphasis on learning by doing. In this way the teacher becomes a guide and places the responsibility for learning on the student. When students are engaged in meaningful and challenging activity, they are more likely to learn.

Fitting Your Classroom Needs

With *Experiencing Choral Music*, your students will be clear about purpose and direction, have multiple routes to success, and be involved in their own learning. The lessons will guide you and your students to share in the excitement of music making, and help you to grow together. The lessons are written the way you teach, and allow you to maintain and strengthen your routines, while adding flexibility, variety and depth.

ORGANIZATION AND FLEXIBILITY

Each *Experiencing Choral Music* text is divided into the following sections:

- Lessons
- Music & History
- Choral Library

Lessons

The Lessons are designed to be taught over a period of time. They are divided into three categories: Beginning of the Year, Mid-Winter, and Concert/Festival. Each lesson is developed around a piece of authentic and quality music literature. The lesson includes background information, vocal examples, sight-reading and rhythmic or melodic drills, all of which are directly related to preparation of the piece. Objectives are clearly stated, and a motivational opening activity or discussion is provided. The Teacher Wraparound Edition outlines a carefully sequenced approach to the piece and clear assessment opportunities to document achievement and growth.

Music & History

Music & History provides narrative and listening experiences for each of the five main historical periods. A *narrative lesson* provides a brief and interesting exposition of the main characteristics of the period outlining the achievements and new styles that emerged. A time line guides the student to place the musical characteristics into a larger historical and cultural context. The listening lesson includes both vocal and instrumental *listening selections* from the period, with a guide to student listening. A listing of the historical pieces to be sung from the period are cross-referenced from the Music & History divider page. Combined, these components give historical context of the period across the arts, then apply the context to musical literature.

Choral Library

The Choral Library provides the same comprehensive student lesson featured in the Lessons. The additional literature features multicultural selections, patriotic and seasonal selections, American folk music, African American spirituals, Broadway show tunes, and light concert pieces that can be used to enhance the repertoire of your choral music performance.

Overview of Lesson Objectives

Each lesson has objectives that emphasize and build conceptual understanding and skills across the lessons. The objectives in this book are:

LESSON OBJECTIVES	
Title	**Objective**
Adoramus Te	• Exhibit appropriate small-ensemble performance techniques. • Describe, classify and perform music representing the Renaissance period. • Define concepts of chord structure using standard terminology (Picardy third).
The Little Beggarman	• Compare the elements of a Mixolydian scale and a major scale. • Read and perform rhythmic patterns in simple meter. • Perform music representing Irish folk music.
The Earth Adorned	• Demonstrate good breath support while singing phrases. • Identify melodic and harmonic parts when performing music. • Define homophony using standard terminology.
God's Gonna Set This World On Fire	• Perform music representing the African American spiritual. • Identify and perform tonic, dominant and subdominant chords.
Cantate Domino	• Describe and perform homophony and polyphony. • Identify and sing a melisma. • Classify and perform music representing the late Renaissance period.
Erev Shel Shoshanim	• Demonstrate ensemble performance techniques (staggered breathing). • Define the relationship between the process of imagery as used in visual art and music. • Sing music representing the Israeli culture.
Sicut Locutus Est	• Identify, describe and perform a fugue. • Listen to and describe music of the Baroque period. • Perform music representing the Baroque period.
Ya Viene La Vieja	• Perform music representing Spanish culture. • Read and write rhythmic patterns in compound meter.
Esto Les Digo	• Read and perform music that contains suspensions and dissonance. • Demonstrate how to sing phrases expressively. • Discover music-related vocations in music.
Sanctus	• Sing a Latin text with correct syllabic stress. • Perform music representing the Classical period.
Der Tanz	• Perform music representing the Romantic period. • Read and perform music in 6/8 meter. • Relate music to poetry.
Laudate	• Read and perform music written in mixed meter. • Identify, analyze and perform music in ABA form. • Describe and perform music from the Contemporary period.

LESSON OBJECTIVES

Title	Objective
Fiddler Man	• Analyze the form of a composition. • Read and perform rhythmic patterns in simple meter. • Define timbre. Use the voice to imitate the sounds of musical instruments.
Finale from The Gondoliers	• Sing music using clean and crisp articulation. • Perform music representing the Victorian operetta.
Holy, Holy, Holy	• Perform rhythmic patterns that contain syncopation. • Describe and perform music representing gospel style.
In Flanders Fields	• Demonstrate musical artistry through musical phrasing. • Use standard terminology to describe a suspension. • Relate music to poetry.
Jabula Jesu	• Perform ostinato and polyrhythm patterns accurately. • Respond to music by creating movement. • Perform music representing the Zulu culture.
New York State Of Mind	• Perform music that contains close harmony. • Use musical terminology to describe scat singing and upbeat. • Perform music representing vocal jazz style.
O My Luve's Like A Red, Red Rose	• Demonstrate musical artistry through expressive phrasing. • Use standard terminology to describe dissonance and consonance. • Relate music to history and culture.
Plaisir d'amour	• Sing in a legato style with accurate intonation and rhythm. • Identify and perform music that contains modulations. • Perform music representing the Classical period.
Salmo 150	• Read and perform rhythmic patterns in compound meter. • Write and perform music in minor tonality. • Perform music representing the Brazilian culture.
Seasons Of Love	• Read and perform melismatic passages. • Sing an improvised melodic line.
The Star-Spangled Banner	• Describe and sing an accidental accurately. • Read and perform rhythmic patterns that contain dotted rhythms. • Relate the music to history, to society and to culture.
Tunggare	• Sing intervals with good intonation. • Identify and perform an ostinato pattern in music written in mixed meter. • Sing with artistic expressing appropriate for the style and structure.

STUDENT TEXT

The comprehensive student lessons are structured as follows:

- **FOCUS** . . . tells the student the main concepts and skills addressed in the lesson. By having only a few main goals, students and teacher will keep focused on these objectives as work progresses.

- **VOCABULARY** . . . gives the student an opportunity to build a musical vocabulary essential for clarity of thought in communicating about music to others.

- **LINKS TO LEARNING**

Vocal . . . allows the student to explore the melodic and vocal skills that are directly related to some aspect of the upcoming musical selection. Also includes melodic sight-singing examples.

Theory . . . builds rhythmic, theory and basic reading skills through exercises that are directly related to the musical selection about to be learned. Through sight-reading practice every day, students gain confidence and skills to become independent readers.

Artistic Expression . . . provides interpretive aspects of music making, such as phrasing, dynamics, stylistic performance practices, movement, and artistic expression through drama, writing and the visual arts. Through interest and active participation, the student is then led logically into the piece.

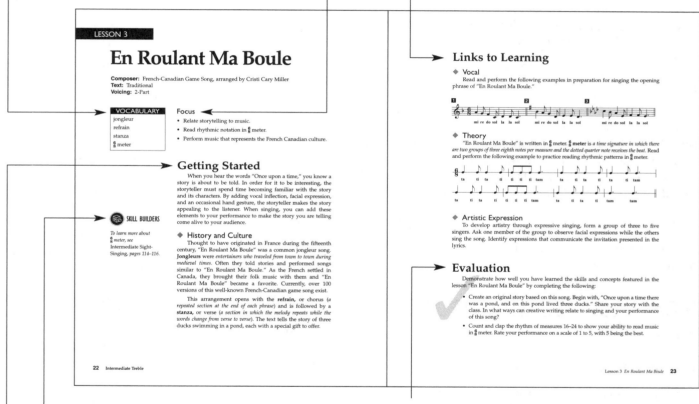

- **SIDEBAR REFERENCES** . . . provide additional information about the lesson through:
  Skill Builders . . . reference to *Sight-Singing* textbook
  Music & History . . . reference to the History section
  Spotlights . . . reference to a featured Spotlight page

- **GETTING STARTED.** . . provides a motivating introduction to the piece of music, related to the student's perspective. The History and Culture provides background information on the selection, the composer and/or the cultural context.

- **EVALUATION** . . . gives the student ways to assess accomplishment, growth and needs, for both self and group. Through careful listening and constructive critique of their own work, they will gradually become more discriminating about the quality of performance and the impact of that performance on the audience.

Lessons

The student lessons, through which students systematically build musical skills and conceptual understanding, comprise the first twelve selections of the text. They are presented in three general categories: Beginning of the Year, Mid-Winter, and Concert/Festival.

Music & History

The Historical section of the text provides a survey of Western music history through exploration of the culture and music of the five overarching periods: Renaissance, Baroque, Classical, Romantic and Contemporary. Each period is addressed in the following ways:

- **Historical Narrative Lesson** . . . provides a brief, student-oriented historical context of the period through visual art, architecture, historical events, musical developments, artistic characteristics, musical personalities and listening selections.
- **Historical Listening Lesson** . . . provides one choral and one instrumental listening selection to give students an aural experience with the styles, sounds and forms of the period. Recordings are provided to aid student learning.

Choral Library

The Choral Library maintains the same comprehensive lesson format of the Lessons and comprises the final twelve selections of the text. The additional literature features multicultural selections, patriotic and seasonal selections, American folk music, African American spirituals, Broadway show tunes and light concert pieces.

Glossary

The glossary provides brief, accurate definitions of musical terms used in the text.

TEACHER WRAPAROUND EDITION

National Standards Connections

Experiencing Choral Music affords multiple opportunities to address the National Standards. Correlations among lesson content, extension activities and bottom-page activities are listed to make obvious the relationship between lesson activities and the standards.

Suggested Teaching Sequence

Each lesson is organized to follow a logical progression from Getting Started through Evaluation, while providing maximum flexibility of use for your individual situation. Each lesson is linked to one musical selection, and provides learning opportunities based on the inherent concepts and skills required to understand and perform the piece. The lessons of the Teacher Wraparound Edition are structured as follows.

- **Overview** . . . Gives the teacher a brief analysis of the music being taught, including composer, text, voicing, key, meter, form, style, accompaniment, programming ideas and vocal ranges for each voice part.
- **Objectives** . . . Two or three concrete, measurable objectives form the skeletal structure for the lesson, allowing an interconnected approach to lesson segments.
- **Vocabulary** . . . Vocabulary terms are those used during the lesson and music terms used in the music to build understanding and skills.
- **Links to Learning** . . . The Links to Learning of the lesson includes exercises that focus on vocal, theory and artistic expression elements of the upcoming song. It provides rhythm and vocal, as well as sight-singing exercises. They are designed to sequentially develop vocal and sight-singing skills, and lead directly into the upcoming piece. These exercises may all be done before the piece is introduced, or they may be presented cumulatively, one each day, and concurrent with developing understanding of the piece.
- **The Lesson Plan: Suggested Teaching Sequence** . . . The Suggested Teaching Sequence is divided into three sections: Introduce, Rehearse, and Refine. At the end of each section, Progress Checkpoints are provided for quick informal assessment of the materials covered to that point. Introduce often refers to the Links to Learning exercises on the student page and provides meaningful ways to introduce a new song to students. Rehearse includes a list of recommended steps to teach the piece through a variety of teaching techniques. Refine puts it all together and prepares the students for performance of the piece. The Performance Tips provide teachers with the polishing nuances that transform the notes on the page into an expressive performance experience.

Informal Assessment, Student Self-Assessment, and Individual and Group Performance Evaluation

Informal Assessment is done by teacher observation during the lesson. Each objective is observable, and the text indicates the checkpoint for teacher assessment.

Student Self-Assessment is accomplished through student evaluation of their individual performance based on an established set of criteria.

Individual and Group Performance Evaluation requires the student to demonstrate a skill or understanding through individual or group evaluation. This is directly related to the Evaluation found in the student lesson. Individual and Group Performance Evaluation can be done by the teacher, student, peers or a combination thereof. Frequent audio- or videotaping is suggested as an effective means of evaluation. The tapes may be compiled into a portfolio that shows growth and developing understanding over time.

Bottom-Page Activities

Bottom-page activities in each lesson afford a plethora of background information, teaching strategies and enrichment opportunities.

- *Teacher 2 Teacher* provides a brief description of the main features of the lesson.
- *Enrichment activities* provide musical activities that go beyond the basic lesson, including composition, improvisation, and so forth.
- *Extension activities* expand the lesson to the other arts or other disciplines.
- *Teaching strategies* reinforce concepts or skills presented in the lesson, or elaborate on classroom management techniques.
- *More about* boxes provide background historical, cultural, and/or biographical information.
- *Curriculum connections* provide strategies to help students build bridges between music and other disciplines.
- *Vocal development strategies* give detailed information about specific techniques that facilitate vocal production and style.
- *Music literacy strategies* help students expand their ability to read and analyze music.
- *Cultural connections* provide cultural information related to the lesson.
- *Connecting to the arts* boxes provide strategies to help students connect music to the other arts.
- *Community connections* provide activities that extend into the community.
- *Careers in music* boxes provide information about career opportunities in music.
- *Online* directs students and teachers to **music.glencoe.com**, the Web site for *Experiencing Choral Music.*

TEACHER RESOURCE BINDER

The *Teacher Resource Binder* contains teaching materials designed to reduce teacher preparation time and maximize students' learning. The following categories are provided to assist with meeting the individual needs and interests of your students.

- **Teaching Masters.** The *Teaching Masters* support, extend and enhance the musical concepts and skills presented in the text lessons. Included are strategied focusing on composing, arranging, evaluating, analyzing, writing, multi-arts, culture and language pronunciation guides.
- **Evaluation Masters.** The *Evaluation Masters* provide performance assessment criteria, rubrics and other pages to help teachers and students with individual group, and ensemble assessment.
- **Music & History.** The *Music & History Masters* include full-color overhead transparencies of the visual art pieces introduced in each of the historical sections. They also include characteristics of the period, biographies of composers and other teaching strategies.
- **Vocal Development Masters.** The *Vocal Development Masters* provide important information about the voice. Included are numerous warm-up exercises that may be used throughout the year. Each exercise is recorded and included on the *Sight-Singing CD.*
- **Skill Builders Masters.** The *Skill Builders Masters* reinforce the development of fundamental skills, knowledge and understanding in areas such as rhythm, notation, music symbols, conducting patterns, improvisation, Kodály hand signs, time signatures and meter.
- **Sight-Singing Masters.** The *Sight-Singing Masters* are directly correlated to the *Sight-Singing* textbooks. They provide reproducible evaluation activity sheets for assessment and review.
- **Kodály, Dalcroze, Interdisciplinary.** Teaching strategies with a focus on Kodály, Dalcroze and Interdisciplinary are presented in this section.
- **Reference Resources.** The *Reference Resource Masters* serve as a resource bank for the teacher and provides a library of resource materials useful in supporting instruction.
- **Listening Selections CD.** The *Listening Selections CD* provides full recordings of the vocal and instrumental historical listening lessons from the student text.
- **Sight-Singing CD.** The *Sight-Singing CD* provides a piano accompaniment track for practice songs and sight-singing exercises found in the student text of *Experiencing Choral Music: Sight-Singing.* The CD also includes the accompaniment track to the vocal warm-up exercises in the Vocal Development section.

EFFECTIVE TEACHING CHECKLIST

Teaching can be a rewarding as well as a challenging experience. The following is a compilation of suggestions and tips from experienced teachers. Review this list often.

Preparation

- Good planning leads to a successful rehearsal.
- Establish high expectations from the start—students want to succeed.
- Establish a routine and basic standards of behavior—and stick to it!
- Follow your planned routine every rehearsal (e.g. opening cue that rehearsal has begun, warm-up, sight-reading, repertoire, evaluation). Younger choirs in particular respond well to structure in a rehearsal.
- Plan, plan, plan.
- Develop long-range planning (the entire year's goals and activities, the semester, the month) and short-range planning (weekly plans and the daily lesson as they fit within the entire year's goals).
- Vary teaching strategies: modeling, peer coaching, large group, small group, cooperative learning, individual instruction, student conductors, independent practice and so forth.
- Study the score well. Anticipate problem areas.
- Be able to sing any one part while playing another.
- Know the vocal ranges of each member of the chorus.
- Select appropriate music to fit those vocal ranges.
- Remember: out-of-range results in out-of-tune singing.
- Select music of appropriate difficulty for the group.
- Plan evaluation techniques in advance.
- Have all necessary supplies and equipment ready (music in folders or ready to pass out, tapes cued, director's folder handy, recording equipment set, and so forth.) before the lesson begins.
- Plan to make beautiful music at least once during every rehearsal.

Presentation

- Begin each lesson with singing rather than talking.
- Make all parts of the lesson musical—including warm-ups and sight-reading.
- Rehearse a cappella. Use the piano as little as possible.
- Remember: Delivering information is not necessarily teaching.
- Display a positive attitude.
- Communicate effectively and concisely.
- Enthusiasm is essential.
- Make learning an enjoyable experience.
- Respect legitimate effort on the part of every student.
- Be the best musician you can be.
- Laugh often.

Pacing

- Be 30 seconds mentally ahead of the class at all times.
- Know where the lesson is going before it happens.
- Vary activities and standing/sitting positions.
- Plan a smooth transition from one activity to the next.
- Avoid "lag" time.
- If a "teachable" moment occurs, make the most of it.
- Avoid belaboring any one exercise, phrase or activity—come back to it at another time.
- Always give students a reason for repeating a section.
- Provide at least one successful musical experience in every rehearsal.

Evaluation

- Assess student learning in every lesson (formally or informally).
- Vary the assessment activities.
- Consider evaluating individual as well as group effort.
- Tape the rehearsals often (audio and/or video).
- Study the rehearsal tapes: (1) to discover where overlooked errors occur, (2) to assist in planning the next rehearsal, or (3) to share findings with the students.
- Provide students with opportunities to evaluate themselves.
- Teach critical listening to the students by asking specific students or a group of students to listen for a specific thing (balance of parts in the polyphonic section, a correct uniform vowel sound on a particular word or words, rise and fall of phrase, and so forth).
- Constantly evaluate what's really happening. (We often hear what we want to hear!)
- Listen, listen, listen.

TEACHER WRAPAROUND EDITION
PROFICIENT

Experiencing
Choral Music

MIXED

Developed by

HAL•LEONARD®
CORPORATION

Mc Graw Hill **Glencoe**

New York, New York   Columbus, Ohio   Chicago, Illinois   Peoria, Illinois   Woodland Hills, California

The portions of the National Standards for Music Education included here are reprinted from *National Standards for Arts Education* with permission from MENC—The National Association for Music Education. All rights reserved. Copyright © 1994 by MENC. The complete National Standards and additional materials relating to the Standards are available from MENC, 1806 Robert Fulton Drive, Reston, VA 20191 (telephone 800-336-3768).

A portion of the sales of this material goes to support music education programs through programs of MENC—The National Association for Music Education.

Printed in the United States of America.

Send all inquiries to:
Glencoe/McGraw-Hill
21600 Oxnard Street, Suite 500
Woodland Hills, CA 91367

ISBN 0-07-861119-9 (Student Edition)
ISBN 0-07-861120-2 (Teacher Wraparound Edition)

4 5 6 7 8 9   045   09 08 07

Credits

LEAD AUTHORS

Emily Crocker
Vice President of Choral Publications
Hal Leonard Corporation, Milwaukee, Wisconsin
Founder and Artistic Director, Milwaukee Children's Choir

Michael Jothen
Professor of Music, Program Director of Graduate Music Education
Chairperson of Music Education
Towson University, Towson, Maryland

Jan Juneau
Choral Director
Klein Collins High School
Spring, Texas

Henry H. Leck
Associate Professor and Director of Choral Activities
Butler University, Indianapolis, Indiana
Founder and Artistic Director, Indianapolis Children's Choir

Michael O'Hern
Choral Director
Lake Highlands High School
Richardson, Texas

Audrey Snyder
Composer
Eugene, Oregon

Mollie Tower
Coordinator of Choral and General Music, K-12, Retired
Austin, Texas

AUTHORS

Anne Denbow
Voice Instructor, Professional Singer/Actress
Director of Music, Holy Cross Episcopal Church
Simpsonville, South Carolina

Rollo A. Dilworth
Director of Choral Activities and Music
  Education
North Park University, Chicago, Illinois

Deidre Douglas
Choral Director
Labay Junior High, Katy, Texas

Ruth E. Dwyer
Associate Director and Director of Education
Indianapolis Children's Choir
Indianapolis, Indiana

Norma Freeman
Choral Director
Saline High School, Saline, Michigan

Cynthia I. Gonzales
Assistant Professor of Music Theory
Texas State University, San Marcos, Texas

Michael Mendoza
Professor of Choral Activities
New Jersey State University
Trenton, New Jersey

Thomas Parente
Associate Professor
Westminster Choir College of Rider University
Princeton, New Jersey

Barry Talley
Director of Fine Arts and Choral Director
Deer Park ISD, Deer Park, Texas

CONTRIBUTING AUTHORS

Debbie Daniel
Choral Director, Webb Middle School
Garland, Texas

Roger Emerson
Composer/Arranger
Mount Shasta, California

Kari Gilbertson
Choral Director, Forest Meadow Junior High
Richardson, Texas

Tim McDonald
Creative Director, Music Theatre International
New York, New York

Christopher W. Peterson
Assistant Professor of Music Education (Choral)
University of Wisconsin-Milwaukee
Milwaukee, Wisconsin

Kirby Shaw
Composer/Arranger
Ashland, Oregon

Stephen Zegree
Professor of Music
Western Michigan State University
Kalamazoo, Michigan

EDITORIAL

Linda Rann
Senior Editor
Hal Leonard Corporation
Milwaukee, Wisconsin

Stacey Nordmeyer
Choral Editor
Hal Leonard Corporation
Milwaukee, Wisconsin

Table of Contents

Lessons

Music & History

Choral Library

TO THE STUDENT

Welcome to choir!

By singing in the choir, you have chosen to be a part of an exciting and rewarding adventure. The benefits of being in choir are many. Basically, singing is fun. It provides an expressive way of sharing your feelings and emotions. Through choir, you will have friends that share a common interest with you. You will experience the joy of making beautiful music together. Choir provides the opportunity to develop your interpersonal skills. It takes teamwork and cooperation to sing together, and you must learn how to work with others. As you critique your individual and group performances, you can improve your ability to analyze and communicate your thoughts clearly.

Even if you do not pursue a music career, music can be an important part of your life. There are many avocational opportunities in music. **Avocational** means *not related to a job or career*. Singing as a hobby can provide you with personal enjoyment, enrich your life, and teach you life skills. Singing is something you can do for the rest of your life.

In this course, you will be presented with the basic skills of vocal production and music literacy. You will be exposed to songs from different cultures, songs in many different styles and languages, and songs from various historical periods. You will discover connections between music and the other arts. Guidelines for becoming a better singer and choir member include:

- Come to class prepared to learn.
- Respect the efforts of others.
- Work daily to improve your sight-singing skills.
- Sing expressively at all times.
- Have fun singing.

This book was written to provide you with a meaningful choral experience. Take advantage of the knowledge and opportunities offered here. Your exciting adventure of experiencing choral music is about to begin!

Lessons

Lessons for the Beginning of the Year

Lessons for Mid-Winter

Lessons for Concert/Festival

Adoramus Te

OVERVIEW

Composer: Giovanni Pierluigi da Palestrina (c. 1525–1594), edited by John Leavitt
Text: Liturgical Latin
Voicing: SATB
Key: A minor
Meter: 4/4
Form: ABA
Style: Italian Renaissance Motet
Accompaniment: A cappella
Programming: Sacred, Concert

Vocal Ranges:

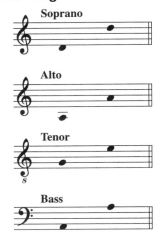

OBJECTIVES

After completing this lesson, students will be able to:

- Exhibit appropriate small-ensemble performance techniques.
- Describe, classify and perform music representing the Renaissance period.
- Define *Picardy third*.

VOCABULARY

Have students review vocabulary in student lesson. Introduce terms found in the music. A complete glossary of terms is found on page 260 of the student book.

Adoramus Te

Composer: Giovanni Pierluigi da Palestrina (c. 1525–1594), edited by John Leavitt
Text: Liturgical Latin
Voicing: SATB

VOCABULARY

Renaissance period
motet
madrigal
a cappella
Picardy third

Focus

- Exhibit appropriate small-ensemble performance techniques.
- Describe, classify and perform music representing the Renaissance period.
- Define concepts of chord structure using standard terminology (Picardy third).

Getting Started

Which choice from the following pairs do you prefer?

- *football or soccer*
- *dogs or cats*
- *vanilla or chocolate*
- *paper or plastic*

If you were a singer during the **Renaissance period** *(c. 1430–1600)* in Italy, you would have two basic choices for music—sacred or secular. Vocal music flourished during the Renaissance as an important part of religious services, pageants, ceremonies and daily life. The short pieces that composers wrote for singers consisted mainly of **motets** *(short, sacred choral pieces with Latin texts that are used in religious services, but are not a part of the regular mass)* and **madrigals** *(short, secular choral pieces with texts in the common language).* Because the text is from the Latin Vesper Service, "Adoramus Te" is classified as a motet. Renaissance singers didn't have much of a choice about the accompaniment because Renaissance vocal music, including this song, was primarily written **a cappella** *(without instrumental accompaniment).*

MUSIC & HISTORY

To learn more about Renaissance music, see page 106.

◆ History and Culture

Although he also wrote madrigals, Giovanni Pierluigi da Palestrina (c. 1525–1594) is mainly remembered for his extraordinary sacred music. He lived and worked in Rome his entire life, holding many important positions in the major chapels and churches. His music was held in the highest regard during his lifetime, as it is still today. Palestrina's music features long, flowing phrases and a smooth melodic and rhythmic connection between the notes in every voice part.

2 Proficient Mixed

RESOURCES

Proficient Sight-Singing

Sight-Singing in A Minor, pages 36–39
Reading Rhythms in 4/4 Meter, pages 2–7

Teacher Resource Binder

Teaching Master 1, *Pronunciation Guide for "Adoramus Te"*

Teaching Master 2, *Introducing "Adoramus Te"*

Evaluation Master 15, *Diction Check-up*

Music and History 2, *Giovanni Pierluigi da Palestrina, a Renaissance Composer*

For additional resources, see TRB Table of Contents.

Links to Learning

◆ **Vocal**

Since "Adoramus Te" is an example of an a cappella Renaissance motet, learn measures 1–4 without the assistance of the piano. Perform the following:

1. Sing an A minor scale to establish minor tonality.

2. Read the solfège syllables for the notes in your voice part. The starting pitches are as follows: *la* for Sopranos; *mi* for Altos; *do* for Tenors; *la* for Basses.

3. Sing your voice part on solfège syllables at a very slow, but steady, tempo.

4. Sing all four parts together.

A minor scale

A   B   C   D   E   F   G   A
la ti do re mi fa sol la

◆ **Theory**

A **Picardy third,** or *tierce de picardie* (French), is *an interval of a major third used in the final, tonic chord of a piece written in a minor key.* The history of this practice is not precisely known, but dates back to around 1500. Perform the following example to practice singing a Picardy third.

Soprano

Alto

Tenor

Bass

Evaluation

Demonstrate how well you have learned the skills and concepts featured in the lesson "Adoramus Te" by completing the following:

• Sing "Adoramus Te" from memory in an SATB quartet. Evaluate the quality of your performance based on: 1) singing in tune, 2) using appropriate Latin diction, 3) singing long, flowing phrases, 4) demonstrating correct memorization.

• Write program notes for "Adoramus Te" and include a short description of Renaissance vocal music. Based on this information, why should "Adoramus Te" be classified as a Renaissance motet?

LINKS TO LEARNING

Vocal

The Vocal section is designed to prepare students to:

• Sing the A minor scale with good intonation.

• Sing their part in a homophonic texture.

Have students:

• Sing the A minor scale on note names first, and then on solfège syllables.

• Chant the first four measures of "Adoramus te" using solfège syllables.

• Sing their part independently in measures 1–4 on solfège syllables at a slow tempo.

• Sing all parts together on solfège syllables.

Theory

The Theory section is designed to prepare students to:

• Understand a Picardy third.

• Perform a Picardy third.

Have students:

• Read the definition of a Picardy third.

• Sing the four-part vocal example on a neutral syllable such as "loo."

• Determine which part sings the interval of the major third, thus creating a Picardy third.

LESSON PLAN

Suggested Teaching Sequence and Performance Tips

1. Introduce

Direct students to:

- Read and discuss the information found in the Getting Started section on student page 2.
- Sing measures 1–4 as suggested in the Vocal section on page 3 to practice homophonic texture.
- Practice singing a Picardy third as shown in the Theory section on page 3.
- Read through the Latin text and its translation to learn its meaning. The Latin pronunciation guide can be found in the Teacher Resource Binder, Teaching Master 1.

Progress Checkpoints

Observe students' progress in:

✓ Their ability to sing homophonic music with precision.

✓ Their ability to understand and perform to a Picardy third.

✓ Their ability to pronounce the Latin text properly.

2. Rehearse

Direct students to:

- Phrase-by-phrase, count the homophonic rhythm, noticing those few places where one part has an ornamented rhythmic part.
- When rhythms are secure, add pitches one part at a time, using solfège syllables.
- Finally, add the Latin text.

Adoramus Te

For SATB, a cappella

Edited by
JOHN LEAVITT

GIOVANNI PIERLUIGI da PALESTRINA
(c. 1525–1594)

4   Proficient Mixed

TEACHER 2 TEACHER

"Adoramus Te" is a wonderful introduction to the music of Palestrina and the music of sixteenth-century Italy. When learning the Latin text, focus on pronouncing the pure vowels correctly. Also learn proper word stress, so that the flow of the language highlights the accented syllables naturally.

Observe students' progress in:

✓ Their ability to perform rhythms accurately.

✓ Their ability to perform rhythms and pitches correctly.

3. Refine

Direct students to:

- Sing with precise and accurate intonation on every chord.
- Sing with correct syllabic stress when pronouncing the Latin text.

Progress Checkpoints

Observe students' progress in:

✓ Their ability to sing their part in the chord with good intonation.

✓ Their ability to sing the Latin text with proper word stress.

ASSESSMENT

Informal Assessment

In this lesson, students showed the ability to:

- Participate in creating a homophonic texture.
- Sing Latin with proper pronunciation and syllabic stress.
- Understand and perform a Picardy third.

MORE ABOUT...

Artistic Expression

In singing Latin, it is important to place the accent on the correct syllable. Use the following as a guide:

Adorámus te, Chríste,	We adore you, O Christ,
et benedícimus tíbi:	and we bless you
Quia per sánctam crúcem	For by your holy cross
et passiónem túam redemísti múndum.	and passion you have redeemed the world.
Dómine, miserére nóbis.	O Lord, have mercy upon us.

5

Student Self-Assessment

Have students evaluate their individual performances based on the following:

• Posture
• Phrasing
• Foreign Language
• Tall Vowels
• Intonation

Have each student rate his/her performance of this song in the areas above on a scale of 1–5, 5 being the best.

Individual and Group Performance Evaluation

To further measure growth of musical skills presented in this lesson, ask students to complete the Evaluation section on page 3.

• Have students form quartets with one person on each part. Each quartet should rehearse individually and then perform for the rest of the class. The class and the group should evaluate the performance based on the elements listed in the Evaluation section.

• Have each student write a short paragraph on Renaissance vocal music. Based on that information, explain why "Adoramus te" is classified as a Renaissance motet. Choose the best paragraph and use it as program notes at your next concert.

• Listen to the motet "O Magnum Mysterium" (page 109). Compare and contrast the form of these two motets. Discuss their similarities and differences.

MORE ABOUT...
Giovanni Pierluigi da Palestrina (c. 1525–1594)

Palestrina is the leading musical figure in sixteenth-century Rome, Italy. He composed more than 100 masses, almost 400 motets and other liturgical works, and more than 150 madrigals. What is truly unique about Palestrina in musical history is that his prestige as a composer remained steady and even increased in the years after his death. This is due not only to his prominence as a composer of church music, but also because his compositional style became the model for teaching counterpoint that remains in effect even today. Mozart, Haydn and Beethoven, among countless others, learned to compose in the style of Palestrina.

SPOTLIGHT

Posture & Breath Management

There are some basic techniques to help you sing higher, lower, louder, softer and for longer periods of time without tiring. First, a singer needs to have proper posture. Try the following exercise:

1. Stand with your feet shoulder width apart and knees unlocked.
2. Balance your head effortlessly on the top of your spine.
3. Exhale all of your air.
4. Raise your arms up over your head.
5. Take in a deep breath as if you were sipping through a straw.
6. Slowly lower your arms down to your sides.
7. Let out your air on a breathy "pah" without letting your chest drop.

Now that you have discovered proper posture, try this for discovering how a singer should breathe and manage the breath:

1. Place your hands on your waist at the bottom of your ribcage.
2. Take in an easy breath without lifting your chest or shoulders.
3. Feel your waist and ribcage expand all the way around like an inflating inner tube.
4. Let your breath out slowly on "sss," feeling your inner tube deflating as if it has a slow leak.
5. Remember to keep your chest up the entire time.
6. Take in another easy breath over four counts before your inner tube has completely deflated, then let your air out on "sss" for eight counts.
7. Repeat this step several times, taking in an easy breath over four counts and gradually increasing the number of release counts to sixteen.
8. Once you have reached sixteen counts, try to see how many times you can repeat it without getting tired.

Practice this every day, gradually working up to five minutes of repetition. If you become lightheaded, you are taking in too much air for the number of counts you are exhaling.

A "catch breath," which is required when you don't have much time to breathe, should feel like the kind of breath you take when you are pleasantly surprised or see something lovely for the first time. It must be silent, though!

RESOURCES

Teacher Resource Binder

Vocal Development 1–6, *Keep the Joy in Singing!*
Vocal Development 13, *Posture and Breathing*
Reference 16, *Expanding a Musical Vocabulary*

National Standards

1. Singing, alone and with others. **(b)**

Objectives

• Demonstrate basic performance techniques including proper singing posture.

Suggested Teaching Sequence

Direct students to:

• Read the Spotlight On Posture & Breath Management on student page 7 and identify the importance of proper posture in singing.

• Perform the exercise for developing posture as presented on page 7.

• Perform the exercise for breathing as presented on page 7.

• Compare the concept of proper posture to basic performance techniques and the effect posture has on breath support, tone quality and overall stage presence.

Progress Checkpoints

Observe students' progress in:

✓ Their ability to stand in correct singing posture.

✓ Their ability to breath using correct breath management.

✓ Their ability to explain the importance of proper posture in singing.

The Little Beggarman

OVERVIEW

Composer: Traditional Irish Folk Song, arranged by Emily Crocker
Text: Traditional Irish Folk Song
Voicing: SATB
Key: D Mixolydian
Meter: 2/4
Form: Verse-Refrain
Style: Irish Folk Song
Accompaniment: Piano
Programming: Multicultural, Folk Music, Concert

Vocal Ranges:

OBJECTIVES

After completing this lesson, students will be able to:

- Define the concept of harmony (scales).
- Read music in simple meters.
- Perform music from diverse cultures.

VOCABULARY

Have students review vocabulary in student lesson. Introduce terms found in the music. A complete glossary of terms is found on page 260 of the student book.

The Little Beggarman

Composer: Traditional Irish Folk Song, arranged by Emily Crocker
Text: Traditional Irish Folk Song
Voicing: SATB

VOCABULARY

ballad
mode
Mixolydian scale

Focus

- Compare the elements of a Mixolydian scale and a major scale.
- Read and perform rhythmic patterns in simple meter.
- Perform music representing Irish folk music.

Getting Started

"The Little Beggarman" is a lively arrangement of a traditional Irish folk song. The lyrics tell the story of a happy-go-lucky beggar named Johnny Dhu who is known up and down the Liffey, the river that flows through Dublin. Arranger Emily Crocker has enhanced the story line by putting Johnny's words in the Tenor and Bass parts, and the flaxen-haired girl's words in the Soprano and Alto parts. By cleverly incorporating the famous fiddle tune "Angeline," the arranger has created an appealing refrain for this **ballad,** *a narrative song dealing with dramatic episodes.*

🎲 **SKILL BUILDERS**

To learn more about the Mixolydian scale, see Proficient Sight-Singing, *page 159.*

◆ History and Culture

Although the key signature indicates the key of D major, "The Little Beggarman" is actually based on a **mode,** or *an early system of pitch organization that was used before major and minor scales and keys were developed.* Modal scales were prevalent in early church music but are also found in folk music. The particular arrangement of pitches used in "The Little Beggarman" consists of D, E, F♯, G, A, B, C, D, and is called a **Mixolydian scale** *(a modal scale that starts and ends on* sol*).* It sounds very much like the major scale except for the seventh degree of the scale. In this instance, C♮ is used in the Mixolydian scale, whereas C♯ is used in the D major scale.

RESOURCES

Proficient Sight-Singing

Sight-Singing in the Mixolydian Scale, page 159

Reading Rhythms in 2/4 Meter, pages 66–67

Reading Sixteenth Notes and Sixteenth and Eighth Note Combinations, pages 62–64

Teacher Resource Binder

Teaching Master 3, *Comparing Modal and Major Scales*

Teaching Master 4, *Lighting Up the Stage!*

Evaluation Master 2, *Analyzing Intonation*

Skill Builder 15, *Major and Minor Scales*

Skill Builder 18, *Modal Scales: An Overview*

For additional resources, see TRB Table of Contents.

Links to Learning

◆ **Vocal**

Perform the following examples and compare the Mixolydian scale to the D major scale.

D Mixolydian scale

D E F♯ G A B C♯ D C♯ B A G F♯ E D
sol la ti do re mi fa sol fa mi re do ti la sol

D major scale

D E F♯ G A B C♯ D C♯ B A G F♯ E D
do re mi fa sol la ti do ti la sol fa mi re do

◆ **Theory**

Fiddle tunes traditionally use different combinations of eighth and sixteenth notes. Perform the following examples to practice reading some of the rhythmic patterns found in "The Little Beggarman."

Evaluation

Demonstrate how well you have learned the skills and concepts featured in the lesson "The Little Beggarman" by completing the following:

- Ask a classmate to sing any pitch. From that pitch, sing a major scale ascending and descending. Then, starting on the same pitch, sing a Mixolydian scale ascending and descending. Evaluate how well you were able to demonstrate the difference between the two scales.

- In an SATB quartet, sing measures 52–61 to demonstrate mastery of eighth and sixteenth note patterns. Assess your ability to sing the rhythms correctly.

Lesson 2 *The Little Beggarman* **9**

RESOURCES

Proficient Mixed Rehearsal/Performance CD

CD 1:3 Voices
CD 1:4 Accompaniment Only
CD 3:2 Vocal Practice Track—Soprano
CD 4:2 Vocal Practice Track—Alto
CD 5:2 Vocal Practice Track—Tenor
CD 6:2 Vocal Practice Track—Bass

National Standards

1. Singing, alone and with others, a varied repertoire of music. **(a, b, c)**
6. Listening to, analyzing, and describing music. **(a, b, c)**
9. Understanding music in relation to history and culture. **(a, d)**

LINKS TO LEARNING

Vocal

The Vocal section is designed to prepare students to:

- Compare and contrast a mixolydian scale and a major scale.
- Sing a Mixolydian scale and a major scale with accuracy.

Have students:

- Sing the D Mixolydian scale on note names and then on solfège syllables.
- Sing the D major scale on note names and then on solfège syllables.
- Compare the two scales and determine what is the same and what is different between them.

Theory

The Theory section is designed to prepare students to:

- Perform eight and sixteenth note combinations with accuracy.
- Locate these patterns in "The Little Beggarman."

Have students:

- Chant or clap the rhythm examples while tapping the quarter note pulse.
- Locate these rhythmic examples in the score. *[(1) measures 26–29, 52–55, 106–109; (2) measures 32–35, 58–61, 112–115]*

LESSON PLAN

Suggested Teaching Sequence and Performance Tips

1. Introduce

Direct students to:

- Read and discuss the information found in the Getting Started section on student page 8.
- Practice the D Mixolydian scale as instructed in the Vocal section on page 9.
- Practice the eighth and sixteenth note rhythm patterns in the Theory section on page 9.
- Read through all the lyrics to learn the story told in this song.

The Little Beggarman

For SATB and Piano

Arranged by EMILY CROCKER incorporating the Appalachian Fiddle Tune "Angeline"

Traditional Irish Folk Song

10 Proficient Mixed

TEACHER 2 TEACHER

"The Little Beggarman" is sure to be a favorite! It provides an excellent opportunity to showcase the Tenor and Bass sections, because they carry the melody throughout and the narrative of the story. The women's part initially imitates the part of an Irish fiddle.

Progress Checkpoints

Observe students' progress in:

✓ Their ability to sing a mixolydian scale.

✓ Their ability to sing harmonies commonly found in mixolydian mode.

✓ Their ability to sing eighth and sixteenth notes rhythm combinations with accuracy.

✓ Their ability to understand the story line of the song.

TEACHING STRATEGY

Performing from Memory

Have students:

1. Memorize this piece by learning shorter phrases at a time.

2. Perform it from memory on a program or in competition.

3. Further develop memorization skills by memorizing other songs and solos to perform for the class informally or at formal concerts.

2. Rehearse

Direct students to:

- Read the lyrics to the verses in rhythm, beginning with a slow tempo and gradually working up to the suggested tempo. When rhythms are precise, return to a slow tempo and add pitches. When pitches are accurate, increase the tempo.
- Learn the interludes: measures 26–35, 52–61, 78–89, 106–128. Begin by reading the rhythms. When rhythms are precise, add pitches.
- Sing the piece from beginning to end to put in place the interludes between the verses.

CONNECTING THE ARTS
Dance – Irish Folk Dance

Have students:

- Identify the style of this piece as a traditional Irish folk song with four verses.
- Learn some Irish dance steps to gain a repertoire of familiar steps and formations. Perhaps there is an Irish dancer among choir members or in the school arts program.
- Explore Irish dance movements that might fit with the melody.
- Explore variations of that movement that would show contrast between the verses and the refrain.
- Create a dance that stylistically matches the piece and shows contrast between the verses and the refrain.

Progress Checkpoints

Observe students' progress in:

✓ Their ability to recite the lyrics in rhythm.

✓ Their ability to sing the verses correctly.

✓ Their ability to sing their part in the interludes, giving attention to precise rhythm and pitches.

TEACHING STRATEGY

Musical Elements of Style

The combination of musical elements determines the style of a piece. Have students:

1. Compile a list of musical elements that might affect style.

2. Share the lists to compile one master list.

3. Sing known songs, trying out different styles, and then try to describe the musical elements that are characteristic of that style. (For example, try salsa, opera, Broadway, rock, military, lullaby, and so forth.)

4. Select appropriate literature for a particular style.

3. Refine

Direct students to:

- Sing the entire piece, giving special attention to the dynamic markings.
- Listen for in-tune open fifths and parallel major chords that are commonly found in music based on the Mixolydian scale.

rain was com-in' through, and the cats and the rats they were play-in' peek-a-boo. When

rain was com-in' through, and the cats and the rats they were play-in' peek-a-boo. When

who should a-wa-ken but the wo-man of the house with her white spot-ted a-pron and her

who should a-wa-ken but the wo-man of the house with her white spot-ted a-pron and her

14 Proficient Mixed

ENRICHMENT

Analyzing Form

Form relates to the structure or musical design of a composition. If students can identify and analyze the form of a composition, they are able to perform with greater comprehension and understanding. Listen to a recording of this song. Direct students to:

- Identify the form of "The Little Beggarman" as strophic.
- Show where each verse begins.
- Analyze the form and discuss how each verse is treated differently. Have students discuss the differences in texture, harmony, placement of melody, dynamics, tempo and so forth.

Progress Checkpoints

Observe students' progress in:
- ✓ Their ability to sing the notated dynamic markings such that changes are audible.
- ✓ Their ability to sing in-tune open fifths and parallel major chords.

MORE ABOUT...

Arranger Emily Crocker

Emily Holt Crocker, Director of the Milwaukee Children's Choir, is recognized nationally as one of the leading experts in children's choirs. After a successful 15-year career as a music teacher and choral director in her native Texas, she joined the music publishing industry, and now holds the position of Vice President of Choral Publications for Hal Leonard Corporation in Milwaukee and is Senior Author and Editor of the *Essential Elements for Choir* textbook series.

She holds degrees from the University of North Texas and Texas Woman's University, and has done additional study at UNT (choral conducting), Westminster Choir College (conducting and voice-building), TWU (vocal pedagogy) and Sam Houston State University (Kodály methods).

ASSESSMENT

Informal Assessment

In this lesson, students showed the ability to:

- Sing a Mixolydian scale and the harmonies typically found in music based on the Mixolydian scale.
- Sing with clear and crisp diction.
- Perform eighth and sixteenth note combinations accurately.
- Interpret the story line of the text.

TEACHING STRATEGY

Mixolydian Scales vs. Major Scales

To familiarize students with the similarities and differences between mixolydian and major scales, have students write out the D major scale. Then, write out the D Mixolydian scale. After they are finished, they should make two columns labeling one "Similarities" and the other "Differences." Have them make a list of attributes for each scale in both columns.

Have students evaluate their individual performances based on the following:

- Posture
- Diction
- Expressive Singing
- Accurate Pitches
- Accurate Rhythms

Have each student rate his/her performance of this song in the areas above on a scale of 1–5, 5 being the best.

Lesson 2 *The Little Beggarman* **17**

Individual and Group Performance Evaluation

To further measure growth of musical skills presented in this lesson, direct students to complete the Evaluation section on page 9.

- Have students pair up and complete the first exercise in the Evaluation section. Assist them in evaluating their ability to demonstrate the difference between the Mixolydian and major scales.

- Have students divide into SATB quartets with one singer on a part. Each quartet should sing measures 52–61 on their own or for the rest of the class. Assist them in evaluating their ability to perform eighth and sixteenth note rhythmic patterns correctly.

18 Proficient Mixed

TEACHING STRATEGY

Concert Etiquette

Have students:

1. Identify appropriate concert etiquette in a variety of settings (formal concerts, informal concerts, large concert halls, small concert halls, and so forth).
2. Attend a variety of live performances.
3. Discuss the appropriate and inappropriate concert behaviors observed.
4. Write a short analysis of appropriate concert etiquette for each setting.

18

EXTENSION

Improvise a Tune

Have students improvise a melody in based on the Mixolydian scale. Begin by mapping out a four-measure harmonic progression in which each measure features one harmony. Start the improvisation by singing the triad of each supporting harmony. When comfortable, move on to add other pitches. Strive to make the improvisation consistent by drawing on a small number of rhythmic patterns.

MORE ABOUT...

Creating an Assessment Rubric for "The Little Beggarman"

Have students:

- Discuss the characteristics of a desirable performance of this piece, using their knowledge of performance.
- Identify the criteria by which they think an adjudicator might assess the performance of the piece.
- For each criterion, decide what characteristics will comprise an "adequate", "good", "very good" and "excellent" performance.
- Create a rubric chart and reproduce it for each student.
- Use the rubric to assess quartets or double quartets performing all or part of "The Little Beggarman."

VOCAL DEVELOPMENT

Relaxation Techniques for Singers

Pulling together many singers whose minds and bodies are diverted to many different places is a real challenge for the choral music director! A common focus and clearing of tension from body and mind needs to occur before effective music making can take place. Use natural body movements and vivid imagery to develop a central focus.

Encourage your students to expore **music.glencoe.com**, the Web site for *Experiencing Choral Music*. You may wish to preview the rich content before directing your students online. Options available on the Web site include:

• Web Link Exercises

• Interactive Projects

• Audio Samples

"Skin-a-ma-rink a doo-dle with my

"Skin-a-ma-rink a doo-dle with my

holes in my shoes and my toes a-peek-in' through, Sing-ing "Skin-a-ma-rink a doo-dle with my

holes in my shoes and my toes a-peek-in' through, Sing-ing "Skin-a-ma-rink a doo-dle with my

old rig-a-doo." Now it's time for bed, for it's get-ting late at night.

old rig-a-doo." Now it's time for bed, for it's get-ting late at night.

old rig-a-doo." The

old rig-a-doo." The

Have students:
- Imagine waking up in the morning, stretching and yawning. Stretch in all different directions.
- Roll the shoulders forward and backward; lift the shoulders to the ears, pressing hard. Drop the shoulders back and down.
- Turn sideways in a line and massage the back of the person in front of you. Reverse and have your back massaged.
- Close eyes and imagine picking up a penny by the toes—feel only that sensation, concentrating on it intently. (Use any kind of imagery to focus the mind.)
- Bring singers back to reality with easy respiration and phonation exercises.

MORE ABOUT...

Careers in Music: Teaching

There are many career opportunities in the field of music teaching. High school and junior high music educators often specialize in one performance area such as choir, band or orchestra. They may also teach general music, music theory and music appreciation. An elementary music teacher enjoys working with young children. They teach singing, dancing, how to play instruments, listening, and much more. A college professor trains students to become professional musicians and teachers. Most music teaching positions require a college degree.

ENRICHMENT

Listening and Classifying

Prepare a listening activity for your choir using the Rehearsal/Performance CDs. Have students listen to the following recordings and then identify/classify them as folk songs or classical songs. Ask students to explain why they classified each listening example as they did.

1. "The Little Beggarman" (page 10—Irish folk song)
2. "Sicut Locutus Est" (page 60—classical—Bach)
3. "Sanctus" (page 86—classical—Mozart)
4. "Jabula Jesu" (page 180—Zulu folk song)
5. "Der Tanz" (page 94—classical—Schumann

CURRICULUM CONNECTIONS

Vocabulary

Have students research the words in "The Little Beggarman" that are unfamiliar to them, such as: three score (three times twenty, or sixty years); Liffey (a river in Eastern Ireland that runs through Dublin); Basin and Zoo (not clear, but could be reference to two well-known locations in Dublin); rigadoo (not clear, but a *rigadoon* is a lively dance or music of the seventeenth and eighteenth centuries); Currabawn (a *bawn* is a defended courtyard with walls surrounding the barn and house on a farm. This name or location is different in other versions of the song.); flaxey-haired (*flaxen* refers to a golden blonde color).

ENRICHMENT

Arranging Musical Melodies

Direct students to:

1. Select one phrase from this song that they know and enjoy singing.

2. Think of creative ways to perform this phrase differently, for example, by using different dynamics, altering the word stress, changing the articulation, and so forth.

3. Create an arrangement of the phrase by adding a descant, adding a simple accompaniment, re-voicing the phrase, adding instruments, writing a new text, changing the meter, and so forth.

4. Have students take turns performing their arrangements for the class.

ASSESSMENT

Evaluating the Quality of a Performance

Have students:

1. Watch a video or listen to an audio recording of this piece as performed by the choir.

2. Compare this performance to exemplary models such as other recordings or other live performances of the piece.

3. Develop constructive suggestions for improvement based on the comparison.

ENRICHMENT

Performing Solos

Solo performance is an important element of vocal development. Encourage students to perform solos whenever possible. When preparing to sing a solo, have students first identify all musical symbols and terms for dynamics, tempo and articulation found in the music. Have them make decisions about how they should interpret those markings. As students perform their solos for the class, evaluate their performance based on the following criteria:

• Did they sing with expression?

• Were all pitches and rhythms accurate?

• Was the solo memorized?

• Did they interpret in an appropriate manner the musical symbols and terms found in the music?

Below is a suggested list of solos that may be used for solo performances.

Treble Voices—Easy

"The Lamb" by Chanler

"The Lass for the Low Countree" by Niles

"Love Has Eyes" by Bishop

"Homeward Bound" arranged by Althouse

Tenor Base Voices—Easy

"All Through the Night" by Welsh

"You Gentlemen of England" written in the Time of Elizabeth

"Rio Grande" by Dougherty

"Swing Low, Sweet Chariot" by Burleigh

Additional National Standards

The following National Standards are addressed through the Assessment, Extension, Enrichment and bottom-page activities:

1. Singing, alone and with others, a varied repertoire of music. **(f)**

3. Improvising melodies, variations and accompaniments. **(b)**

5. Reading and notating music. **(a)**

7. Evaluating music and music performances. **(a, b)**

8. Understanding relationships between music, the other arts, and disciplines outside the arts. **(a, c)**

Physiology Of The Voice

Physiology is a branch of biology that deals with living organisms and their parts. It is interesting to see how the parts of the human body work together to produce vocal sound. Vocal production requires the following elements:

The Actuators

The actuators are parts of the body involved in the breathing process. The parts of the airway include (1) head airways (the nose and mouth), (2) pharynx (throat tube), (3) larynx (voice box), (4) trachea (windpipe), (5) bronchi (two branches of trachea that lead into the lungs), and (6) lungs. The muscles used in breathing include (1) the abdominals (belly muscles), (2) intercostals (muscles attached to the ribs), and (3) diaphragm (a horizontal, dome-shaped muscle separating the chest and abdominal cavities).

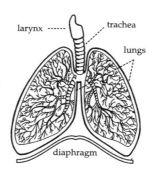

The Vibrators

The vocal folds (or "vocal cords") are housed in the larynx (the voice box) at the top of the trachea and vibrate when air from the lungs passes between them.

The Resonators

The sound waves produced by the vocal folds are enhanced and amplified by the resonators or natural cavities located in the pharynx, larynx, mouth, nasal passages and sinus passages.

The Articulators

The articulators are the parts of the body used in speech, namely the lips, teeth, tongue, jaw and soft palate. To find the soft palate, place the tip of your tongue on the roof of your mouth and slide it toward your throat just past the bony ridge of your hard palate.

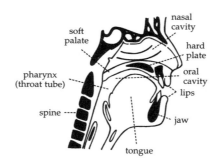

Spotlight *Physiology Of The Voice* **25**

RESOURCES

Teacher Resource Binder

Vocal Development 1–6, *Keep the Joy in Singing!*
Reference 16, *Expanding a Musical Vocabulary*
Reference 22, *Monitoring My Voice*

National Standards

1. Singing, alone and with others. **(b)**
8. Understanding relationship between music, the other arts, and disciplines outside the arts. **(a, b)**

PHYSIOLOGY OF THE VOICE

Objectives

• Define the relationship between the content of other subjects and those of music.
• Demonstrate knowledge and awareness of vocal physiology as important to musical vocal performance.

Suggested Teaching Sequence

Direct students to:

• Read the Spotlight On The Physiology Of The Voice on student page 25 and identify the four main elements of vocal production and the parts of the body used for speech.
• Listen and observe as teacher demonstrates various pitches on a stringed instrument—guitar, violin, and so forth.
• Comment on the correlation between string length, thickness as it affects pitch and tone color.
• Draw parallels between the human voice and musical instruments as it relates to pitch, timbre and tone color.
• Relate the information about physiology of the parts of the voice to what they have studied in science class.

Progress Checkpoints

Observe students' progress in:

✓ Their ability to identify the parts of the body used for speech and for singing.
✓ Knowing the importance of how the voice works in relationship to how they sing.

The Earth Adorned

OVERVIEW

Composer: Waldemar Ahlén (1894–1982), edited by Kenneth Jennings

Text: Waldemar Ahlén, translated by Carolyn and Kenneth Jennings

Voicing: SATB

Key: A major

Meter: 3/4

Form: Strophic

Style: Contemporary Swedish Anthem

Accompaniment: A cappella

Programming: Concert, Festival

Vocal Ranges:

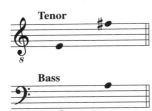

OBJECTIVES

After completing this lesson, students will be able to:

- Demonstrate good breath support while performing.
- Identify melodic and harmonic parts when performing music.
- Define *homophony* using standard terminology.

VOCABULARY

Have students review vocabulary in student lesson. Introduce terms found in the music. A complete glossary of terms is found on page 260 of the student book.

The Earth Adorned

Composer: Waldemar Ahlén (1894–1982), edited by Kenneth Jennings
Text: Waldemar Ahlén, translated by Carolyn and Kenneth Jennings
Voicing: SATB

VOCABULARY

hymn
homophony
strophic form
avocation
unison

Focus

- Demonstrate good breath support while singing phrases.
- Identify melodic and harmonic parts when performing music.
- Define *homophony* using standard terminology.

Getting Started

The earth adorned in verdant robe sends praises upward surging…

If you painted a landscape to visually portray these words, what would you include? How would you adorn the earth in summer greens that seem to reach for the sky? The musical setting of this graceful Swedish **hymn** (*a song of praise or adoration for God*) is also "adorned" in beauty. Although the Soprano line is the melody, the other voice parts surround and adorn the melody with resonant harmonic support. "The Earth Adorned" is an example of **homophony,** or *music in which melodic interest is concentrated in one voice part and may have subordinate accompaniment.* It is written in **strophic form,** *a form in which the melody repeats while the words change from verse to verse.*

◆ History and Culture

Besides untouched wilderness and a midnight sun that never sets in June or July, Sweden can also boast of a rich and impressive choral music tradition. Even today, with a population of nine million, Sweden has almost 700,000 citizens who sing weekly in a choir as an **avocation** (*not related to job or career*). The capital, Stockholm, is currently home to fifteen professional choruses and has a high school, the Stockholm Musikgymnasium, which specializes in choral singing. The Stockholm native, Waldemar Ahlén (1894–1982), an organist and composer of choral and organ works, wrote "The Earth Adorned," or "Sommarpsalm," as it is known in Sweden.

SPOTLIGHT

To learn more about posture and breath management, see page 7.

RESOURCES

Proficient Sight-Singing

Teacher Resource Binder

Links to Learning

◆ **Vocal**

Perform the following example in only one breath while demonstrating the rise and fall of the phrase. In order to sustain the "sss" sound throughout the phrase, you must take a good breath and use proper breath management.

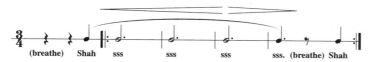

(breathe) Shah   sss   sss   sss   sss. (breathe) Shah

Perform the following example on an "ah" vowel. Shape the phrase by beginning softly, then gradually singing louder to the peak of the phrase, and finally tapering off to the end of the phrase. Repeat as desired, changing the dynamic levels and the vowels.

◆ **Artistic Expression**

The sound of homophonic music is one reason that singers are attracted to choral ensembles. Try this experiment. Have everyone in your choir sing the Soprano melody in a comfortable range. Listen carefully to the sound of the voices. Now sing the song as written. Compare the difference in sound between singing the melody in **unison** *(all parts singing the same notes at the same time)* and supporting the melody with harmony.

Evaluation

Demonstrate how well you have learned the skills and concepts featured in the lesson "The Earth Adorned" by completing the following:

• Perform measures 1–8 individually to demonstrate artistic shaping of the phrases and proper breath support. Evaluate how well you did.

• Identify your voice part as melody or accompaniment to the melody. How does your voice part add to the overall performance of the piece? Why are both important in choral ensemble singing?

RESOURCES

Proficient Mixed Rehearsal/Performance CD

CD **1:5** Voices

CD **1:6** Accompaniment Only

CD **3:3** Vocal Practice Track—Soprano

CD **4:3** Vocal Practice Track—Alto

CD **5:3** Vocal Practice Track—Tenor

CD **6:3** Vocal Practice Track—Bass

National Standards

1. Singing, alone and with others, a varied repertoire of music. **(a, b)**

5. Reading and notating music. **(a, b)**

6. Listening to, analyzing, and describing music. **(b)**

Vocal

The Vocal section is designed to prepare students to:

• Perform a four-measure phrase with good breath control.

• Properly shape a phrase with good intonation.

Have students:

• Take a deep breath on the first two beats of the first example.

• Shape the phrase as indicated by the dynamic markings.

• Sing the four-part choral example, shaping the phrase as indicated.

Artistic Expression

The Artistic Expression section is designed to prepare students to:

• Hear the difference between unison singing and homophonic sound.

• Sing both homophony and unison singing with good intonation.

Have students:

• All sing the Soprano melody in a comfortable range throughout the entire piece.

• Sing all parts as written after the piece has been learned.

• Compare the two styles: unison singing verses homophony.

LESSON PLAN

Suggested Teaching Sequence and Performance Tips

1. Introduce

Direct students to:

- Read and discuss the information found in the Getting Started section on page 26.
- Practice performing the breath control exercise as shown in the Vocal section on page 27.
- Practice singing in four-part harmony with good intonation and phrase shaping as also shown in the Vocal section on page 27.
- Speak the first verse in rhythm with proper syllabic stress.

Progress Checkpoints

Observe students' progress in:

- ✓ Their ability to sustain the breath throughout a four-measure phrase.
- ✓ Their ability to sing in four-part harmony with accuracy.

2. Rehearse

Direct students to:

- Numerically label each of the seven phrases with the terms "Phrase 1, Phrase 2, Phrase 3," etc. Use the breath marks in the score as a guide to locate phrase endings.
- Sight-sing the Soprano part on Phrases 1 and 2 using a neutral syllable. After secure, add the Alto part. Repeat until two parts are secure.
- Sight-sing Bass part on Phrases 1 and 2 using a neutral syllable. When parts are secure, add the Tenor part on a neutral syllable as the Basses continue to sing.

The Earth Adorned
(Psalm of Summer)

For SATB, a cappella

Edited by
KENNETH JENNINGS

WALDEMAR AHLÉN

* Stanza 2 may be sung as a soprano solo with the other voice parts humming.

28   Proficient Mixed

TEACHER 2 TEACHER

"The Earth Adorned" is structured like a hymn in that all of its verses are set to the same music. The composer has carefully marked each of the four measure phrases with dynamics. This piece will assist students in developing good breath control while singing a musical phrase. Clear communication of the text will also be key; therefore, careful attention must be given to syllabic stress.

- Add the text in all voices and perform Phrases 1 and 2.
- Repeat this same procedure for Phrases 3 and 4.
- When pitches are secure, sing Phrases 1 through 4.
- Repeat the above procedure for Phrases 5–7.

Progress Checkpoints

Observe students' progress in:

✓ Singing with good intonation in four parts.

✓ Singing with appropriate breath control throughout each phrase.

3. Refine

Direct students to:

- Discuss the dynamic markings that are indicated in each phrase.
- Sing the Soprano part through the entire piece with expression. Challenge the other sections to do the same and discuss strengths and weaknesses of each performance.

Progress Checkpoints

Observe students' progress in:

✓ Their ability to sing in four-part harmony, with occasional divisi.

✓ Their ability to sustain the breath over a four-bar phrase.

✓ Their ability to sing expressively, following all dynamic markings.

✓ Their ability to articulate the text with proper syllabic stress.

EXTENSION

Improvising Rhythmic Variations

The music indicates that verse two may be sung as a Soprano solo with the other voice parts humming the supporting harmony (accompaniment). Using the neutral syllable *noo*, have students improvise the rhythms of the Alto, Tenor and Bass parts. They may sing some note durations as written, or they may choose to subdivide and sing a half note as two quarter notes, or as four eighth notes, as long as they keep the pitches and the overall beat durations the same. In this way, each choir member may improvise his or her own part by subdividing and the entire choir will stay together rhythmically. Experiment with this technique, and discuss your opinions about the results.

ASSESSMENT

Informal Assessment

In this lesson, students showed the ability to:

- Sing all phrases with good breath control.
- Observe all dynamic markings and perform them with accuracy.
- Sing with proper shaping of phrases.

Student Self-Assessment

Have students evaluate their individual performances based on the following:

- Breath Management
- Phrasing
- Expressive Singing
- Intonation
- Correct Part-Singing

Have each student rate his/her performance of this song in the areas above on a scale of 1–5, 5 being the best.

Individual and Group Performance Evaluation

To further measure growth of musical skills presented in this lesson, direct students to complete the Evaluation section on page 27.

- Have students perform their part in measures 1–8. Have them evaluate their ability to shape phrases and sing with proper breath support. Ask students to record their evaluations and turn them in.
- Have students analyze the music score and identify which voice part has the melody. Have them make a list of the measures in which they sing the melody and the measures in which they sing the harmony. Then list why both are important.

TEACHING STRATEGY

Performing a Solo

To gain experience in performing a solo, direct students to learn the Soprano part to "The Earth Adorned." Have students identify the musical symbols and terms relating to tempo, dynamics and articulation found in the music. Then, have students take turns performing "The Earth Adorned" as a solo for the class. Assess how well the singers were able to interpret the musical symbols and terms for tempo, dynamics and articulation as they sang the solo.

SPOTLIGHT

Diction

Singing is a form of communication. To communicate well while singing, you must not only form your vowels correctly, but also say your consonants as clearly and cleanly as possible.

There are two kinds of consonants: voiced and unvoiced. Consonants that require the use of the voice along with the **articulators** (*lips, teeth, tongue, and other parts of the mouth and throat*) are called voiced consonants. If you place your hand on your throat, you can actually feel your voice box vibrate while producing them. Unvoiced consonant sounds are made with the articulators only.

In each pair below, the first word contains a voiced consonant while the second word contains an unvoiced consonant. Speak the following word pairs, then sing them on any pitch. When singing, make sure the voiced consonant is on the same pitch as the vowel.

Voiced:	Unvoiced Consonants:	More Voiced Consonants:
[b] bay	[p] pay	[l] lip
[d] den	[t] ten	[m] mice
[g] goat	[k] coat	[n] nice
[dʒ] jeer	[tʃ] cheer	[j] yell
[z] zero	[s] scenic	[r] red
[ʒ] fusion	[ʃ] shun	
[ð] there	[θ] therapy	More Unvoiced Consonants:
[v] vine	[f] fine	[h] have
[w] wince	[hw] whim	

The American "r" requires special treatment in classical choral singing. To sing an American "r" at the end of a syllable following a vowel, sing the vowel with your teeth apart and jaw open. In some formal sacred music and English texts, you may need to flip or roll the "r." For most other instances, sing the "r" on pitch, then open to the following vowel quickly.

Spotlight *Diction* **31**

RESOURCES

Teacher Resource Binder

Evaluation Master 6, *Diction Check-up*
Vocal Development 8, *Articulation*
Vocal Development 9, *Diction*
Reference 20, *Diction Guide*

National Standards

1. Singing, alone and with others, a varied repertoire of music. **(b)**

8. Understanding relationships between music, the other arts, and disciplines outside the arts. **(b)**

DICTION

Objectives

- Demonstrate basic performance techniques using proper diction.

Suggested Teaching Sequence

Direct students to:

- Read the Spotlight On Diction on student page 31 and identify the importance of diction in singing.
- Define articulators.
- Describe the difference between voiced and unvoiced consonants.
- Speak the voiced and unvoiced consonants out loud and find examples in music.
- Compare the concept of proper diction to effective performance practices.
- Discuss on the proper use of the "r" consonant when singing.

Progress Checkpoints

Observe students' progress in:

✓ Their ability to speak voiced and unvoiced consonants properly.

✓ Their ability to name the parts of the body that are the articulators.

✓ Their ability to recognize voiced and unvoiced consonants in other music they are studying.

✓ Their ability to relate the importance of proper diction in other areas such as drama, speech and public speaking.

God's Gonna Set This World On Fire

OVERVIEW

Arranger: Traditional Spiritual, arranged by Moses Hogan (1957–2003) and Edwin B. Hogan

Text: Traditional Spiritual

Voicing: SATB

Key: G major

Meter: 4/4

Form: Strophic

Accompaniment: A cappella

Programming: Multicultural, Concert, Contest, Festival, Appropriate for large or small ensemble

Vocal Ranges:

Soprano

Alto

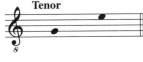
Tenor

Bass

OBJECTIVES

After completing this lesson, students will be able to:

• Perform expressively from notation a varied repertoire of music including the African American spiritual.

• Identify and define concepts of chord structure using standard terminology.

VOCABULARY

Have students review vocabulary in student lesson. Introduce terms found in the music. A complete glossary of terms is found on page 260 of the student book.

God's Gonna Set This World On Fire

Composer: Traditional Spiritual, arranged by Moses Hogan (1957–2003) and Edwin B. Hogan

Text: Traditional Spiritual

Voicing: SATB

VOCABULARY

spiritual

chord

tonic chord

dominant chord

subdominant chord

Focus

• Perform music representing the African American spiritual.

• Identify and perform tonic, dominant and subdominant chords.

Getting Started

If you wanted to hear a deeply emotional and inspirational performance of "God's Gonna Set This World On Fire," you might listen to:

Marian Anderson—concert singer (1897–1993)
Harry Thacken Burleigh—composer and singer (1866–1949)
Mahalia Jackson—gospel singer (1911–1972)
Paul Robeson—singer, actor, political activist (1898–1976)

These four talented African American artists were renowned for their interpretations of spirituals.

As part of the African American tradition, a **spiritual** is *a song that was first sung by slaves and is often based on a biblical theme or story.* Spirituals were probably sung while the slaves were working in the fields, engaging in social activities or participating in worship.

 SPOTLIGHT

To learn more about arranging, see page 145.

◆ History and Culture

Moses Hogan (1957–2003) was born in New Orleans, Louisiana. Primarily a pianist, he became well known throughout the world for his choral arrangements of African American spirituals, which were recorded and often premiered by his ensembles, the Moses Hogan Chorale and the Moses Hogan Singers. Featuring syncopated rhythms, gospel-style harmonies, and call-and-response patterns, Mr. Hogan brought a new and fresh perspective to this historic genre of music.

RESOURCES

Proficient Sight-Singing

Sight-Singing in G Major, pages 71–73

Reading Rhythms in 4/4 Meter, pages 2–6

Reading Dotted Notes and Sixteenth Notes, pages 51, 63–64, 76

Teacher Resource Binder

Teaching Master 6, *Head Start on a Career*

Evaluation Master 9, *Evaluating Rhythmic Accuracy*

Skill Builder 1, *Building Harmony*

Skill Builder 2, *Chord Challenge in Major*

Vocal Development 12, *Intonation and Choral Blend*

For additional resources, see TRB Table of Contents.

Links to Learning

◆ Vocal

Arranger Moses Hogan has used **chords** *(the combination of three or more notes played or sung at the same time)* to create the harmony in this spiritual. The three principal chords of the scale—the **tonic chord** *(a chord built on the home tone of a scale)*, the **dominant chord** *(a chord built on the fifth note of a scale)*, and the **subdominant chord** *(a chord built on the fourth note of a scale)*—are used extensively in this spiritual. In major keys, these three chords are often designated by Roman numerals (tonic—I, dominant—V, subdominant—IV). Sing the following example and listen to the sound of each chord.

◆ Theory

Each verse begins with the same rhythmic pattern (a dotted quarter note followed by two sixteenth notes), but then varies because the words are different in each verse. Clap, tap or chant the following rhythmic patterns. Match the rhythmic pattern with the appropriate verse.

Evaluation

Demonstrate how well you have learned the skills and concepts featured in the lesson "God's Gonna Set This World On Fire" by completing the following:

• Sing the first two measures of each verse demonstrating the correct rhythm for each. Evaluate how well you were able to sing the correct rhythms.

• Make three flash cards that represent the tonic, dominant and subdominant chords. In a small group, sing measures 17–24 and hold up the correct flash card when you sing each chord. How well were you able to identify the three chords?

Lesson 4 God's Gonna Set This World On Fire **33**

RESOURCES

Proficient Mixed Rehearsal/Performance CD

CD **1:7** Voices

CD **1:8** Accompaniment Only

CD **3:4** Vocal Practice Track—Soprano

CD **4:4** Vocal Practice Track—Alto

CD **5:4** Vocal Practice Track—Tenor

CD **6:4** Vocal Practice Track—Bass

National Standards

1. Singing, alone and with others, a varied repertoire of music. **(a, b, c)**

6. Listening to, analyzing, and describing music. **(a, c)**

9. Understanding music in relation to history and culture. **(b)**

LINKS TO LEARNING

Vocal

The Vocal section is designed to prepare students to:

• Understand chords and the three principal chords of the scale: tonic, dominant, subdominant.

• Perform these chords in tune and locate them in the music.

Have students:

• Read the definitions of chords, tonic chord, dominant chord and subdominant chord.

• Sing the four-part choral example listening to the sounds of each chord.

• Locate this chord pattern in the music.

Theory

The Theory section is designed to prepare students to read and perform the various rhythmic patterns found in this piece.

Have students:

• Tap or clap the quarter note pulse.

• Chant or clap the rhythm examples, while tapping the quarter note pulse.

• Locate these rhythm patterns in the music.

LESSON PLAN

Suggested Teaching Sequence and Performance Tips

1. Introduce

Direct students to:

- Read and discuss the information found in the Getting Started section on student page 32.
- Practice singing the tonic, dominant and subdominant chords as found in the Vocal section on page 33.
- Practice chanting the rhythm patterns as found in the Theory section on page 33.

Progress Checkpoints

Observe students' progress in:

✓ Their ability to understand and perform tonic, dominant and subdominant chords in tune.

✓ Their ability to perform rhythmic patterns found in this piece with accuracy.

God's Gonna Set This World On Fire

For SATB, a cappella

Arranged by MOSES HOGAN
and EDWIN B. HOGAN

Traditional Spiritual

Traditional Spiritual

34   Proficient Mixed

TEACHER 2 TEACHER

Strophic form is a common form that every student should be able to identify. Many hymns and folk songs are written in strophic form. The origins of the spiritual are somewhat controversial but may have been influenced by the structure of the hymn since many are composed in strophic form.

2. Rehearse

Direct students to:

• Chant measures 1–8 in rhythm using accents where written.

• Sing measures 1–8 in rhythm with all parts together at first, and then, rehearsing each part individually to secure accurate pitches.

• Sing all stanzas with correct rhythms using accents where written.

• Sing all stanzas with correct pitches and unified vowels.

• Sing all stanzas in correct style.

Progress Checkpoints

Observe students' progress in:

✓ Singing correct rhythms and pitches.

✓ Singing with the correct usage of accents.

✓ Singing with proper pronunciation and unified vowels.

✓ Singing in the correct style.

CULTURAL CONNECTIONS

Spirituals

Spirituals are songs first sung by African American slaves. Considered to be one of the first American musical forms, these songs of sorrow and songs of hope were important tools for motivating and sustaining African Americans during the slavery experience. Many of these songs were composed in the fields during labor, which means that movement often coincided with the rhythms and expressions of these pieces. The texts of spirituals often carry multiple meanings, depicting religious desires for heavenly peace, as well as physical desires for freedom and equality.

3. Refine

Direct students to:

- Review all dynamic markings in the piece and observe them.
- Bring out the "yes yes yes" phrase in the Bass part each time it occurs.
- Practice the *sforzando-piano* in measure 31, holding the fermata at *piano* until the director guides them to the next beat.
- Watch for the *rallentando* in measure 31, last beat followed by a fermata. Watch closely as the director guides them to the last accented whole note.
- Be careful not to oversing throughout. The sound should be rich and full, not overbearing and forced.

Progress Checkpoints

Observe students' progress in:

✓ Singing with expression observing all dynamic markings and accent marks.

✓ Bringing out the Bass part where indicated.

✓ Watching the director in the final two bars and observing all tempo changes.

✓ Creating a full, rich sound that it not pushed.

MORE ABOUT...

Arranger Moses Hogan (1957–2003)

Moses George Hogan, born in New Orleans, Louisiana, on March 13, 1957, earned an international reputation as one of America's most gifted African-American pianists and arrangers. The American Choral Directors Association, Gramophone Magazine and choral directors of churches and schools praised his contemporary choral settings of spirituals and other works across America. Audiences have been moved to respond with standing ovations upon hearing these unique and sensitive arrangements. He died of cancer at the age of forty-six in 2003.

ASSESSMENT

Informal Assessment

In this lesson, students showed the ability to:

- Understand and perform a tonic, dominant and subdominant chords in the key of G major.
- Perform rhythms accurately in 4/4 meter.
- Sing a cappella in tune and stylistically correct.
- Create a full, rich sound without over-singing.

Student Self-Assessment

Have students evaluate their individual performances based on the following:

- Posture
- Tall Vowels
- Expressive Singing
- Intonation
- Correct Part-Singing

Have each student rate his/her performance of this song in the areas above on a scale of 1–5, 5 being the best.

MORE ABOUT...

Pronunciation in Spirituals

Since the early African American slaves did not speak English, they were approximating the English language as they spoke. The "th" sound did not exist in their language, therefore the "th" became "d." The word "the" was spoken as "duh" and "these" was spoken as "dese." They were not familiar with the "ing" sound, and therefore the "g" sound was dropped as in "mumblin' word." We perform spirituals this way to preserve that cultural heritage.

Individual and Group Performance Evaluation

To further measure growth of musical skills presented in this lesson, direct students to complete the Evaluation section on page 33.

- Have each student sing the first two measures of each verse on their own voice part. Evaluate their ability to sing the correct rhythms.
- After students have made flashcards that represent the tonic, dominant and subdominant chords, have them sing measures 17–24 and hold up the correct flash card when they sing each chord. How many students held up the correct cards and the correct time?

EXTENSION

Have students write out the I (tonic), IV (subdominant) and V (dominant) chord progressions in every major key. Collect them and play selected student samples on the keyboard. Have the students listen carefully and determine if the sample is correct.

Additional National Standards

The following National Standards are addressed through the Assessment, Extension, Enrichment and bottom page activities:

5. Reading and notating music. **(a)**

6. Listening to, analyzing, and describing music. **(a)**

7. Evaluating music and music performances. **(b)**

SPOTLIGHT

Gospel Music

Gospel music is *religious music that originated in the African American churches of the South.* Characteristics of gospel music include improvisation, syncopation and repetition. Following the Civil War, African American churches began to emerge. The spirituals sung by the early slaves served as their main source of sacred music. By the early 1900s, some sectors of the church moved to more spirited songs accompanied by tambourines, drums and piano. These were the earliest versions of gospel music.

African American gospel music gained national recognition during the 1940s and the 1950s with the recordings and live concerts by the singing great Mahalia Jackson. Also influential was Thomas Andrew Dorsey (1899–1993). He published over 400 gospel songs and is known as the father of gospel music. His gospel music used lively rhythms and syncopated piano accompaniments. "Precious Lord, Take My Hand" is probably his most famous song.

When asked about the correct way to sing gospel music, contemporary composer Rollo Dilworth shared these thoughts. He said that singers often debate about the appropriate use of chest voice and head voice registers when performing gospel style. While some believe that excessive use of the chest voice might cause vocal damage, others believe that singing in the African American idiom is not "authentic" if performed in head voice. Dilworth suggests that successful singing in most any genre requires a balanced, healthy singing tone in both head and chest registers.

Vocal techniques used in gospel singing include (1) percussive singing (a style that lies between legato and staccato styles); (2) swell (an exaggerated crescendo that adds weight and breadth to an accented syllable); and (3) pitch bending (or the scooping up to a pitch, often coupled with a swell or a "falling off" of a pitch). The rhythm is felt in an accurate yet relaxed style. Basic movements may include stepping, clapping and rocking. Improvisation of melody is frequently heard in gospel music.

Listen to a recording of other gospel music and identify characteristics of gospel-style singing.

RESOURCES

Teacher Resource Binder

Reference 2, *Listening Guide*
Reference 16, *Expanding a Musical Vocabulary*
Reference 37, *Quiz Master: Rubric Construction Form*

National Standards

1. Singing, alone and with others, a varied repertoire of music. **(a, b, c)**
7. Evaluating music and music performances. **(a, b)**

GOSPEL MUSIC

Objective

- Classify aurally-presented music representing diverse styles.

Suggested Teaching Sequence

Direct students to:

- Read the Spotlight On Gospel Music on student page 39 and list the characteristics.
- Make a list of familiar gospel songs or artists/composers. If possible, play an example of Thomas Dorsey's "Precious Lord, Take My Hand."
- List and demonstrate the vocal techniques used in gospel singing.
- Demonstrate movements often seen in performances of gospel music.
- Listen to the recording of "Holy, Holy, Holy" on student page 160 and identify the characteristics of gospel-style singing that is heard.
- Share with the class any experience they may have had with gospel music, such a performing, attending a concert, and so forth.
- Listen to exemplary recordings of gospel groups and determine what makes them exemplary examples.

Progress Checkpoints

Observe students' progress in:

✓ Their ability to define and classify gospel music.
✓ Their ability to list the characteristics of gospel music.
✓ Their ability to list and demonstrate the vocal techniques used in gospel singing.

39

Cantate Domino

OVERVIEW

Composer: Hans Leo Hassler (1564–1612), edited and arranged by John Leavitt

Text: from Psalm 96

Voicing: SATB

Key: C major

Meter: 2/2, 3/4

Form: ABB'CC'D

Accompaniment: A cappella

Programming: Contest, Festival, Concert, Sacred

Vocal Ranges:

OBJECTIVES

After completing this lesson, students will be able to:

• Identify homophony and polyphony when listening to and performing music.

• Perform expressively from notation a varied repertoire of music representing styles from diverse periods including the late Renaissance.

VOCABULARY

Have students review vocabulary in student lesson. Introduce terms found in the music. A complete glossary of terms is found on page 260 of the student book.

Cantate Domino

Composer: Hans Leo Hassler (1564–1612), edited and arranged by John Leavitt
Text: from Psalm 96
Voicing: SATB

VOCABULARY

polyphony

homophony

High Renaissance

melisma

Focus

• Describe and perform *homophony* and *polyphony*.

• Identify and sing a melisma.

• Classify and perform music representing the late Renaissance period.

Getting Started

"Cantate Domino" has much in common with "Adoramus Te," the first song in this book found on page 2. Both songs are motets with Latin texts that are sung a cappella. How are they different? Which piece has a major tonality? Which piece has a minor tonality? Which piece has more than one time signature?

Both works are wonderful examples of well-written Renaissance sacred music. They also highlight the late Renaissance trend of moving away from **polyphony** *(music that consists of two or more independent melodies that combine to create simultaneous voice parts with different rhythms)* to **homophony** *(music in which melodic interest is concentrated in one voice part and may have a subordinate accompaniment)*. Some church leaders of the time felt that congregations could not understand the words in complex polyphonic music, so they encouraged composers to write in a more straightforward style with all voices singing the same words at the same time.

SPOTLIGHT

To learn more about melismas, see page 258.

◆ History and Culture

Hans Leo Hassler (1564–1612) was born in Nürnberg, Germany. His father, Isaac, was an organist and his first music teacher. He left Germany in 1584 to study with the great Venetian composer Andrea Gabrieli. Hassler, an accomplished master of polyphony, composed during the **High Renaissance**, considered *the latter part of the Renaissance (c. 1430–1600).*

RESOURCES

Proficient Sight-Singing

Sight-Singing in C Major, pages 13, 26, 34–35

Reading Rhythms in 2/2 Meter, page 147

Reading Rhythms in 3/4 Meter, page 14

Teacher Resource Binder

Teaching Master 7, *Pronunciation Guide for "Cantate Domino"*

Teaching Master 8, *Compositional Contrasts*

Evaluation Master 8, *Evaluating Musical Expression*

Evaluation Master 15, *Diction Check-up*

Skill Builder 8, *Composing in Mixed Meter*

For additional resources, see TRB Table of Contents.

Links to Learning

◆ Vocal

A **melisma** is *a group of notes sung on one syllable of text.* Composers sometimes used melismas to give a word or syllable emphasis. In "Cantate Domino," all voice parts sing a melisma on the word *cantate,* or "sing." Use proper breath support to connect the notes in a smooth and flowing style when you sing the following melismas.

◆ Theory

When changing meter in "Cantate Domino," the eighth note subdivision should remain steady and constant from the $\frac{2}{2}$ to the $\frac{3}{4}$ sections. Clap, tap or chant the following example while maintaining a steady eighth note pulse.

◆ Artistic Expression

If you are not familiar with Latin, memorize the English translation of the text. When performing, keep in mind the translation so that you can communicate the meaning of "Cantate Domino" to your audience.

Evaluation

Demonstrate how well you have learned the skills and concepts featured in the lesson "Cantate Domino" by completing the following:

- Identify the following sections in "Cantate Domino" as either homophonic or polyphonic: (1) measures 1–4, (2) measures 8–13, (3) measures 14–23, (4) measures 24–31. What indicators did you use to arrive at your answers? How well did you do?

- In an SATB quartet, sing measures 8–13 using a smooth and legato style. Evaluate how well you are able to sing a melisma in a smooth, legato style while making each note clearly understood.

Lesson 5 *Cantate Domino* **41**

RESOURCES

Proficient Mixed Rehearsal/Performance CD

CD 1:9 Voices
CD 1:10 Accompaniment Only
CD 3:5 Vocal Practice Track—Soprano
CD 4:5 Vocal Practice Track—Alto
CD 5:5 Vocal Practice Track—Tenor
CD 6:5 Vocal Practice Track—Bass

National Standards

1. Singing, alone and with others, a varied repertoire of music. **(a, b, c)**
6. Listening to, analyzing, and describing music. **(b)**
9. Understanding music in relation to history and culture. **(a)**

LINKS TO LEARNING

Vocal

The Vocal section is designed to prepare students to:
- Understand a *melisma*.
- Sing a melisma with proper breath support.

Have students:
- Read the definition of melisma.
- Sing the vocal example concentrating on good breath support and a smooth, flowing line.

Theory

The Theory section is designed to prepare students to sing the change of meter seamlessly.

Have students:
- Tap or clap the eighth note pulse.
- Speak the rhythm example moving from 2/2 meter to 3/4 meter keeping the eighth note pulse constant.

Artistic Expression

The Artistic Expression section is designed to prepare students to sing the Latin text with knowledge of the English translation.

Have students:
- Read the Latin text throughout the piece.
- Listen as you translate the words. See bottom box on page 43.

LESSON PLAN

Suggested Teaching Sequence and Performance Tips

1. Introduce

Direct students to:

• Read and discuss the information found in the Getting Started section on student page 40.

• Practice the melismatic passage in the vocal section on page 41.

• Practice moving from 2/2 meter to 3/4 meter seamlessly by keeping the eighth note constant as in the Theory example on page 41.

• Speak the Latin text. A pronunciation guide can be found in the Teacher Resource Binder, Teaching Master 7.

• Practice saying Latin text in rhythm.

Progress Checkpoints

Observe students' progress in:

✓ Singing a melisma in a smooth and flowing style.

✓ Moving from 2/2 meter to 3/4 meter seamlessly by keeping the eighth notes constant.

✓ Correctly pronouncing the Latin text.

Cantate Domino

For SATB, a cappella

Edited and Arranged by
JOHN LEAVITT

Words from Psalm 96
Music by HANS LEO HASSLER (1564–1612)

42   Proficient Mixed

TEACHER 2 TEACHER

The Renaissance era produced choral music that was truly conducive for the voice. This period saw the development of syllabic along with a melismatic style writing to convey or enhance the meaning of text.

2. Rehearsal

Direct students to:

- Sight-sing measures 1–8 in Latin, rehearsing parts individually as necessary. Move on when this section is secure.
- Sing the melismatic section, measures 8–13 on *doo*, giving every eighth and sixteenth note a syllable for now. When comfortable, sing on *doo* with all the notes in a slur on one syllable and then move to the Latin text. Rehearse parts individually as necessary.
- Sight-sing measures 14–23 in Latin, rehearsing parts individually as necessary. Move on when this section is secure.
- Practice singing measures 8–18 in Latin and in rhythm keeping an even eighth note subdivision from the 2/2 to 3/4 sections.
- Sight-sing measures 23–37 in Latin, rehearsing parts individually as necessary. Move on when this section is secure.

MORE ABOUT...

Cantate Domino Translation

The English translation of "Cantate Domino" is as follows:

Sing to the Lord a new song and praise his name, for He has done marvelous things. Make music to the Lord with the harp and the sound of singing.

–Psalm 96

- Practice singing measures 19–31 keeping an even eighth note subdivision from the 3/4 to 2/2 sections.
- Sight-sing measures 38–end in Latin, rehearsing parts individually as necessary. Move on when this section is secure.
- Sing entire song in Latin, rhythmically correct and in tune.

Progress Checkpoints

Observe students' progress in:

✓ Their ability to sight-sing their parts independently and with the ensemble.

✓ Their ability to sing melismas with accuracy and proper breath support.

✓ Their ability to properly pronounce the Latin text with tall, pure vowels.

44   Proficient Mixed

MORE ABOUT...

Composer Hans Leo Hassler

Hans Leo Hassler (1564–1612) was born in Nürnberg, Germany. He is considered a transitional composer in the sense that he also is an early Baroque composer. He studied with Andrea Gabrieli in Venice, and was an accomplished master of the Venetian polychoral (multichoral) style as well as polyphony.

3. Refine

Direct students to:

- Locate and identify syllabic and melismatic sections.
- Define and discuss characteristics of the Renaissance period.
- Use accurate diction, unified vowel sounds and proper syllabic stresses.
- Listen to a recording of a reputable Renaissance group and challenge students to imitate that sound and style.
- Sing through entire piece, focusing on stylistic qualities, dynamic fluctuations, seamless meter changes, pure Latin vowels and smooth, flowing, accurate melismas.

Progress Checkpoints

Observe students' progress in:

- ✓ Their ability to locate and identify syllabic and melismatic sections.
- ✓ Their ability to define and discuss the Renaissance era.
- ✓ Their ability to sing the entire work in Latin, with correct rhythms and accurate pitches yet stylistically correct.

MUSIC LITERACY

When Does Polyphonic Texture Work?

To help students expand their music literacy, have them:

- Identify several familiar melodies and sing them as rounds, raising a hand when the melodies stop sounding good.
- Identify several familiar melodies that they know will work as rounds, for example, "Frère Jacques" and "Row, Row, Row Your Boat."
- Discuss the reason some melodies work better than others as rounds.
  (They are based on one chord, or a repeating chord sequence, that allows the harmony to remain consonant.)

ASSESSMENT

Informal Assessment

In this lesson, students showed the ability to:

- Sing melismatic passages with proper breath support and a smooth flowing line.
- Move through a meter change seamlessly by keeping the eighth note constant.
- Sing the Latin text correctly with tall, pure vowels and proper syllabic stress.
- Sing a Renaissance motet stylistically correct.

Student Self-Assessment

Have students evaluate their individual performances based on the following:

- Breath Management
- Latin Text
- Tall Vowels
- Accurate Pitches
- Accurate Rhythms

Have each student rate his/her performance of this song in the areas above on a scale of 1–5, 5 being the best.

TEACHING STRATEGY

Extra Help – Tuning Chords

To help students listen to one another, have one student in each section choose a pitch and hold it out until everyone in the section is singing the same pitch, using a neutral syllable such as "oo" or "ah." Point to one student from one of the sections. That student changes the section's pitch, and everyone must listen and move to that pitch. Continue to point to individual students in each of the four vocal sections, waiting each time until the group has tuned to the new pitch. The chords will be very interesting, sometimes dissonant, which requires even more careful listening. Encourage soft singing, and very careful listening within and between sections.

To further measure growth of musical skills presented in this lesson, direct students to complete the Evaluation section on page 41.

- After all students have identified the sections indicated as either homophonic or polyphonic, ask for volunteers to share their answers and explain how they arrived at those answers. The other students should evaluate how they did based on the discussion.

- Have students divide into SATB quartets with one on a part. Have the quartets sing measures 8–13 for the rest of the class. Assist them in evaluating how well they sang melismas in a smooth and legato style. Offer suggestion for improvement if necessary.

EXTENSION

Other Settings of "Cantate Domino"

Have students look at other settings of this text to see how other composers treated this text, for example: Giuseppe Pitoni (1657–1743)—late Baroque; Claudio Monteverdi (1567–1643)—Renaissance; Daniel Pinkham (b. 1923)—Contemporary; and so forth.

Additional National Standards

The following National Standards are addressed through the Assessment, Extension, Enrichment and bottom-page activities:

1. Singing alone and with others, a varied repertoire of music. **(f)**

7. Evaluating music and music performances. **(a, b)**

Erev Shel Shoshanim

OVERVIEW

Composer: Josef Hadar, arranged by Jack Klebanow

Text: "Song of Songs," additional text by Moshe Dor

Voicing: SATB

Key: C minor

Meter: 4/4

Form: AABB Coda

Style: Contemporary Israeli Anthem

Accompaniment: Piano

Programming: Multicultural, Concert

Vocal Ranges:

OBJECTIVES

After completing this lesson, students will be able to:

• Demonstrate basic performance techniques, including staggered breathing while performing.

• Define the relationships between the processes of the other fine arts, such as visual art and those of music.

VOCABULARY

Have students review vocabulary in student lesson. Introduce terms found in the music. A complete glossary of terms is found on page 260 of the student book.

Erev Shel Shoshanim

Composer: Josef Hadar, arranged by Jack Klebanow

Text: "Song of Songs," additional text by Moshe Dor

Voicing: SATB

VOCABULARY

folk song

natural minor scale

staggered breathing

phrase

Focus

• Demonstrate ensemble performance techniques (staggered breathing).

• Define the relationship between the process of imagery as used in visual art and music.

• Sing music representing the Israeli culture.

Getting Started

Sometimes composed songs become so popular in a national culture that they take on the familiarity of a **folk song** *(a song that has been passed down by word of mouth from generation to generation).* Can you pick the composed songs out of the following list?

> "Home On The Range"
> "Let There Be Peace On Earth"
> "This Land Is Your Land"
> "Shenandoah"

"Erev Shel Shoshanim" was originally composed in 1956 but is so popular that it is often mistaken for an Israeli folk song. The beautiful and sensitive melody captures the essence of the poetry it serves and evokes strong feelings of nostalgia and love for the land of Israel.

◆ History and Culture

The words of "Erev Shel Shoshanim" are largely taken from the "Song of Songs" found in the Old Testament of the Bible. The following translation is literal but is not meant to be sung. It allows the original poetry to shine through.

Verse: *Evening of roses, let us go out to the grove*
Myrrh, fragrant spices and incense are a threshold for your feet.

Chorus: *Night falls slowly and the wind of roses is blowing*
Let me whisper you a song, secretly a song of love.

Verse: *Dawn, a dove is cooing, your head is filled with dew*
Your mouth is a rose unto the morning; I will pick it for myself.

🔲 SKILL BUILDERS

To learn more about the key of C minor, see Proficient Sight-Singing, page 122.

RESOURCES

Proficient Sight-Singing

Sight-Singing in C Minor, pages 122–123

Reading Rhythms in 4/4 Meter, pages 2–6

Reading Dotted Eighth and Sixteenth Note Combinations, pages 76–77

Teacher Resource Binder

Teaching Master 9, *Pronunciation Guide for "Erev Shel Shoshanim"*

Teaching Master 10, *The Colors in "Erev Shel Shoshanim"*

Evaluation Master 15, *Diction Check-up*

Skill Builder 15, *Major and Minor Scales*

Skill Builder 17, *Minor Scales: An Overview*

For additional resources, see TRB Table of Contents.

Links to Learning

◆ Vocal

This arrangement of "Erev Shel Shoshanim" is in the key of C minor and is based on the C natural minor scale. A **natural minor scale** is *a scale that has* la *as its keynote, or home tone.*

Sing the C minor scale.

C natural minor scale

C	D	E♭	F	G	A♭	B♭	C
la	ti	do	re	mi	fa	sol	la

Staggered breathing is *a technique that creates the overall effect of continuous singing by having each singer take a breath at different times.* Using staggered breathing, read and perform the following example with a classmate. Plan your breathing to create a continuous **phrase**, or *a musical idea with a beginning and an end.*

◆ Artistic Expression

Using the translation of "Erev Shel Shoshanim," create a visual image with pencils, crayons or markers. Choose shapes and colors that represent the long, sustained tones in the music.

Evaluation

Demonstrate how well you have learned the skills and concepts featured in the lesson "Erev Shel Shoshanim" by completing the following:

- As a small group, perform measures 1–25. Have the rest of the choir listen and decide if they can hear the proper use of staggered breathing. Were they able to hear continuous singing with no audible breaks for breathing? Switch roles.

- Share your artwork of "Erev Shel Shoshanim" with the choir and explain how it interprets the musical imagery.

Lesson 6 *Erev Shel Shoshanim* **49**

RESOURCES

Proficient Mixed Rehearsal/Performance CD

CD 1:11 Voices

CD 1:12 Accompaniment Only

CD 3:6 Vocal Practice Track—Soprano

CD 4:6 Vocal Practice Track—Alto

CD 5:6 Vocal Practice Track—Tenor

CD 6:6 Vocal Practice Track—Bass

National Standards

1. Singing, alone and with others, a varied repertoire of music. **(a, b, c)**

8. Understanding relationships between music, the other arts, and disciplines outside the arts. **(c)**

9. Understanding music in relation to history and culture. **(a)**

- Perform expressively from notation a varied repertoire of music representing styles from diverse cultures, including Israeli.

LINKS TO LEARNING

Vocal

The Vocal section is designed to prepare students to:

- Understand and perform a natural minor scale.
- Understand and perform with staggered breathing.

Have students:

- Read the definition of a natural minor scale.
- Sing the C natural minor scale first on note names and then on solfège syllables.
- Read the definition of staggered breathing.
- Perform the example using staggered breathing to create a long, flowing phrase without audible breaks.

Artistic Expression

The Artistic Expression section is designed to prepare students to relate to the meaning of the text and the images it portrays.

Have students:

- Read the English translation in the Getting Started section on page 48.
- Create a visual image on paper with pencils, crayons or markers that represent the meaning of the text and the long, sustained tones in the music.

LESSON PLAN

Suggested Teaching Sequence and Performance Tips

1. Introduce

Direct students to:

- Read and discuss the information found in the Getting Started section on student page 48. *(composed songs are "Let There Be Peace On Earth" and "This Land Is Your Land")*

- Practice the C natural minor scale in the Vocal section on page 49 to establish the key of this piece.

- Practice the technique of staggered breathing with the Vocal example on page 49.

- Review the English translation of the Hebrew text at the bottom of page 48.

- Listen to the recording of "Erev Shel Shoshanim" and create a visual image that represents the meaning of the text and the long sustained tones in the music.

Progress Checkpoints

Observe students' progress in:

✓ Familiarizing themselves with the C natural minor scale.

✓ Understanding and using the concept of staggered breathing.

✓ Understanding and feeling the meaning of the text.

Erev Shel Shoshanim

For SATB and Piano

Arranged by
JACK KLEBANOW

Words by MOSHE DOR based on Song Of Songs
Music by JOSEF HADAR

50 Proficient Mixed

TEACHER 2 TEACHER

Aural and visual recognition of musical phrases contribute to the concept that individual notes in tonal music are not isolated sound units but are integral parts of a larger whole (phrases and melody). The ability to recognize what notes "belong to each other" contributes to the learning efficiency and the understanding of the musical sense of the work. This wonderful Israeli anthem will allow students to recognize the necessity to create smooth continuous phrases with proper shape and beauty.

2. Rehearse

Direct students to:

- Sight-sing measures 6–13 on "loo" using the technique of staggered breathing to create two flowing phrases. Note the breath mark before measure 10. Rehearse parts as necessary until all notes are correct.

- Locate different phrases in measures 6–14 that make up the melody.

- Learn the Hebrew text for verse 1. A pronunciation guide can be found in the Teacher Resource Binder, Teaching Master 9. Speak first, then speak in rhythm, then sing.

- Learn the Hebrew text for verse 2. Speak first, then speak in rhythm, then sing.

- Sight-sing measures 18–25/26 on "loo." Rehearse parts as necessary until all notes are correct.

- Determine which part is singing the melody in what measures.

Encourage your students to expore **music.glencoe.com**, the Web site for *Experiencing Choral Music.* You may wish to preview the rich content before directing your students online. Options available on the Web site include:

- Web Link Exercises
- Interactive Projects
- Audio Samples

- Learn the Hebrew text for the chorus, measures 18–25/26. Speak first, then speak in rhythm, then sing.
- Sight-sing measures 27–end on *loo*. Rehearse parts as necessary until all notes are correct.
- Review the Hebrew text as this section is the Coda and is a repeat of all text sung before. Speak first, then speak in rhythm, then sing.

Progress Checkpoints

Observe students' progress in:

✓ Recognizing where the melody is at all times.

✓ Singing accurate rhythms and pitches.

✓ Singing long flowing phrases using the technique of staggered breathing.

✓ Pronouncing the Hebrew text with accuracy.

TEACHING STRATEGY

Solo and Small Ensemble Performances

Have students:

1. Prepare solos and small ensembles for performance or competition.
2. Interpret music symbols and terms referring to dynamics, tempo and articulation during the performance.
3. Critique and analyze the quality of the performance using standard terminology.

va — Ha - va el-chash lach shir ba - lat

va — Ha - va el-chash lach shir ba - lat

va — Ah —

va Sho - shan nosh-va Ah —

Ah — a - ha - va. a - ha - va.

Ze - mer shel a - ha - va. va.

Ah —

Ah — Ze - mer

3. Refine

Direct students to:

- Review the dynamic markings and tempo indications throughout the piece. Even though the voices are not marked with a dynamic level at the beginning, we can assume they begin at a *piano*, move to a *mezzo-forte* at the Chorus section at measure 18 and varies during the Coda section, measures 27–end. Note the tempo variation in measure 37 and 43.

- Sing the entire piece observing all dynamic markings and tempo indications, concentrating on creating long phrases using staggered breathing.

- Refine the Hebrew text using tall vowels and reviewing the syllabic stress intended.

- Create an expressive interpretation of this piece recalling the English translation and the visual imagery created in the Artistic Expressions section.

Progress Checkpoints

Observe students' progress in:

✓ Creating smooth long phrases using staggered breathing.

✓ Creating audible differences in dynamic levels between and within sections of the piece.

✓ Singing the Hebrew text with proper vowels and syllabic stresses.

✓ Singing with appropriate expression for the style of the piece.

TEACHING STRATEGY

Staggered Breathing

"Erev Shel Shoshanim" calls for the use of staggered breathing. Have students:

- Practice holding out chord tones, each person breathing at a different time than either neighbor, and then joining back in without any accent.

- Continue to hold the chord indefinitely, each section changing their pitch as indicated by the teacher, but sustaining the tone through staggered breathing. (Note: By changing tones one at a time, you can help students become accustomed to sustaining dissonant relationships between parts, then resolving them.)

ASSESSMENT

Informal Assessment

In this lesson, students showed the ability to:

- Sing the entire work in tune with the correct rhythms and Hebrew pronunciation.
- Identify and locate the different phrases within the melody and supporting parts.
- Sing long flowing phrases using the technique of staggered breathing.
- Create an expressive interpretation of the piece based on their knowledge of the English translation and style of the piece.

VOCAL DEVELOPMENT

Have students:

- Sing with tall vowels in Hebrew.
- Lift the tone on melodic leaps by increasing the space in the mouth and pharynx.
- Energize sustained tones by increasing the breath support and dynamic level.
- Sustain phrases by staggering the breathing through the phrases.
- Increase intensity on repeated notes to feel forward movement of the melodic lines.
- Feel the contour of musical phrases.
- Note when the voices move from parts to unison singing to adjust the dynamic attack.

Student Self-Assessment

Have students evaluate their individual performances based on the following:

- Breath Management
- Phrasing
- Hebrew Language
- Tall Vowels
- Expressive Singing

Have each student rate his/her performance of this song in the areas above on a scale of 1–5, 5 being the best.

TEACHING STRATEGY

Performance Techniques for Large-Ensembles

Have students:

- Identify appropriate performance techniques to be used with " (phrasing, articulation, intonation, diction, tempo, dynamic contrast, interpretation, tone, blend, balance, and so forth).
- Explain/describe these performance techniques in relationship to this song.
- Perform this piece from memory at a formal concert.
- Critique the performance techniques observed at the formal concert.

Individual and Group Performance Evaluation

To further demonstrate musical growth, direct students to complete the Evaluation section on page 49.

- Have small groups of students perform measures 1–25 to demonstrate the proper use of staggered breathing for the rest of the class. Ask the class, "Were you able to hear continuous singing with no audible break for breathing?"

- Have each student share their artwork as created in the Artistic Expression assignment with the rest of the class. Ask them to explain how it interprets the musical imagery of this piece. Display their artwork when you perform this piece in a concert.

ENRICHMENT

Composing Music in Asymmetric Meter

After students can successfully read the rhythms of this song in simple meter, challenge them to create a complex rhythmic pattern in asymmetric meter such as 5/8 and 7/8. Explain that asymmetric meter is a meter in which the strong beats create combinations of groups of two and three. See *Proficient Sight Singing* pages 166–167 for additional information on asymmetric meter.

Additional National Standards

The following National Standards are addressed through the Assessment, Extension, Enrichment and bottom-page activities:

7. Evaluating music and music performances. **(b)**

SPOTLIGHT

Vowels

The style of a given piece of music dictates how we should pronounce the words. If we are singing a more formal, classical piece, then we need to form taller vowels as in very proper English. If we are singing in a jazz or pop style, then we should pronounce the words in a more relaxed, conversational way. To get the feeling of taller vowels for classical singing, do the following:

- Let your jaw gently drop down and back as if it were on a hinge.
- Place your hands on your cheeks beside the corners of your mouth.
- Sigh on an *ah* [ɑ] vowel sound, but do not spread the corners of your mouth.
- Now sigh on other vowel sounds—*eh* [ɛ], *ee* [i], *oh* [o] and *oo* [u]—keeping the back of the tongue relaxed.
- As your voice goes from higher notes to lower notes, think of gently opening a tiny umbrella inside your mouth.

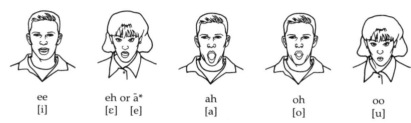

ee [i]   eh or ā* [ɛ] [e]   ah [a]   oh [o]   oo [u]

Other vowel sounds used in singing are diphthongs. A **diphthong** is *a combination of two vowel sounds.* For example, the vowel *ay* consists of two sounds: *eh* [E] and *ee* [i]. To sing a diphthong correctly, stay on the first vowel sound for the entire length of the note, only lightly adding the second vowel sound as you move to another note or lift off the note.

I = *ah*_____(ee) [ɑi]

boy = *oh*_____(ee) [oi]

down = *ah*_____(oo) [ɑu]

*Note: This is an Italian "ā," which is one sound, and not an American "ā," which is a diphthong, or two sounds.

Spotlight *Vowels* **57**

RESOURCES

Teacher Resource Binder

Vocal Development 10, *Diphthongs*
Vocal Development 15, *Vowels*
Reference 29, *IPA Vowels*

National Standards

1. Singing, alone and with others. **(b)**

VOWELS

Objectives

- Demonstrate basic performance techniques through proper use of vowels.

Suggested Teaching Sequence

Direct students to:

- Read the Spotlight On Vowels on student page 57 and identify the importance of uniform vowels in singing.
- Practice the exercise as presented on page 57.
- Identify the five basic vowels. Practice speaking and singing each.
- Define diphthong and demonstrate the proper and improper way to sing a diphthong.
- Find examples of each of the five basic vowels and diphthongs in music they are currently studying.
- Compare the concept of uniform vowels to appropriate large- and small-ensemble performance techniques.

Progress Checkpoints

Observe students' progress in:

✓ Their ability to speak the five basic vowels properly and uniformly.
✓ Their ability to define diphthong, find examples in the music and sing them properly.
✓ Their ability to relate the importance of uniform vowels in ensemble singing.

57

Sicut Locutus Est

OVERVIEW

Composer: Johann Sebastian
Bach (1685–1750), edited by
John Leavitt
Text: Liturgical Latin
Voicing: SSATB
Key: D major
Meter: Cut Time
Form: AB
Style: German Baroque Fugue
Accompaniment: Piano
Programming: Concert,
Contest, Festival

Vocal Ranges:

OBJECTIVES

After completing this lesson,
students will be able to:

• Compare and contrast music
forms including a fugue.

• Define texture of music
listened to and performed
using standard terminology.

• Perform a varied repertoire
of music representing genres
from diverse periods,
including Baroque.

VOCABULARY

Have students review
vocabulary in student lesson.
Introduce terms found in the
music. A complete glossary
of terms is found on page
260 of the student book.

Sicut Locutus Est

Composer: Johann Sebastian Bach (1685–1750), edited by John Leavitt
Text: Liturgical Latin
Voicing: SSATB

VOCABULARY

fugue
counterpoint
Baroque period
subject
answer

Focus

• Identify, describe and perform a fugue.

• Listen to and describe music of the Baroque period.

• Perform music representing the Baroque period.

Getting Started

Can you complete this musical analogy?

A yellow cupcake is to a wedding cake as a round/canon is to a _____.

The answer is **fugue,** *a polyphonic composition consisting of a series of successive melody imitations.* If you think of the difference between a plainly frosted cupcake and a highly decorated, multi-layered wedding cake, you will see how a simple round could be transformed into a complex, multi-voiced fugue. A fugue, which has a specific set of compositional rules, is an example of how the polyphony of Renaissance music (c. 1430–1600) evolved into the **counterpoint** *(the combination of two or more melodic lines)* during the **Baroque period** *(1600–1750).* "Sicut Locutus Est" is a fugal chorus from the *Magnificat* (canticle of Mary), by the great Baroque composer Johann Sebastian Bach (1685–1750). After you learn this festive chorus, think of how it must have sounded in a gilded, ornate, European Baroque church. That performance could have been a wedding cake for your eyes as well as your ears.

MUSIC & **HISTORY**

To learn more about the Baroque period, see page 108.

◆ History and Culture

Although his musical genius is undisputed, Bach was first and foremost a commercial composer. There was a practical reason for almost everything he wrote. He was primarily a church musician and composed for Sunday and feast-day services. Born in Eisenach, Germany, Bach spent much of his life in Leipzig. The *Magnificat,* one of his few works with a Latin text, was first performed on Christmas Day in 1723 at the Church of St. Nicholas in Leipzig.

RESOURCES

Proficient Sight-Singing

Sight-Singing in D Major,
  pages 104–106
Reading Rhythms in Cut Time,
  page 147
Reading Eighth Notes, pages 23–24

Teacher Resource Binder

Teaching Master 11, *Pronunciation
  Guide for "Sicut Locutus Est"*
Evaluation Master 15, *Diction Check-up*
Music and History 5, *Characteristics of
  Baroque Music: 1600–1750*
Music and History 8, *Johann Sebastian
  Bach, a Baroque Composer*
Music and History 9, *Fine Art Teaching
  Strategy—Baroque*

Links to Learning

◆ **Vocal**

The first melody in a fugue is called the **subject.** The **answer** is *the subject of a fugue that appears later in the fugue, usually starting on a different pitch or having a different tonal center.* Using solfège syllables, read and perform the following examples from "Sicut Locutus Est." Discuss the similarities and differences between the subject and the answer.

◆ **Theory**

Fugues are both challenging and appealing to singers because all voice parts share the responsibility for presenting the melody. All voice parts must cleanly sing the large skips found in the melodic patterns. Perform the following examples that contain skips.

Evaluation

Demonstrate how well you have learned the skills and concepts featured in the lesson "Sicut Locutus Est" by completing the following:

- Locate all statements of the subject and the answer in your voice part of "Sicut Locutus Est." Share your findings with a classmate. How well did you do?
- Find another setting of the Magnificat (by title, score or recording) and describe how it is similar to or different from the Magnificat by J.S. Bach.

RESOURCES

Proficient Mixed Rehearsal/Performance CD

CD 1:13 Voices

CD 1:14 Accompaniment Only

CD 3:7 Vocal Practice Track—Soprano I

CD 3:8 Vocal Practice Track—Soprano II

CD 4:7 Vocal Practice Track—Alto

CD 5:7 Vocal Practice Track—Tenor

CD 6:7 Vocal Practice Track—Bass

National Standards

1. Singing, alone and with others, a varied repertoire of music. **(a, b, c, d, e)**
6. Listening to analyzing, and describing music **(a, c)**
9. Understanding music in relation to history and culture. **(a, d)**

LINKS TO LEARNING

Vocal

The Vocal section is designed to prepare students to:

- Understand the subject and answer of a fugue.
- Perform the subject and answer of the fugues in this piece and locate them in the choral score.

Have students:

- Read the definition of subject and answer of a fugue.
- Sing the Subject example on solfège syllables.
- Sing the Answer example on solfège syllables.
- Located these two examples in their choral scores and count how many times each occurs.

Theory

The Theory section is designed to prepare students to sing the large leaps required to sing this fugue.

Have students:

- Sing the example slowly at first, concentrating on tuning each pitch and being accurate on each interval leap.
- Gradually increase the tempo as the leaps begin to feel more comfortable and are accurate.
- Locate and mark these leaps in their vocal parts in their choral scores to prepare for these large intervals when sight-singing the piece.

LESSON PLAN

Suggested Teaching Sequence and Performance Tips

1. Introduce

Direct students to:

- Read and discuss the information found in the Getting Started section on student page 58.
- Practice singing the primary subject and answer as found in the Vocal section on page 59.
- Locate and mark in their scores with a bracket and an "S" wherever the primary subject occurs and with a bracket and an "A" wherever the primary answer occurs.
- Practice the large interval skips as found in the Theory section on page 59. Locate and mark those skips in their choral scores to prepare for sight-singing them.

Progress Checkpoints

Observe students' progress in:

✓ Their ability to comprehend the subject and answer of a fugue and locate them in their scores.

✓ Their ability to sing the large leaps with tonal accuracy and mark them in their vocal parts.

Sicut Locutus Est

from Magnificat, BWV 243

For SSATB and Piano

Edited by JOHN LEAVITT

JOHANN SEBASTIAN BACH
(1685–1750)

60   Proficient Mixed

TEACHER 2 TEACHER

The fugue was a common form of composition during the Baroque era. Understanding the sections of the fugue helps the efficiency of the learning rate as well as providing the student the opportunity to sing music that is contrapuntal. "Sicut Locutus Est" is a wonderful opportunity for students to study the fugue and for each vocal part to sing the melody and to shine.

2. Rehearse

Direct students to:

- Locate and all sight-sing the subject on "doo." *(measures 1–9 in Bass, measures 9–17 in Alto, again partially in measures 33–37 in Bass)* Sing one syllable per note for now. Concentrate on tuning the large leaps learned in the Theory section. Start slowly at first and increase tempo as notes and rhythms become more secure.

- Locate and all sight-sing the answer on "doo." *(measures 5–13 in Tenor, measures 13–21 in Soprano II, measures 21–29 in Soprano I)* Sing one syllable per note for now. Concentrate on tuning the large leaps learned in the Theory section. Start slowly at first and increase tempo as notes and rhythms become more secure.

- Return to the beginning and each voice part sings as written, still on the neutral syllable "doo," one syllable per note, slowly at first and increasing the tempo gradually. Stop singing after their subject or answer measures are complete. Do not sing the connecting material for now, but follow along.

Encourage your students to expore **music.glencoe.com**, the Web site for *Experiencing Choral Music*. You may wish to preview the rich content before directing your students online. Options available on the Web site include:

- Web Link Exercises
- Interactive Projects
- Audio Samples

- Sing again from the beginning once the subject and answer measures are secure. Now sight-sing the connecting material on "doo." Rehearse individual parts as necessary until rhythms and pitches are secure.
- Learn the Latin text. A pronunciation guide can be found in the Teacher Resource Binder, Teaching Master 9. First speak the text, then speak the text in rhythm, then sing.
- Sing from the beginning to measure 37 on the Latin text.
- Sight-sing from measures 37–end on "doo" or the Latin text if comfortable. Note the Latin text in this section is repeated from what has already been learned. Rehearse parts individually as necessary to secure all notes and rhythms.

62   Proficient Mixed

CONNECTING THE ARTS

Musical Theater Fugue

Have students listen to the fugue in the musical *Guys and Dolls* ("Fugue For Tinhorns") and discuss what they heard. What similarities does it have to "Sicut Locutus Est"? Play the beginning of "Fugue For Tinhorns" and identify the subject. How many measures does it last? Once they are familiar with it, sing it as a group.

Progress Checkpoints

Observe students' progress in:

✓ Their ability to locate and sing the subject in tune on a neutral syllable with correct rhythms.

✓ Their ability to locate and sing the answer in tune on a neutral syllable with correct rhythms.

✓ Their ability to pronounce the Latin text correctly.

✓ Their ability to sing the entire work in Latin.

MORE ABOUT...

Composer Johann Sebastian Bach

Bach created masterpieces of choral and instrumental music. Bach wrote both sacred and secular music. Bach's music is regarded as the high point of the Baroque era, which lasted from 1600 to 1750. Bach married twice and was the father of 20 children. Several of his children became well-known composers. Johann Sebastian Bach died July 28, 1750.

3. Refine

Direct students to:

- Locate all dynamic markings throughout the piece. Note they are in parenthesis as these are editor's suggested dynamics, not the composer's.
- Sing through the piece observing all dynamic marking as suggested by the editor.
- Review the tall pure vowels and syllabic stresses of the Latin text.
- Sing through the piece concentrating on using tall pure vowels and proper syllabic stresses.
- Listen to a reputable, professional Baroque ensemble perform this piece to be familiar with the vocal style and energy needed to perform this piece. Emulate that style when performing.

Progress Checkpoints

Observe students' progress in:

- ✓ Their ability to sing with correct Latin pronunciation, with tall pure vowels and proper syllabic stress.
- ✓ Their ability to observe and perform all suggested dynamic markings.
- ✓ Their ability to sing this piece in a Baroque style.

TEACHING STRATEGY

Singing High Pitches in Tune

Have students:

- Reach high pitches by vocalizing gradually up to the pitch.
- Always use the *awh* vowel sound on high pitches. Add the resonance of the *oo* vowel on the high pitches for tone quality and to sing in tune.
- Zero in on the precise pitch after phonating above it on an *awh* or *oo* sound. Feel the sensation of the vocal tract when reaching the exact pitch.
- Modify the vowel sound of the word to be sung to achieve the best tone quality and intonation.
- Use full breath support to sing the tops of the high pitches.
- When singing descending lines, think or gesture with upward motions.

Informal Assessment

In this lesson, the students showed the ability to:

- Sing melodies from a fugue (subjects).
- Sight-sing in the key of D major.
- Perform a Latin text.

CONNECTING THE ARTS

Processes in the Arts

Have students:

1. Find examples of artwork or art forms from the Baroque period, describing how they exhibit the characteristics of the period. (Choose from visual art, architecture, dance, drama, poetry or literature.)

2. Discuss how the processes used in the other areas are the same and different from music, taking into consideration the roles of artists, performers and audience.

3. Find other examples from the same art category, but from a different style, period or culture.

4. Discuss similarities and differences between the examples.

Have students evaluate their individual performances based on the following:

- Phrasing
- Diction
- Foreign Language
- Tall Vowels
- Correct Part-Singing

Have each student rate his/her performance of this song in the areas above on a scale of 1–5, 5 being the best.

66   Proficient Mixed

ASSESSMENT
Creating an Assessment Rubric

Have students:

1. Discuss the characteristics of a desirable performance of this piece, using all their knowledge of performance techniques.
2. Identify the criteria by which they think an adjudicator might assess the performance of this piece.
3. For each criterion, decide what characteristics will comprise an adequate, good, very good and excellent performance.
4. Create a rubric chart.
5. Use the rubric to assess quartets or small ensembles performing all or part of this song.

Individual and Group Performance Evaluation

To further measure growth of musical skills presented in this lesson, direct students to complete the Evaluation section on page 59.

- After locating all statements of the subject and answer from one vocal part in "Sicut Locutus Est," compare the answers with a friend from the same section. Review the findings by asking, "Did both students agree or disagree? Were all examples found?"

- After finding a score or recording of another *Magnificat*, evaluate the differences by asking, "What is the same between these two pieces? What is different? Do both have musical merit and why or why not?"

MORE ABOUT...

Editor John Leavitt

John Leavitt is a Kansas native, born and raised in Leavenworth, Kansas. He completed doctoral work in choral conducting at the University of Missouri-Kansas City Conservatory of Music. At Wichita State University he pursued a Master of Music degree in Piano Performance with significant study in composition. He served on the faculty at Friends University where he won the faculty award for teaching excellence in 1989. Leavitt now devotes himself full-time to composing and conducting. He is the artistic director and conductor of a professionally trained vocal ensemble known as The Master Arts Chorale and an associated children's choir, The Master Arts Youth Chorale.

EXTENSION

The Art of Expression

The *Magnificat* has been an attractive text for classical composers to set to music because of its short length and joyful nature. The *Magnificat* by Johann Sebastian Bach is one of the most popular of all settings. Listen to a recording of Bach's *Magnificat*. What is heard before and after "Sicut locutus est"? Read the entire text of the *Magnificat* to become familiar with the complete message. How might this background information improve your overall performance?

Additional National Standards

The following National Standards are addressed through the Assessment, Extension, Enrichment and bottom-page activities:

5. Reading and notating music. **(a, b)**

8. Understanding relationships between music, the other arts, and disciplines outside the arts. **(a)**

SPOTLIGHT

Physiology Of Singing

Physiology is a branch of biology that deals with living organisms and their parts. It is interesting to see how the parts of the human body affect our singing. Familiarize yourself with "Physiology of the Voice" on page 25 before studying this page.

Vocal Pitch, Range and Timbre

- Pitch is related to the length of the vocal folds. The longer and more stretched the folds are, the higher the pitch; the shorter and more relaxed, the lower the pitch.

- Range is related to the length and thickness of the vocal folds. Longer, thinner folds vibrate more easily at higher pitches; shorter, thicker folds vibrate more easily at lower pitches.

- Timbre or "tone color" of the voice is related to the size of the larynx, the relative thickness of the vocal folds, and resonance factors (see below). A large larynx with thicker vocal folds produces a deeper, richer sound; a small larynx with thinner vocal folds produces a lighter, simpler sound.

Resonance

- Resonance is related to the size, shape and texture; of the surface of the resonators and how we utilize them.

- Some resonators are fixed in size, shape and texture; for example, the sinus and nasal cavities (except when you have a cold!).

- Others such as the oral, pharyngeal and laryngeal cavities change depending on how we utilize the articulators in shaping the vowels and defining the consonants.

Projection

- Projection is related to many factors. Some of these factors include (1) the amount of air pressure used at the onset of the tone and throughout the phrase, (2) the utilization of the resonators, (3) the amount of tension in the body, (4) the health of the vocal mechanism, (5) the physical and emotional energy level of the singer, and (6) the acoustics of the room.

Spotlight *Physiology Of Singing*   **69**

RESOURCES

Teacher Resource Binder

Vocal Development 11, *Flexibility and Range*
Vocal Development 14, *Resonance*
Reference 16, *Expanding a Musical Vocabulary*

National Standards

1. Singing, alone and with others. **(b)**
8. Understanding the relationships between music, the other arts, and disciplines outside the arts. **(b)**

PHYSIOLOGY OF SINGING

Objectives
- Sing individually.
- Define the relationship between the content of other subjects and those of music.

Suggested Teaching Sequence
Direct students to:
- Read the Spotlight On The Physiology Of Singing on student page 69 and identify *pitch, range* and *timbre*. Discuss the relationship between the vocal folds and pitch.
- Discuss the difference between fixed resonators and changeable resonators. Identify parts of the body for each.
- Identify five factors that have an effect on projection of the voice.
- Sing or speak into a microphone to record their voices. Play the recording and identify the person speaking or singing based on the timbre of the voice.
- Relate this information to what they have studied in science class.

Progress Checkpoints
Observe students' progress in:
- ✓ Their ability to identify the parts of the body used for speech and for singing.
- ✓ Their ability to identify the elements of the human body that affect pitch, range and timbre in the voice.
- ✓ Their ability to understand the importance of knowing how the voice works in becoming a better singer.

Ya Viene la Vieja
OVERVIEW

Composer: Nineteenth-Century Andalusian Carol, arranged by Audrey Snyder

Text: Nineteenth-Century Andalusian Carol, arranged by Audrey Snyder

Voicing: SATB

Meter: 6/8

Form: ABABAB coda

Style: Romantic Andalusian Carol

Accompaniment: Piano

Programming: Multicultural, School assembly, Seasonal or Winter Concert

Vocal Ranges:

OBJECTIVES

After completing this lesson, students will be able to:

- Perform a varied repertoire of music representing styles from diverse cultures.
- Create music within specified guidelines.
- Relate music to society.

VOCABULARY

Have students review vocabulary in student lesson. Introduce terms found in the music. A complete glossary of terms is found on page 260 of the student book.

Ya Viene la Vieja

Composer: Nineteenth-Century Andalusian Carol, arranged by Audrey Snyder
Text: Nineteenth-Century Andalusian Carol, English Text by Audrey Snyder
Voicing: SATB

VOCABULARY
carol
villancico
compound meter
ostinato

Focus
- Perform music representing Spanish culture.
- Read and write rhythmic patterns in compound meter.

🎲 **SKILL BUILDERS**

To learn more about $\frac{6}{8}$ *meter, see* Proficient Sight-Singing, *pages 114 and 117.*

Getting Started

Can you match each carol with the correct country?

a. "Joy To The World"   1. Austria
b. "O Christmas Tree"   2. England
c. "Still, Still, Still"   3. Spain
d. "Ya Viena la Vieja"   4. Germany

The Andalusian carol "Ya Viena la Vieja" is from the southern region of Spain. As you learn this song, look for ways in which the melody and rhythms create a Spanish dance-like feel.

◆ History and Culture

A **carol** is *a song of English origin dating back to the Middle Ages with subject matter pertaining to the Virgin Mary or Christmas.* Christmas carols are usually strophic in nature with a recurring refrain between verses. Similar songs exist in other cultures—*noël* in France, *Weinachtlied* in Germany and *villancico* in Spain—although today all of these Christmas songs are referred to as carols.

Villancico is *a type of Spanish music consisting of several verses and a refrain usually dealing with Christmas.* "La Viene La Vieja" is a quick, dancelike villancico from the southernmost Spanish province of Andalusia. The text describes the Feast of the Three Kings that takes place on January 6. In this whimsical folk song, the first presenter is not a king but an old woman!

RESOURCES

Proficient Sight-Singing

Reading in D Major, pages 104–106
Reading in 6/8 Meter, page 113–114

Teacher Resource Binder

Teaching Master 12, *Pronunciation Guide for "Ya Viene la Vieja"*

Teaching Master 13, *Creating Rhythmic Ostinatos*

Evaluation Master 9, *Evaluating Rhythmic Accuracy*

Evaluation Master 15, *Diction Check-up*

For additional resources, see TRB Table of Contents.

Links to Learning

◆ **Theory**

$\frac{6}{8}$ meter is an example of **compound meter,** or *any meter in which the dotted quarter note receives the beat and the division of the beat is based on three eighth notes.* Perform the following examples by clapping the upper notes in a circular motion, one circle per beat, and stepping the lower notes to the beat. Begin at a slow tempo.

◆ **Artistic Expression**

To add authenticity and interest to the performance of this piece, add simple **ostinato** *(a rhythmic or melodic passage that is repeated continuously)* patterns on hand percussion instruments. Here is an example:

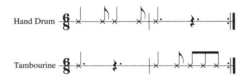

Evaluation

Demonstrate how well you have learned the skills and concepts featured in the lesson "Ya Viene la Vieja" by completing the following:

- With a partner, take turns clapping the rhythm of the music in measures 24–36. Evaluate each other's performance based on precision and accurate rhythm in $\frac{6}{8}$ meter.

- Write a short ostinato in $\frac{6}{8}$ meter. Use the examples in the Artistic Expression above as a guide. How well were you able to write notation in $\frac{6}{8}$ meter correctly? Perform your ostinato on a percussion instrument while the class sings "Ya Viene la Vieja."

Lesson 8 Ya Viene la Vieja **71**

RESOURCES

Proficient Mixed Rehearsal/Performance CD

CD 1:15 Voices
CD 1:16 Accompaniment Only
CD 3:9 Vocal Practice Track—Soprano
CD 4:8 Vocal Practice Track—Alto
CD 5:8 Vocal Practice Track—Tenor
CD 6:8 Vocal Practice Track—Bass

National Standards

1. Singing, alone and with others, a varied repertoire of music. **(a)**
4. Composing and arranging music within specific guidelines. **(a)**
9. Understanding music in relation to history and culture. **(a, d)**

LINKS TO LEARNING

Theory

The Theory section is designed to prepare students to:

- Read, write and perform various rhythms in compound meter including eighths, quarters and dotted quarters.
- Experience the difference between the basic beat, or pulse, and the dance-like flow of 6/8 rhythms.

Have students:

- Step to the beat as they walk around the room.
- Clap the rhythm in a circular clapping motion, one circle per beat.
- Combine the stepping motion with the clapping motion to experience doing two patterns simultaneously with the upper and lower parts of the body.

Artistic Expression

The Artistic Expression section is designed to prepare students to play an ostinato pattern on a hand percussion instrument.

Have students:

- Clap and chant the rhythm of each ostinato pattern.
- Add a hand percussion instrument.
- Perform the ostinato pattern with instrument as the choir sings.

LESSON PLAN

Suggested Teaching Sequence and Performance Tips

1. Introduce

Direct students to:

- Read and discuss the information found in the Getting Started section on the student page. *[Answers: a. "Joy To The World" is from England (2); b."O Christmas Tree" is from Germany (4); c. "Still, Still, Still" is from Austria (1); d. "Ya Viene la Vieja" is from Spain (3).]*

- After listening to a recording of "Ya Viene la Vieja," discuss the character of the music.

- Read and clap the rhythmic patterns in the Theory section on page 71.

- Experience the dotted quarter as the basic pulse.

Progress Checkpoints

Observe students' progress in:

✓ Reading and clapping rhythmic patterns in 6/8 meter.

✓ Their ability to step the quarter note pulse while clapping the rhythm.

Ya Viene la Vieja

For SATB and Piano

English Text by
AUDREY SNYDER

Nineteenth-Century Andalusian Carol

* Like a pitched drum, pronounced somewhere between "Toon" and "Doon." Go to the n.

72   Proficient Mixed

TEACHER2TEACHER

This arrangement is strong and musically solid, yet it retains the simple beauty of the original folk song. The tessitura falls well within the midrange of each singer. It is mainly diatonic and rhythmically uncomplicated yet full of vitality. Students will enjoy learning this sweet, unassuming expression of Christmas joy.

2. Rehearse

Direct students to:

- Analyze the musical score and identify measures that contain rhythms similar to those found in the Theory section on page 71. (*Answers: example 1—measures 17, 19, 32, 34, 47, 49; example 2—measures 28–29, 44–45; example 3—measures 9–16, 24–31, 39–46*)

- Use a metronome to help maintain a steady beat while performing the examples in the Theory section. Gradually increase the tempo. As the tempo increases, the stepping of the beat should become lighter and buoyant.

- Perform example 1 as six light, quick steps that must be quite small.

- Perform example 2 with a skip on the first beat followed by three light, running steps on the second beat.

- Perform example 3 as a skip followed by a limp followed by another limp.

Progress Checkpoints

Observe students' progress in:

- ✓ Their ability to maintain a positive response to moving.
- ✓ Clapping, stepping and skipping expressively and accurately.
- ✓ Their ability to move in a free and uninhibited manner.

MORE ABOUT...

Characteristics of Spanish Music

There is not a singular list of characteristics that represents all Spanish music, since Spanish music encompasses many styles and genres, historical periods, and different cultural groups. There are some characteristics that are found frequently in Spanish music, and are found in "Ya Viene la Vieja." These include 6/8 meter, the shifting of accents, a strong rhythmic pulse, a dance-like melody, harmony written in thirds or triads, and descending sequences of melodic thirds. Guitar-like accompaniments are a common characteristic, also. In addition, of course, is the use of the Spanish language. Although many of these characteristics are found in other types of music, the combination is frequently found in Spanish folk music.

3. Refine

Direct students to:

- Sing one verse at a time (verse 1 is measures 9–21; verse 2 is measures 24–36; verse 3 is measures 39–53).
- Step the underlying dotted quarter note pulse while singing the three verses.
- Reverse tasks by stepping the rhythm of the words while singing the three verses.
- Divide into two groups within each section. Have half of the section step the beat while the other half steps the rhythm simultaneously.
- Form two circles in the room, one within the other. The outer circle will step the rhythm while the inner circle will step the beat.

Progress Checkpoints

Observe students' progress in:

✓ Their ability to demonstrate spatial relations—the quarter note step should be twice as big as the eighth note step, while the dotted quarter step should be even longer.

✓ Their ability to maintain focus and stay on their part while other parts are doing something different.

✓ Their ability to express the mood of the music while stepping the pulse or the rhythm of the song.

74   Proficient Mixed

COMMUNITY CONNECTIONS

Spanish Music in Your School Community

Have students:

- Search for performance of Spanish music within your community.
- Explore recordings of Spanish music available in the record store.
- Make plans to attend a live performance of Spanish music.
- Invite a Spanish music performer, composer, or other artist from the community to come to the class and discuss Spanish music with them.

ASSESSMENT

Informal Assessment

In this lesson, students showed the ability to:

- Maintain a steady and eurhythmic beat.
- Move to the rhythm of their part while others were moving to a different part.
- Read, perform and identify the rhythms found in the Theory section on page 71.

Student Self-Assessment

Have students evaluate their individual performances based on the following:

- Precise Diction
- Expressive Movement
- Accurate Rhythms
- Intonation
- Phrasing

Have each student rate his/her performance of this song in the areas above on a scale of 1–5, 5 being the best.

MORE ABOUT...

Careers in Music: The Job of the Translator

When a piece of music is translated from another language into English, there are several considerations for the translator. A word-for-word translation seems like it would be best, but there are several issues that suggest otherwise. The translated text should match the meaning of the piece. This is not always accomplished through a word-for-word translation because word order syntax is often different in any two languages. Next, the syllabic stress of languages is different. In order to make a translation fit the notation, the translator must have freedom to select the best combination of words to fit the rhythm and stresses. A good translation is often difficult to achieve.

Individual and Group Performance Evaluation

To further measure growth of musical skills presented in this lesson, direct students to complete the Evaluation section on page 71.

- With a partner, have students clap the rhythms of measures 24–36. Ask them to evaluate each other's performance, and identify the rhythms that were performed incorrectly. Repeat the process until students can perform the rhythms correctly.

- Have students write a short ostinato pattern in 6/8 meter. Ask them to check their work for rhythmic accuracy. Ask students to answer these questions: Are there six beats in every measure? Are you able to perform the ostinato on a percussion instrument? After students are able to perform their patterns correctly, have them individually perform their ostinato while the class sings "Ya Viene la Vieja." Ask students to evaluate how well they were able to perform their ostinato while the class was singing.

76   Proficient Mixed

CURRICULUM CONNECTIONS

Mime and Creative Dance

Have students:

- Discuss possibilities for movement interpretation to go with "Ya Viene la Vieja" considering both mime and creative dance.
- Discuss the advantages and disadvantages of each for this piece.
- In two groups, create two different movement settings for the piece.
- Share, revise and refine each, and then prepare them to be performed.
- Compare the creative process in dance (choreography and performance) to music (composition and performance), citing similarities and differences in the creative, preparation and performance process.

EXTENSION

Improvising Movement

Direct students to:

- Listen to a recording of the choir singing "Ya Viene la Vieja."
- As they hear the music, improvise movements that interpret the meaning of the words.
- Discuss how movement can enhance a performance of a song.
- Discuss how movement helps a singer better understand the text.

Additional National Standards

The following National Standards are addressed through the Assessment, Extension, Enrichment and bottom-page activities:

1. Singing, alone and with others, a varied repertoire of music. **(a, c)**

4. Composing and arranging within specific guidelines. **(a)**

6. Listen to, analyze and describe music. **(e)**

Esto Les Digo

OVERVIEW

Composer: Kinley Lange (b. 1951)
Text: Matthew 18:19–20
Voicing: SATB
Key: C major
Meter: 3/4
Form: Through-composed
Style: Contemporary American Anthem
Accompaniment: A cappella
Programming: Concert, Festival

Vocal Ranges:

OBJECTIVES

After completing this lesson, students will be able to:

- Define harmony using standard terminology.
- Perform expressively a varied repertoire of music.
- Identify music-related vocations and avocations within the community.

VOCABULARY

Have students review vocabulary in student lesson. Introduce terms found in the music. A complete glossary of terms is found on page 260 of the student book.

Esto Les Digo

Composer: Kinley Lange (b. 1951)
Text: Matthew 18:19–20
Voicing: SATB

VOCABULARY

suspension
dissonance
composer
lyricist
head voice

SPOTLIGHT

To learn more about careers in music, see page 83.

Focus

- Read and perform music that contains suspensions and dissonance.
- Demonstrate how to sing phrases expressively.
- Discover music-related vocations in music.

Getting Started

What grabs your attention first when you learn a song? Is it the music, the words, or both? The renowned German recital singer Dietrich Fischer-Dieskau made this observation:

> *Words are the marriage of sound and expression, and both should thus enjoy equal importance in the elevated language of song. If either is neglected, the result tends either towards instrumental music or towards pure speech.*

While learning "Esto Les Digo," you will be treated to the fusion of the beautiful Spanish language and the expressive musical writing of Kinley Lange.

◆ History and Culture

Texas composer Kinley Lange uses **suspensions** (*the holding over of one or more musical tones in a chord into the following chord, producing a momentary tension*) and **dissonance** (*a combination of pitches or tones that clash*) to enhance the beauty of the song. The composer had this to say about his use of different compositional techniques: "In my own mind, I've purposely blurred the line between contemporary and traditional music. To me, they are not at odds. What matters is quality and purity of purpose."

Have you ever considered a career in writing music? Whether your interests lie in being a **composer** (*one who writes music*) or a **lyricist** (*one who writes the words to a song*), you need to ask these questions—What grabs your attention first? Is it the music, the words, or both?

78 Proficient Mixed

RESOURCES

Proficient Sight-Singing

Reading in C Major, pages 13, 26–27, 34–35

Reading in 3/4 Meter, page 14–16

Consonant and Dissonant Intervals, page 175

Teacher Resource Binder

Teaching Master 14, *Pronunciation Guide for "Esto Les Digo"*

Teaching Master 15, *A Life in Music*

Evaluation Master 8, *Evaluating Musical Expression*

Evaluation Master 15, *Diction Check-up*

Skill Builder 20, *Naming Intervals*

For additional resources, see TRB Table of Contents.

Links to Learning

◆ **Vocal**

With a sustained and supported breath, sing the following example in your **head voice** *(the higher part of a singer's range)*. Raise the pitch a half step on each repetition. Perform first on an "oo" vowel, and then with words. Find this pattern in the music.

◆ **Theory**

The frequent use of the interval of a major second (two notes a whole step apart) in the harmony is used to create dissonance. As you perform the following example, make sure the intensity of the dissonant note carries through to the resolution. How many major seconds, or dissonances, can you identify in this example?

Evaluation

Demonstrate how well you have learned the skills and concepts featured in the lesson "Esto Les Digo" by completing the following:

• In an SATB quartet with one singer on a part, perform measures 40–47 to show that you can sing the dissonant notes in tune. How well were you able to maintain the intensity of the dissonance notes through the resolution before getting softer?

• Perform "Esto Les Digo" expressively. In what ways did you show the meaning of the text through your emphasis of the dissonance and overall stage presence? How well were you able to sing the phrases expressively?

Lesson 9 Esto Les Digo **79**

RESOURCES

Proficient Mixed Rehearsal/Performance CD

CD 1:17 Voices

CD 1:18 Accompaniment Only

CD 3:10 Vocal Practice Track—Soprano

CD 4:9 Vocal Practice Track—Alto

CD 5:9 Vocal Practice Track—Tenor

CD 6:9 Vocal Practice Track—Bass

National Standards

1. Singing, alone and with others, a varied repertoire of music. **(a)**

6. Listening to, analyzing and describing music. **(b)**

9. Understanding music in relation to history and culture. **(c)**

LINKS TO LEARNING

Vocal

The Vocal section is designed to prepare students to sing in their head voice.

Have students:

• Sing the example on an *oo* vowel.

• Discuss the difference between the chest voice and head voice in singing.

• Sing again with the Spanish text maintaining tall, pure vowels sounds.

Theory

The Theory section is designed to prepare students to:

• Perform the interval of a major second in tune.

• Identify dissonance in notation and performance.

Have students:

• Identify the interval of a major second in the example. *(Answer: Soprano/Alto—measure 2 (E and F); measure 4 (F and G). Tenor/Bass—measure 1 (C and D); measure 2 (C and D, Tenor with the Alto); measure 3 (C and D, Tenor with the Alto)*

• Sing the example using solfège syllables.

• Stress the dissonance notes.

• Perform again on words. Maintain the intensity of the dissonant note through to the resolution before decreasing the dynamic level.

LESSON PLAN

Suggested Teaching Sequence and Performance Tips

1. Introduce

Direct students to:

• Read and discuss the information found in the Getting Started section on student page 78.

• Describe *suspension, dissonance* and *resolution*.

• Listen to a recording of "Esto Les Digo." Discuss ways in which the composer expresses the text "Where two or three are gathered in My name, there will I be also" through the music.

• Discuss other career opportunities in the field of music.

Progress Checkpoints

Observe students' progress in:

✓ Their ability to describe the importance of the text to a song.

✓ Their ability to identify dissonance in music notation.

2. Rehearse

Direct students to:

• Perform the Theory section on page 79 to perform and identify dissonance in music.

• Sing the melody to feel the flow of the melodic line.

• Sing measures 1–6 using solfège syllables to work on pitch accuracy. Hold each chord for tuning before moving on to the next chord.

• Identify the intervals that create the dissonance. *(Answer: In measure 1, C-D-E; in measure 2, E-F, C-D; in measure 3, C-D; in measure 4, F-G-A; in measure 5, C-D-E; C-B; in measure 6, A-G, F-G)*

80

Dedicado a Daniel y Alicia Vergarra

Esto Les Digo

For SATB, a cappella

Text: Matthew 18:19–20   Where two or three are gathered in My name, there will I be also.

Music by
KINLEY LANGE

80   Proficient Mixed

TEACHER 2 TEACHER

Students will enjoy learning this gorgeous anthem that shares words of comfort. As the singers work together to blend in close harmony, a sense of community may emerge. Students may come to realize that the group is greater than the individual.

- Shape each phrase with a gradual *crescendo* to the peak of the phrase, and a gradual *diminuendo* to the end of the phrase.
- Practice the Spanish text phrase-by-phrase before adding to the music.

Progress Checkpoints

Observe students' progress in:

✓ Their ability to sing chords in tune.

✓ Their ability to identify and perform dissonance.

✓ Singing dissonance chords in tune.

3. Refine

Direct students to:

- Focus on the phrasing of this piece. Have students divide into two groups with an equal number on each voice part in both groups.
- Perform for each other to listen for the phrasing (an obvious rise and fall in dynamics and intensity).
- Continue to refine the phrasing, diction and musical expression of this piece.

Progress Checkpoints

Observe students' progress in:

✓ Their ability to perform the piece, observing all dynamic and expression markings.

✓ Their ability to sing dissonance chords in tune.

✓ Their ability to sing with clear Spanish diction.

MORE ABOUT...

Texas Composer

"Esto Les Digo" was written by Texas composer Kinley Lange. As a composer, he has published works for choirs, orchestra, organ and handbells. He earned his bachelor's of music degree from the University of Hawaii with an emphasis in ethnomusicology, and later studied composition at the University of Texas-Austin. He currently lives and works as a church musician in Houston, Texas.

ASSESSMENT

Informal Assessment

In this lesson, students showed the ability to:

- Define and apply their knowledge of dissonance.
- Perform phrases expressively.
- Discuss careers opportunities in the field of music.

Student Self-Assessment

Have students evaluate their individual performances based on the following:

- Diction
- Expressive Singing
- Phrasing
- Intonation
- Accurate Pitches

Have each student rate his/her performance of this song in the areas above on a scale of 1–5, 5 being the best.

Individual and Group Performance Evaluation

To further measure growth of musical skills presented in this lesson, direct students to complete the Evaluation section on page 79.

- Have students get into small SATB ensembles to sing measures 40–47. As each quartet performs, have them assess how well they were able to sing the dissonance chords in tune.
- Record the class performing "Esto Les Digo." As the students listen to the recording, have them answer the following questions: How well was the choir able to sing the phrases expressively? How well was the choir able to sing the dissonant chords in tune?

TEACHING STRATEGY
Performing a Solo

Direct students tolocate the solo found in measures 41–47 of "Esto Les Digo." Have them identify the musical terms and symbols for dynamics and tempo such as *mp*, *ritard (rit.)*, and fermata. Have students take turns performing the solo, intrpreting the musical terms and symbols as they sing.

SPOTLIGHT

Careers In Music

Music Industry

The music industry provides career opportunities that encompass the area of business as well as music. This article will focus on music publishing, retail sales and instrumental sales.

Music publishing involves the process of finding music to publish, preparing the music for print (editing and proofreading), marketing and distributing the music for sales, and supporting the composers for their contribution. The skills required for this type of job may vary greatly. On the business side of the company, training in business, accounting, marketing, advertising and sales would be necessary. The ability to communicate, both in writing and orally, is vital in business. On the editorial side, there are job opportunities as editors, proofreaders, graphic designers, and music engravers. Some of these jobs require a music background, as well as writing skills and possible specific computer skills. Quite often there will be on-the-job training to learn the mechanical techniques and specialized software systems used at the company.

Music retail sales requires music experience or training specific to the area of sales. Music stores may feature different instruments, pianos, vocal music, textbooks or accessories. Anyone considering a career in instrumental sales should have a working knowledge of the instruments and be able to demonstrate on the instrument for the customer. The same is true for the other area of sales—one must have a working knowledge of the item being sold. Another job position in music retail sales is that of the store manager, who oversees the entire operation of the store. This would require skills in business, management and inventory control. It would also require the hiring and training of new employees. Anyone interested in this field should have a background in business and a working knowledge of music.

An instrument sales representative is someone who represents an instrument manufacturing company. While the position requires skills in sales, it is also important to have an in-depth knowledge of the instrument, skill in playing the instrument, and a passion for the instrument or music in general. The salesperson will most likely be required to work in the field. This involves hard work and possibly time away from home. In addition to music training, a sales representative must also have skills in sales, accounting and bookkeeping.

Spotlight *Careers In Music* **83**

RESOURCES

Teacher Resource Binder

Reference 9, *Career: Music Education*
Reference 10, *Career: Comparing Performance Opportunities*
Reference 16, *Describing: Expanding a Musical Vocabulary*

National Standards

8. Understanding relationship between music, the other arts, and disciplines outside the arts. **(b)**
9. Understanding music in relation to history and culture. **(c)**

CAREERS IN MUSIC

Objective

- Identify and describe music-related career opportunities.
- Define the relationship of the processes of other subjects and those of music.

Suggested Teaching Sequence

Direct students to:

- Read the Spotlight On Careers in Music on page 83 and identify the career opportunities in the music industry.
- Divide into small groups and make a list of as many different career opportunities available in the music business or industry. Share the list with the rest of the class.
- Discuss the training requirements needed to enter a career in music business.
- Compare and contrast a career in music business versus a career in nonmusical business. Include training, job market, salary, specialized skills, and so forth.
- Search the Internet or research the library to find other job opportunities in the field of music.

Progress Checkpoints

Observe students' progress in:

✓ Their ability to identify what is meant by the music industry.
✓ Their ability to describe the training and job opportunities available in the music industry.

Sanctus

OVERVIEW

Composer: Wolfgang Amadeus Mozart (1756–1791), edited by Patrick M. Liebergen

Text: Liturgical Latin, English text by Patrick M. Liebergen

Voicing: SATB

Key: B♭ major

Meter: 4/4, Cut Time

Form: AB

Style: Classical German Anthem

Accompaniment: Piano

Programming: Concert opener, Contest, Festival

Vocal Ranges:

OBJECTIVES

After completing this lesson, students will be able to:

- Demonstrate independently and in ensembles, fundamental skills while performing.

- Perform expressively a varied repertoire of music representing styles from diverse periods including Classical.

VOCABULARY

Have students review vocabulary in student lesson. Introduce terms found in the music. A complete glossary of terms is found on page 260 of the student book.

Sanctus

Composer: Wolfgang Amadeus Mozart (1756–1791), edited by Patrick M. Liebergen

Text: Liturgical Latin, English text by Patrick M. Liebergen

Voicing: SATB

VOCABULARY

missa brevis

mass

Classical period

syllabic stress

Focus

- Sing a Latin text with correct syllabic stress.

- Perform music representing the Classical period.

Getting Started

The year 1776 has special significance for all Americans, for it is the year that America won its independence from England. It is also the year that Wolfgang Amadeus Mozart (1756–1791) wrote his 258th composition, a **missa brevis** *(a brief mass)*, which contained this "Sanctus."

It is interesting that as young American soldiers in the Revolutionary War were fighting for independence from England, a very polished and refined male choir was performing the "Missa Brevis K. 258" in Salzburg, Austria.

In 1776, twenty-year-old Mozart had just returned to Salzburg from an unsuccessful trip to Munich and Vienna to obtain commissions. Mozart was serving as a court musician and concertmaster in the orchestra of the archbishop while refining his skills as a pianist, violinist and composer. Like most young adults, he was extremely restless for his independence and wanted to be as far away from Salzburg and his parents as possible!

MUSIC & HISTORY

To learn more about the Classical period, see page 112.

◆ History and Culture

A **mass** is *the main religious service of the Roman Catholic Church.* There are two divisions of the mass: the Proper of the mass, in which the text changes for each day, and the Ordinary of the mass, in which the text remains the same for every mass. The Ordinary includes the *Kyrie, Gloria, Credo, Sanctus* and *Agnus Dei.* One opinion is that Mozart wrote "Missa Brevis K. 258" for the consecration of Friedrich Franz Joseph Count von Spaur, who later became the dean of the cathedral in Salzburg. Mozart lived and worked during the **Classical period** *(1750-1820).*

84   Proficient Mixed

RESOURCES

Proficient Sight-Singing

Sight-Singing in B♭ Major, pages 90–93

Reading Rhythms in 4/4 Meter, pages 2–6

Reading Rhythms in Cut time, page 147

Reading Eighth Notes, pages 23–24

Teacher Resource Binder

Teaching Master 16, *Pronunciation Guide for "Sanctus"*

Teaching Master 17, *Text Emphasis in "Sanctus"*

Evaluation Master 15, *Diction Check-up*

Music and History 10, *Characteristics of Classical Music: 1750–1820*

Music and History 11, *Wolfgang Amadeus Mozart, a Classical Composer*

Links to Learning

◆ **Vocal**

Vocal music should be sung with **syllabic stress** *(the musical emphasis of the naturally stressed syllable in a word)*. Latin texts, with their pure vowel sounds, are especially good for practicing syllabic stress. Sing the opening measures from "Sanctus," observing the indicated syllabic stresses.

◆ **Theory**

Mozart introduces the text *"Hosanna in excelsis"* (Hosanna in the highest) with a descending scale melody for each voice part. These passages need to be sung clearly and prominently. Practice the following exercises on solfège syllables. Begin with a slow, steady tempo. Gradually increase the tempo until you can sing quickly and cleanly.

◆ **Artistic Expression**

The joyful text of the "Sanctus" has made it a favorite of choral composers for centuries. Even Mozart wrote eighteen masses with "Sanctus" movements. Using the library or the Internet, find another setting of "Sanctus" by Mozart or another choral composer. Play the "Sanctus" for your class and ask the students to discuss similarities and differences between the recorded "Sanctus" and this Mozart "Sanctus."

Evaluation

Demonstrate how well you have learned the skills and concepts featured in the lesson "Sanctus" by completing the following:

- In an SATB quartet, sing measures 1–5 in "Sanctus," demonstrating correct syllabic stress. Assess how well you did.
- In an SATB quartet, sing measures 11–18 in "Sanctus" with the Latin text, demonstrating predominant entrances of *"Hosanna in excelsis."* Evaluate how well you were able to sing the text quickly and cleanly.

LINKS TO LEARNING

Vocal

The Vocal section is designed to prepare students to:

- Understand syllabic stress.
- Perform "Sanctus" with the proper syllabic stress.

Have students:

- Speak the Vocal example in rhythm with the proper syllabic stress as indicated by the all-capped syllables.
- Sing the Vocal example observing the indicated syllabic stresses.

Theory

The Theory section is designed to prepare students to sing the descending scale passages in "Sanctus" accurately and prominently.

Have students:

- Sing the Theory exercise on solfège syllables slowly concentrating on accuracy of intervals. Be careful the downward intervals are not too large.
- Increase tempo when rhythms and intervals are accurate and clean.

RESOURCES

Proficient Mixed Rehearsal/Performance CD

CD 1:19 Voices

CD 1:20 Accompaniment Only

CD 3:11 Vocal Practice Track—Soprano

CD 4:10 Vocal Practice Track—Alto

CD 5:10 Vocal Practice Track—Tenor

CD 6:10 Vocal Practice Track—Bass

National Standards

1. Singing, alone and with others, a varied repertoire of music. **(a, b, c)**
9. Understanding music in relation to history and culture. **(a)**

Artistic Expression

The Artistic Expression section is designed to prepare students to understand the text and setting of Mozart's "Sanctus."

Have students:

- Write down the Latin text and research the translation.
- Find other settings of the "Sanctus" text and locate a recording.
- Play the recording of the other settings and compare them to the Mozart "Sanctus" being studied in this lesson.

LESSON PLAN

Suggested Teaching Sequence and Performance Tips

1. Introduce

Direct students to:

- Read and discuss the information found in the Getting Started section on page 84.
- Practice the Vocal exercise on page 85 concentrating on proper syllabic stress and locate these measures in their choral score.
- Practice the Theory exercise on page 85 concentrating on accuracy of the descending scales and locate these scales in their choral score.
- Learn the Latin text. A pronunciation guide can be found in the Teacher Resource Binder, Teaching Master 16.
- Speak the Latin text of the entire piece concentrating on proper syllabic stress. A text emphasis guide can be found in the Teacher Resource Binder, Teaching Master 17.

From MISSA BREVIS, K. 258

Sanctus

For SATB and Piano

English text by
PATRICK M. LIEBERGEN

WOLFGANG AMADEUS MOZART
(1756–1791)

TEACHER 2 TEACHER

Understanding form facilitates the learning process. This lesson expands this concept by relating the form of literature (Mass) to the form of music; in this case the music (movement) is a part of a larger form. The movement, in turn, has its own form (like a box within a box).

Lesson 10 *Sanctus* **87**

Progress Checkpoints

Observe students' progress in:

✓ Singing descending scales with accuracy.

✓ Their use of accurate diction, unified vowel sounds and stresses.

✓ Their proper use of Latin vowels.

2. Rehearse

Direct students to:

• Sing measures 1–5 in Latin, concentrating on tuning the homophonic chords in this section. Rehearse parts individually if necessary.

• Sight-sing measures 6–18 on the Latin text in a slow but comfortable tempo in cut time.

• Rehearse parts individually if necessary until secure. Increase the tempo as comfort level increases. Bring out the descending scales in each part and make sure they are crisp and accurate.

• Sight-sing measures 19–end on the Latin text in a slow, but comfortable tempo in cut time.

• Rehearse parts individually if necessary until secure. Increase the tempo as comfort level increases. Bring out the descending scales.

MORE ABOUT...

Wolfgang Amadeus Mozart (1756–1791)

As a representative composer of the Classical Period, Mozart embodied the spirit of the classical style: crisp harmonies, exuberant melodies, formal balance and symmetry. He composed in virtually all forms of the time, including symphonies, operas, string quartets, art songs and masses. Mozart died at the early age of 35, cutting short the career of one of the most prolific composers of all times.

Observe students' progress in:

✓ Their ability to sing in Latin with correct pronunciation, rhythm and tempos throughout the entire work.

✓ Their ability to sing descending scales accurately and prominently within the context of a polyphonic section.

3. Refine

Direct students to:

- Sing measures 1–5 concentrating on the proper syllabic stress and pure vowels of the Latin text. Students may underscore stressed syllables in their choral scores if needed.

- Locate the dynamic and tempo indications throughout. Sing entire piece observing those markings.

- Sing the entire work a cappella including time for rests to be sure that they are independent of the accompaniment.

Progress Checkpoints

Observe student's progress in:

✓ Singing the Latin text with proper syllabic stress and pure vowels.

✓ Singing the piece with proper dynamic levels a tempo variations.

✓ Singing the piece a cappella with accuracy and independence of parts.

88   Proficient Mixed

CONNECTING THE ARTS

Processes in the Arts

Have students:

1. Find examples of artwork or art forms from the Classical period, describing how they exhibit the characteristics of the period. (Choose from visual art, architecture, dance, drama, poetry or literature.)

2. Discuss how the processes used in the other areas are the same and different from music, taking into consideration the roles of artists, performers and audience.

3. Find other examples from the same art category, but from a different style, period or culture.

4. Discuss similarities and differences between the examples.

ASSESSMENT

Informal Assessment

In this lesson, students showed the ability to sing the work in Latin with correct pronunciation and syllabic stress.

Student Self-Assessment

Have students evaluate their individual performances based on the following:

- Diction
- Latin Text
- Pure Vowels
- Intonation
- Correct Part-Singing

Have each student rate his/her performance of this song in the areas above on a scale of 1–5, 5 being the best.

Individual and Group Performance Evaluation

To further demonstrate musical growth, direct students to complete the Evaluation section on page 85.

- After each SATB quartet has sung measures 1–5 for the rest of the class, have the class and the quartet evaluate their ability to sing with correct syllabic stress.
- After each SATB quartet has sung measures 11–18 for the rest of the class, have the class and the quartet evaluate their ability to sing the text quickly and cleanly.

TEACHING STRATEGY

Homophonic and Other Styles

The three basic textures are monophony, homophony, and polyphony. Monophony is a single melodic line; homophony is harmony produced by block chords; polyphony is harmony produced by the interweaving of multiple melodic lines.

Have students:

- Look through the pieces in this book to find examples of each texture.
- Discuss the advantages and challenges inherent in each style.
- Suggest a concert program that would be centered on the theme of texture. Challenge students to select pieces and tie the whole program together.

EXTENSION

Movements of the Mass

Have students research the different movements of a Mass and list them. Discuss the differences in mood one might find between the different movements (i.e. Kyrie and Sanctus; Credo and Agnus Dei). They should choose one movement and write a one-page paper on the translation, its function in the mass, its mood and different settings found.

Encourage your students to expore **music.glencoe.com**, the website for *Experiencing Choral Music.* You may wish to preview the rich content before directing your students online. Options available on the Web site include:

- Web Link Exercises
- Interactive Projects
- Audio Samples

Additional National Standards

The following National Standards are addressed through the Assessment, Extension, Enrichment and bottom-page activities:

6. Listening to, analyzing, and describing music. **(a, b, c)**

7. Evaluating music and music performances. **(b)**

SPOTLIGHT

Vocal Health

Since our voices are a result of physical processes in our bodies, we need to learn a few things we can do to ensure that our voices will be healthy and function well for years to come.

To experience, explore and establish good habits for vocal health, try the following:

- Limit shouting and trying to talk over loud noise.
- Do not smoke. Avoid smoky environments.
- Avoid beverages with caffeine and fried foods (acid reflux).
- Limit talking on the telephone. Use a supported voice when you do.
- Avoid whispering if you lose your voice.
- Rest your voice if it is tired or if it takes more muscular effort to sing.
- Keep your voice hydrated. Drink lots of water every day and use nonmentholated, sugar-free lozenges if your throat is dry.
- Gargle with warm salt water if your throat is sore.
- Use a humidifier in your bedroom when the air conditioning or furnace is on.
- Try not to clear your throat. Swallow or clear with a puff of air instead.
- Avoid coughing, if at all possible.
- Cover your nose and mouth with a scarf in cold weather.
- Get plenty of sleep, especially the night before a performance.

As you can see, maintaining good vocal health is a matter of common sense in taking care of your body. By taking good care of yourself, you can continue to enjoy a strong, healthy singing voice. Take care and sing long!

Spotlight *Vocal Health* **91**

RESOURCES

Teacher Resource Binder

Vocal Development 1–6, *Keep the Joy in Singing!*

National Standards

1. Singing, alone and with others, a varied repertoire of music. **(b)**

VOCAL HEALTH

Objectives

- To introduce and experience healthy vocal production as related to musical vocal performance.

Suggested Teaching Sequence

Direct students to:

- Read Spotlight On Vocal Health on student page 91.
- Identify and write down (for their own viewing) any of the directives on the student page that might impact them on a regular or sometimes basis.
- Incorporate as many of the directives as possible for the next six weeks.
- Keep a record of any noticeable improvements in their vocal health.
- Share their results with the choir if they are willing.

Progress Checkpoints

Observe students' progress in:

- ✓ Demonstrating body awareness.
- ✓ Using proper posture and breath management.
- ✓ Shaping vowels correctly with clear diction.
- ✓ Seemingly effortless singing.
- ✓ Vocal projection.
- ✓ Vocal health awareness.

Der Tanz

OVERVIEW

Composer: Franz Schubert (1797–1828), edited by John Leavitt

Text: Kolumban Schnitzer von Meerau

Voicing: SATB

Key: C major

Meter: 6/8

Form: Through-composed

Style: German Romantic Part-song

Accompaniment: Piano

Programming: Contest, Concert Opener

Vocal Ranges:

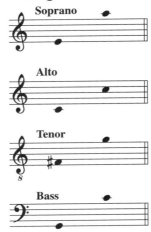

Soprano

Alto

Tenor

Bass

OBJECTIVES

After completing this lesson, students will be able to:

- Sing in groups a varied repertoire of music.
- Demonstrate in ensembles accurate rhythm while performing moderately easy to moderately difficult literature.

VOCABULARY

Have students review vocabulary in student lesson. Introduce terms found in the music. A complete glossary of terms is found on page 260 of the student book.

Der Tanz

Composer: Franz Schubert (1797–1828), edited by John Leavitt
Text: Kolumban Schnitzer von Meerau
Voicing: SATB

VOCABULARY

Schubertiad

Romantic period

6/8 meter

melisma

marcato

MUSIC & HISTORY

To learn more about the Romantic period, see page 116.

Focus

- Perform music representing the Romantic period.
- Read and perform in 6/8 meter.
- Relate music to poetry.

Getting Started

Birthday parties, graduation parties, Christmas parties…
Time spent with family and friends celebrating special occasions can be some of the most memorable times in life.

If you had lived in Vienna, Austria, in 1820, you might have received an invitation to a most memorable party, a **Schubertiad.** These were *parties held in the homes of Vienna's middle-class families that featured amateur performances of the songs and instrumental works by Franz Schubert (1797–1828).* Schubert's circle of friends included poets, authors and artists who were fiercely loyal to their musical colleague and held parties so people could hear his new compositions. You might have been lucky enough to hear "Der Tanz" at your Schubertiad.

◆ History and Culture

The title of this song, "Der Tanz" (The Dance), evokes many ideas, for there are many kinds of dances. The dance Schubert is describing, however, is the dance of life and living. Music describing life, with its ups and downs, sadness and joy, achievements and disappointments would be quite emotional. Inspired by his friend and poet Kolumban Schnitzer von Meerau, Schubert wrote a piece with intense rhythmic drive and an energetic melody.

Schubert wrote over 600 songs with harmonies and rhythms that perfectly capture the mood and meaning of the words. His music is also filled with spinning, lyrical melodies. With its expression and rich sound, Schubert's music is an important part of the early **Romantic period** *(1820–1900).*

92   Proficient Mixed

RESOURCES

Proficient Sight-Singing

Sight-Singing in C Major, pages 7, 9, 13, 26–27, 34–35

Reading Rhythms in 6/8 Meter, pages 113–114, 117

The Division of the Beat, page 127

Teacher Resource Binder

Teaching Master 18, *Pronunciation Guide for "Der Tanz"*

Skill Builder 12, *Conducting in Compound Meter*

Music and History 14, *Characteristics of Romantic Music:1820-1900*

Music and History 17, *Franz Schubert, a Romantic Composer*

For additional resources, see TRB Table of Contents.

Links to Learning

◆ **Vocal**

Perform the following example to extend the vocal range and develop vocal agility.

zing ah,_____ zing ah,_____ zing ah,_____ (etc.)

◆ **Theory**

$^6_8$ **meter** is *a time signature in which there are two groups of three eighth notes per measure and the dotted quarter note receives the beat.* $^6_8$ meter is an example of compound meter. Perform the following example, feeling the beat in two groups of three eighth notes. Conduct in two as you chant.

ti   ti   ti ka ti ka ti   ti   ti   ti ti ti ta   ti   ti ti ka ti ka ti ti ti   tam   ti

◆ **Artistic Expression**

The restless passion of the Romantic period is expressed in "Der Tanz" by using two contrasting compositional styles. The use of **melismas** (*long groups of notes sung on one syllable of text*) gives a lift to the melody and a feeling of freedom. The **marcato** (*emphasized, heavily accented*) section creates a feeling of impatience and despair. Find examples of melismas and marcato in the music.

Evaluation

Demonstrate how well you have learned the skills and concepts featured in the lesson "Der Tanz" by completing the following:

• Sing the Soprano part in your range in measures 4–8 to demonstrate vocal agility. Evaluate how well you were able to sing with a light and flexible tone.

• Chant the text in measures 14–18 while conducting in two to demonstrate your ability to perform compound meter. How well did you do?

RESOURCES

Proficient Mixed Rehearsal/Performance CD

CD **1:21** Voices

CD **1:22** Accompaniment Only

CD **3:12** Vocal Practice Track—Soprano

CD **4:11** Vocal Practice Track—Alto

CD **5:11** Vocal Practice Track—Tenor

CD **6:11** Vocal Practice Track—Bass

National Standards

1. Singing, alone and with others, a varied repertoire of music. **(c)**

8. Understanding relationships between music, the other arts, and disciplines outside the arts. **(c)**

• Define the relationships between the concepts of the other fine arts and those of music.

LINKS TO LEARNING

Vocal

The Vocal section is designed to prepare students to sing arpeggios to help extend the vocal range.

Have students:

• Sing the exercise using solfège syllables.

• Sing the exercise using the syllables written below the staff.

Theory

The Theory section is designed to prepare students to establish rhythmic accuracy in reading 6/8 meter.

Have students:

• Read the exercise using the syllables written below the staff as they are conducting in two.

• Clap the exercise.

Artistic Expression

The Artistic Expression section is designed to prepare students to sing expressively using contrasting techniques.

Have students:

• Find examples of melismas and marcato in the score.

• Perform those sections with the correct articulation.

LESSON PLAN

Suggested Teaching Sequence and Performance Tips

1. Introduce

Direct students to:

- Read and discuss the information found in the Getting Started section on page 92.
- Practice singing the exercise shown in the Vocal section on page 93 to extend their range.
- Practice the rhythmic exercises as shown in the Theory section on page 93 to increase ability to read and perform compound rhythms in 6/8 meter.
- Locate examples of melismas and marcato in the score as described in the Artistic Expression section on page 93. Sing those sections with the appropriate articulation.

Progress Checkpoints

Observe students' progress in:

- ✓ Singing comfortably in extended ranges.
- ✓ Conducting and performing rhythmic patterns in 6/8 meter .
- ✓ Singing melismas and marcato articulatinon.

Der Tanz
(The Dance)

For SATB and Piano

Edited by
JOHN LEAVITT

Words by KOLUMBAN SCHNITZER VON MEERAU
Music by FRANZ SCHUBERT (1797–1828)

94   Proficient Mixed

TEACHER 2 TEACHER

Students will enjoy learning about the Romantic Period through their study of "Der Tanz." The strong emotional drive of the music will encourage your singers to meet the challenges of language and vocal technique.

Jugend so viel, von Tanzen, Galoppen, Ge-

Jugend so viel, von Tanzen, Galoppen, Ge-

Jugend so viel, von Tanzen, Galoppen, Ge-

Jugend so viel, von Tanzen, Galoppen, Ge-

la-gen, auf einmal erreicht sie ein

la-gen, auf einmal erreicht sie ein

la-gen, auf einmal erreicht sie ein

la-gen, auf einmal erreicht sie ein

2. Rehearse

Direct students to:

- Listen to the recorded performance of "Der Tanz" (CD 1:21). Discuss the piece in terms of Romantic style *(emotional, driving rhythm, contrasting emotions)*.
- Locate melismatic passages *(Soprano: measures 5, 7, 9, 10, 12, 21, 25; Alto: measure 8; Tenor: measure 21; Bass: measures 21, 25)* and the contrasting marcato passages *(measures 19–20 in all voices)*.
- Note in measures 4–12 the lower voices accompany the Soprano melody while in measures 15 to the end the voices move in a homophonic (chordal) style.
- Listen to the recording again while conducting in two.
- Discuss and practice the accidentals in each voice part. Practice the Bass and Tenor parts together using solfège syllables while the Sopranos and Altos sign their parts with solfège syllables. Strive for rhythmic grouping in two with accents on the first eighth note in each group, creating a dance-like buoyancy.
- Practice the Soprano and Alto parts while the Tenors and Basses sign their parts with solfège syllables.
- Combine the three lower voices in measures 4–12. Pay particular attention to the tuning of half steps, as created by accidentals.

MORE ABOUT...

Composer Franz Schubert

The music of Franz Schubert (1797–1828) is basically simple, friendly, and heartfelt, and he was a master of finding just the right moment to add an unusual or colorful effect. His small explorations opened the door for the more adventuresome Romantic composers to follow. Schubert was not known as a performer, but rather spent his life composing and teaching. He composed a vast number of works, including operas, masses, symphonies, chamber music, and songs. He was never widely appreciated during his lifetime, and died at the age of 31. His best known works today are the *Unfinished Symphony* and the tone poem *The Erlking*. However, many of his pieces are in the repertoire of choirs, orchestras and solo recitalists around the world.

- Practice the Soprano part in measures 4–12. Strive for clean, accurate sixteenth notes.
- Combine all parts in measures 4–12. Move from using solfège syllbles to a neutral doo syllable.
- Continue practicing with measures 15–26. Practice the Soprano and Bass parts together while Tenors and Altos sign their parts. Practice the Alto and Tenor parts together while the Sopranos and Basses sign.
- Sing the Soprano and Tenor parts together. Note the dissonances (measures 15–16) and the harmony in thirds (measures 17–18). Listen to all of the sections as you sing. Strive to blend with all voices.

Progress Checkpoints

Observe students' progress in:

✓ Their ability to characterize music of the Romantic period.

✓ Their ability to locate melismatic and marcato passages in the score.

✓ Performing with rhythmic precision and pitch accuracy.

ENRICHMENT

Compare and Contrast

Compare the music and words of "Der Tanz" to those of "Shall We Dance" from *The King and I*. In what ways are these two songs similar? In what ways are they different? Discuss other songs on the subject of dancing. Can you think of another song about dancing that is referring to life rather than the physical dance? (e.g., "I Hope You Dance" by Lee Ann Womack)

3. Refine

Direct students to:

- Practice pronouncing the German. Repeat small sections of the text. Work for clarity and precision.
- Sing the text phrase-by-phrase. Stop and repeat any challenging text. Isolate specific voice parts and listen as they sing the text.
- Work to perform the text with rhythmic precision, paying particular attention to the changes in dynamics. Remember: softer passages demand loud diction!
- Sing measures 19–22 in individual voice parts. Decide which voice part best achieved the piano singing with the marcato accents (measures 19–20) contrasted by the forte section (measures 21–22). Add one voice part at a time to the best section.
- Listen to the introduction and practice singing the beginning with quiet energy. Note that the introduction is forte, but the singers enter at the piano level. Keep the energy.

CONNECTING THE ARTS
Creative Dance

If some ensemble members are familiar with modern or creative dance, have them:

- Create a dance that matches the mood and phrases of the piece.
- First explore possible movements that flow with the piece, using the rainbow, rose, moon, and waters on a starry night as images for impressionist or abstract interpretation.
- Move as the piece is sung (perhaps using an audio tape), exploring the phrase lengths and mood. Avoid movements that are too literal.
- Allow each phrase to rise and fall with the pitch and dynamics that shape it.
- Create a dance by choosing the best of their explored movements.
- Perform the dance with the piece.

- Be certain to hold out the final quarter note in measures 12 and 26 full value and with a forward motion rather than a decrescendo.
- Discuss the lifted accent in the feeling of two. Conduct in a light manner as you sing to feel the style of the piece. Perhaps there are dancers in the class who can demonstrate. If not, view a video of a famous dance in this style (such as "Shall We Dance" from *The King and I*).

Progress Checkpoints

Observe students' progress in:

✓ Using correct German diction.

✓ Their energetic presentation in all dynamic levels.

✓ Performing the dynamic contrasts.

✓ Singing the legato melismas and contrasting marcato section.

✓ Secure four-part singing.

✓ A sense of lift on accented beats to capture the style of the dance.

ASSESSMENT

Informal Assessment

In this lesson, students showed the ability to:

- Sing a composition written in the Romantic style.
- Sing contrasting dynamics with energy.
- Read and perform in compound meter.

98   Proficient Mixed

CURRICULUM CONNECTIONS

Translations

Research the English translation of "Der Tanz." Write your interpretation of the text and relate it to events in your own life. Do you think the text describes a realistic aspect of life and human nature? Include your answer in your interpretation.

Student Self-Assessment

Have students evaluate their individual performances based on the following:

- Phrasing
- Diction
- Foreign Language
- Expressive Singing
- Correct Part-Singing

Have each student rate his/her performance of this song in the areas above on a scale of 1–5, 5 being the best.

Individual and Group Performance Evaluation

To further measure growth of musical skills presented in this lesson, direct students to complete the Evaluation section on page 93.

- After singing the Soprano part in measures 4–8 as solos in a comfortable range, review each performance by asking, "Was the tone light and flexible? If not, how could it be improved?"

- Chant the text in measures 14–18 as you conduct in two in front of a friend. Evaluate the performance by asking, "Were the rhythms accurate? Was the conducting clear and rhythmically correct?" Switch roles.

Additional National Standards

The following National Standards are addressed through the Assessment, Extension, Enrichment and bottom-page activities:

1. Singing, alone and with others, a varied repertoire of music. **(a)**

5. Reading and notating music. **(a)**

7. Evaluating music and music performances. **(a)**

8. Understanding relationships between music, the other arts, and disciplines outside the arts. **(a)**

Laudate

OVERVIEW

Composer: Knut Nystedt (b. 1915)
Text: Vesper Psalm
Voicing: SATB divisi
Key: A major
Meter: 3/4, 2/4, 4/4
Form: ABA
Style: Contemporary Norwegian Song
Accompaniment: A cappella
Programming: Concert Opener, Contest, Festival, Special Services

Vocal Ranges:

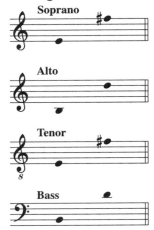

Soprano

Alto

Tenor

Bass

OBJECTIVES

After completing this lesson, students will be able to:

• Read music that incorporates rhythmic patterns in simple meters.

• Interpret music terms.

• Relate music to history.

VOCABULARY

Have students review vocabulary in student lesson. Introduce terms found in the music. A complete glossary of terms is found on page 260 of the student book.

Laudate

Composer: Knut Nystedt (b. 1915)
Text: Vesper Psalm
Voicing: SATB

VOCABULARY

fanfare

Contemporary period

ABA form

Focus

• Read and perform music written in mixed meter.

• Identify, analyze and perform music in ABA form.

• Describe and perform music from the Contemporary period.

Getting Started

Cell phones, voice mail, e-mail, chat rooms—these are modern ways of instantly reaching someone in our world. Nothing, however, can compare to receiving a traditional greeting card in the mail! A short composition that sends a message is like a musical greeting card. The opening section of "Laudate" is a **fanfare,** *a brief celebratory piece performed at the beginning of an event.* You might think of this as a fanfare greeting card of praise.

MUSIC & HISTORY

To learn more about the Contemporary period, see page 120.

◆ History and Culture

"Laudate," by Norwegian composer Knut Nystedt (b. 1915), is a musical composition from the **Contemporary period** *(1900–present).* Some of the characteristics common to this period are the use of mixed meter and innovative harmonies, and the blending of traditional texts with nontraditional harmonies.

The text of "Laudate" is a psalm associated with the ancient liturgical Vespers service.

Laudate Dominum omnes gentes;	O praise the Lord, all ye nations;
Laudate eum, omnes populi	praise Him, all ye peoples.
Quoniam confirmáta est	For His loving kindness
super nos misericordia ejus,	has been bestowed upon us.
et veritas Domini	And the truth of the Lord
manet in aeternum.	endures forever.

RESOURCES

Proficient Sight-Singing

Sight-Singing in A Major, pages 138–139

Reading Rhythms in 3/4 Meter, page 14

Reading Rhythms in 2/4 Meter, pages 66–67

Reading Rhythms in 4/4 Meter, pages 2, 6, 27

Teacher Resource Binder

Teaching Master 20, *Pronunciation Guide for "Laudate"*

Skill Builder 27, *Rhythm Challenge in Mixed Meter*

Music and History 19, *Characteristics of Contemporary Music*

Music and History 22, *Knut Nystedt, a "Contemporary" Composer*

For additional resources, see TRB Table of Contents.

Links to Learning

◆ **Theory**

Read and perform the following examples to practice singing traditional and nontraditional harmonies found in "Laudate."

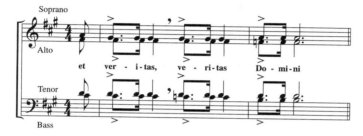

◆ **Artistic Expression**

"Laudate" is written in **ABA form,** or *a form in which an opening section (A) is followed by a contrasting section (B), which leads to the repetition of the opening section (A).* Design a "Laudate" greeting card. Fold a piece of paper into a card and write the text of measures 1–15 (section A) on the cover. Write the text of measures 16–27 (section B) on the inside. Choose a design and colors that illustrate the meaning and strength of the words.

Evaluation

Demonstrate how well you have learned the skills and concepts featured in the lesson "Laudate" by completing the following:

• In a quartet with one singer on a part, perform measures 1–15 to show your ability to sing music in mixed meter. Assess how well you were able to read the rhythms, including the eight meter changes.

• Exchange "Laudate" greeting cards with another student. Discuss the design and colors you used and how they reflect the meaning of the song.

LINKS TO LEARNING

Theory

The Theory section is designed to prepare students to sing traditional and nontraditional harmonies.

Have students:

• Sing the exercises using solfège syllables.

• Sing the exercises using the text.

• Sing the exercises with the text while observing the articulation markings.

• Relate the exercises to measures in the score *(measures 1–2; 23–25).*

Artistic Expression

The Artistic Expression section is designed to prepare students to identify ABA form.

Have students:

• Prepare greeting cards by writing the text for measures 1–15 on the front and measures 16–27 on the inside.

• Select fonts, design and colors for the cards that reflect the lyrics.

RESOURCES

Proficient Mixed Rehearsal/Performance CD

CD 1:23 Voices

CD 1:24 Accompaniment Only

CD 3:13 Vocal Practice Track— Soprano

CD 4:12 Vocal Practice Track—Alto

CD 5:12 Vocal Practice Track—Tenor

CD 6:12 Vocal Practice Track—Bass

National Standards

1. Singing, alone and with others, a varied repertoire of music. **(a, b, c, f)**

5. Reading and notating music. **(a)**

6. Listening to, analyzing, and describing music. **(b)**

7. Evaluating music and music performances. **(b)**

8. Understanding relationships between music, the other arts, and disciplines outside the arts. **(a, b, c)**

LESSON PLAN

Suggested Teaching Sequence and Performance Tips

Direct students to:

- Read and discuss the ideas presented in the Getting Started section on page 100. Review Latin vowel and consonant sounds and learn the Latin text.

- Clap or tap the rhythm in measures 1–15 while counting the subdivided beats.

- Work in voice part sectionals and recite the solfège syllables in rhythm while keeping a steady beat. Sing the solfège syllables in rhythm.

- Repeat the above activities for measures 16–27.

- Recite the Latin text in rhythm. Return to sectionals and rehearse the entire song with the text. Allow each voice part to perform for the class.

- Have two voice parts sing together (i.e., Soprano and Tenor, Alto and Bass).

- Observe all tenuto markings in the score, and recite the Latin text in rhythm with syllabic stress.

- Sing "Laudate" with students standing in sections but in one large circle. Take turns having one section stand in the middle of the circle while singing.

Progress Checkpoints

Observe students' progress in:

✓ Using pure and consistent Latin vowels.

✓ Their ability to work in small-group setting.

✓ Their ability to identify connections between visual images and musical style.

102

Laudate
For SATB and Piano

KNUT NYSTEDT

102   Proficient Mixed

TEACHER 2 TEACHER

It does not take long for young singers to appreciate Latin texts. The pure and unchanging vowels make beautiful tone quality and vocal blend instantly attainable. Two or three English words are often needed to convey the meaning of one Latin word, so texts are usually succinct and easily memorized. "Laudate" is also a wonderful introduction to unconventional harmonies. Nystedt has colored this setting with seconds, sevenths, and ninths that flow easily to and from more traditional sonorities. Along with the ABA setting, "Laudate" packs a lot of teachable moments into 27 measures!

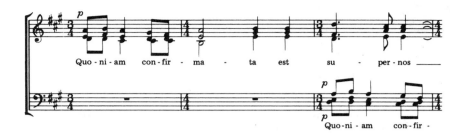

D. C. al FINE

ASSESSMENT

Informal Assessment

In this lesson, students showed the ability to:

- Read mixed meter rhythms.
- Sing with in small ensembles.

Student Self-Assessment

Have students evaluate their individual performances based on the following:

- Diction
- Foreign Language
- Tall Vowels
- Expressive Singing
- Intonation

Have each student rate his/her performance of this song in the areas above on a scale of 1–5, 5 being the best.

Individual and Group Performance Evaluation

To further measure growth of musical skills presented in this lesson, direct students to complete the Evaluation section on page 101.

- After singing measure 1–15 in quartets with one on a part, review each performance by asking, "How accurate were the rhythms? Which section(s) needs more rehearsal to perform rhythms correctly?"
- After exchanging "Laudate" greetings cards, discuss which fonts, design and colors were used and why they were used.

CURRICULUM CONNECTIONS
Visual Arts

This lesson provides the opportunity to compare the processes used in visual arts to those used in music.

- Create greeting cards as described in the Artistic Expression section on page 101. Discuss the rationale for choosing particular fonts and colors by analyzing the look of the score and the meaning of the text.
- Finish the "Laudate" greeting cards, making final decisions about font and color from listening to the choir's performance. Collect cards. Divide choir into groups of six to ten and give each group a card. Ask groups to plan a performance of "Laudate" that reflects the design of the card. Allow groups to perform for each other and critique the contrasts of the A and B sections.

CONCERT ETIQUETTE

Objective

- Exhibit informed concert etiquette in a variety of settings.

Suggested Teaching Sequence

Direct students to:

- Read the Spotlight On Concert Etiquette on student page 104 and discuss the importance of concert etiquette in respecting the efforts of others.
- Identify the six elements that constitute proper concert etiquette.
- Compare the elements of concert etiquette to appropriate performance practices. In what ways are they related to one another?
- Apply concert etiquette during live performances in a variety of settings.
- Divide the class into small groups and assign each group one concert venue. Ask each group to make a list of five appropriate and five inappropriate behavior expectations for the assigned venue. Share findings with the class.

Progress Checkpoints

Observe students' progress in:

- ✓ Their ability to identify the elements of concert etiquette.
- ✓ Their ability to understand the importance of concert etiquette.
- ✓ Their ability to apply concert etiquette in a variety of settings.

SPOTLIGHT

Concert Etiquette

Whether you are attending a rock concert, an athletic event or a musical concert, there are unique criteria for appropriate behavior at each event. The way in which one shows enthusiasm for a school athletic team or a favorite rock band is very different than the way one would express appreciation for a formal musical presentation.

Understanding appropriate expectations specific to individual events is what allows an audience, as well as the performers, to enjoy a presentation. The ultimate goal should be to show consideration and respect to everyone involved in a performance.

The term that describes how one is expected to behave in a formal music concert is *concert etiquette*. Let's examine behavior criteria specific to a formal concert.

- If you arrive late, wait outside the auditorium until a break in the music or until the audience is clapping.
- Wait to exit the hall until a break in the musical selections if a personal emergency occurs.
- Audience members will hear and enjoy the concert if everyone remains quiet and still throughout the performance.
- Take your cue from the performers or conductor and wait for an invitation when it comes to audience participation.
- Affirm your appreciation of the performance by applauding at the end of a selection of music and when the conductor's hands are lowered.
- Cellular telephones and pagers should be set so that no audible sound can be heard. Better yet, turn them off!

Understanding the uniqueness between various events is the first step toward knowing the behavior expectations particular to individual performances. When these guidelines are followed, everyone's enjoyment will be enhanced.

104 Proficient Mixed

RESOURCES

Teacher Resource Binder

Evaluation Master 5, *Concert Etiquette Quiz*
Reference 16, *Expanding a Musical Vocabulary*

National Standards

7. Evaluating music and music performances. **(a, b)**

Music & History

Links to Music

RENAISSANCE

OVERVIEW

Objectives

After completing this lesson, students will be able to:

• Describe the Renaissance period, including important developments.

• Describe characteristics of Renaissance music.

Introduce the Renaissance period through visual art. Analyze the painting by Leonardo da Vinci on page 106. Show Fine Art Transparency 1, *Ginevra de' Benci*, (from the Teacher Resource Binder) and direct students to discuss the costume of the day as depicted in the painting. Review the background information about Renaissance art as found on teacher page 108.

 Italian painter Leonardo da Vinci (1452–1519) was a genius who showed great skill in everything he tried. In *Ginevra de' Benci*, he uses a blending of light and dark values. The subtle changes in the light make the sad face seem three-dimensional. Notice how the figure of the woman stands out dramatically against the dark background. It is interesting to speculate about who this woman is and why she is so sad.

Leonardo da Vinci. *Ginevra de' Benci*. c. 1474. Oil on panel. 38.1 x 37.0 cm (15 x 14 9/16"). National Gallery of Art, Washington, D. C. Ailsa Mellon Bruce Fund.

106 Proficient Mixed

RESOURCES

Teacher Resource Binder

Music and History 1, *Renaissance Music*

Music and History 4, *Giovanni Pierluigi da Palestrina*

Fine Art Transparency 1, *Ginevra de' Benci*, Leonardo da Vinci

Music and History 5, *Fine Art Teaching Strategy—Renaissance*

For additional resources, see Music and History section.

Listening Selections CD

(found in the Teacher Resource Binder)

Track 1: "O Magnum Mysterium"

Track 2: "Canzon XV"

R E N A I S S A N C E   c. 1430–1600

Focus

- Describe the Renaissance period, including important developments.
- Describe characteristics of Renaissance music.

The Renaissance— A Time of Discovery

Renaissance means "rebirth" or "renewal." The **Renaissance period** *(c. 1430–1600)* was a time of rapid development in exploration, science, art and music. Vasco da Gama first rounded the coast of Africa from Europe to reach India. Christopher Columbus found the Americas, and Ferdinand Magellan circumnavigated the globe. The compass and first maps for navigation were developed and were used to find and chart new lands.

The greatest invention of the Renaissance (and perhaps the most important invention to modern civilization) was the movable-type printing press. For the first time, books, music and maps could be created quickly and inexpensively, making them available to larger segments of the population. As a result, news was easily accessible and ideas were embraced, since more people could read and afford printed materials.

The Protestant Reformation, in which various groups of Christians left the Catholic Church to form their own denominations, brought about a significant change in religion. Bibles and music were translated from the Latin used in the Catholic Church to the languages spoken by the people.

Painters and sculptors created images and figures that were more realistic and lifelike. Among these were Leonardo da Vinci's *Mona Lisa* and Michelangelo's paintings on the ceiling of the Sistine Chapel in Rome. Sculpture developed from a craft to an art form. Michelangelo's *David* was created during this time.

Scientists were aided with refinements in the telescope and microscope. Galileo provided proof that the earth revolved around the sun, and Sir Isaac Newton explained the concept of gravity.

COMPOSERS

Josquin des Prez
(c. 1450–1521)

Giovanni Pierluigi da Palestrina
(c. 1525–1594)

William Byrd
(1543–1623)

Tomás Luis de Victoria
(c. 1548–1611)

Giovanni Gabrieli
(1553–1612)

ARTISTS

Sandro Botticelli (1445–1510)

Leonardo da Vinci (1452–1519)

Michelangelo (1475–1564)

Raphael (1483–1520)

El Greco (c. 1541–1614)

Michelangelo Merisi da Caravaggio
(1571–1610)

AUTHORS

Nicolo Machiavelli (1460–1527)

Martin Luther (1483–1546)

Miguel de Cervantes (1547–1616)

William Shakespeare (1564–1616)

René Descartes (1569–1650)

VOCABULARY

Renaissance period

polyphony

mass

motet

chorale

madrigal

lute

National Standards

6. Listening to, analyzing, and describing music. **(a, b, c, e, f)**
8. Understanding relationships between music, the other arts, and disciplines outside the arts. **(a, b, c, d, e)**
9. Understanding music in relation to history and culture. **(a, c, d, e)**

LESSON PLAN

Suggested Teaching Sequence

1. Examine the Renaissance period in a historical perspective.

Direct students to:

- Read and discuss the information found on student page 107.
- Share what they know about the composers, artists and authors listed on this page.
- Turn to the time line on pages 108–109 and read the citations.
- Discuss why these are considered important dates during the Renaissance period.
- Identify specific accomplishments that were made during the Renaissance period and the people associated with those accomplishments.
- Compare each of these events to what occurred after the Renaissance period.

2. Define the musical aspects of Renaissance music.

Direct students to:

- Read and discuss information on Renaissance music found on student page 108.
- Describe the difference between sacred and secular music.
- Define *polyphony, mass, chorale, madrigal, a cappella* and *lute*.

3. Discuss the performance guidelines of Renaissance music.

Direct students to:

- Read the Performance Links found on student page 108.
- Discuss the performance guidelines.

LISTENING LESSONS

This feature is designed to expand students' appreciation of choral and instrumental music of the Renaissance period.

**Choral Selection:
"O Magnum Mysterium" by Tomás de Victoria**

Direct students to:

- Read the information on student page 109 to learn more about Tomás de Victoria and "O Magnum Mysterium."

- Review the meaning of the musical style of the motet. *(a shorter choral work, set to Latin texts and used in religious services, but not part of the regular mass)*

- After listening to the recorded performance, discuss the interplay of major and minor tonality.

- Use signals such as raising their hands, standing/ sitting, holding up appro- priate flash cards to indicate when they hear major and minor tonalities, during a second listening.

**Instrumental Selection:
"Canzon XV" by Giovanni Gabrieli**

Direct students to:

- Read the information on student page 109 to learn more about Giovanni Gabrieli and "Canzon XV."

- After the first listening, discuss the contrast between contrapuntal writing and the sound of big block chords.

- During the second listening, tap a steady beat to find the change in meter and to name the different meters used.

Renaissance Music

During the Renaissance, both sacred and secular music became more complex. The Renaissance period is often referred to as the "golden age of polyphony." **Polyphony**, which literally means "many-sounding," is *a type of music in which there are two or more different melodic lines being sung or played at the same time.* Each line is independent of the other, and often, each line is of equal importance.

In the Catholic Church, the two prominent forms of music were the **mass**, *a religious service of prayers and ceremonies*, and the **motet**, *a shorter choral work, also set to Latin and used in religious services, but not part of the regular mass.* In the Protestant churches, the entire congregation would sing a **chorale**—*a melody that features even rhythms and simple harmonies.* Chorales are sometimes known as hymn tunes, and many hymns still sung in churches today are based on these early chorales.

There were great advances in secular music, as well. For the first time in history, the popularity of secular music rivaled that of sacred music. One of the most common forms of secular music was the **madrigal**, *a musical setting of a poem, generally in three or more parts.* Madrigals were generally performed a cappella, and the text was usually based on a romantic or pastoral theme.

During the Renaissance, there was an awakening of interest in instrumental music. Instruments were not only used to accompany voices, but were also featured in solo and ensemble music. The **lute**, *an early form of the guitar*, was as universally used during the Renaissance as the piano is today.

Performance Links

When performing music of the Renaissance period, it is important to apply the following guidelines:

- Sing with clarity and purity of tone.
- Balance the vocal lines with equal importance.
- In polyphonic music, sing the rhythms accurately and with precision.
- When designated by the composer, sing a cappella.

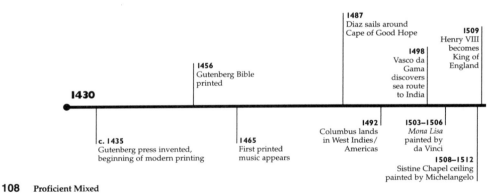

MORE ABOUT

Painting

During the Renaissance, there was a renewed focus back to the ancient culture of the Roman Empire and the classical spirit. In visual art, this was represented by a shift from sacred symbolism to realistic art. Leonardo da Vinci, one of the foremost painters and sculptors of the Renaissance, was also an architect, a scientist, an engineer and a musician. Perspective was explored as a result of interest in geometry, and the flat canvas now represented three-dimensional perspective from one point of view outside the plane of the art. The human form was celebrated, and the ideal was a realistic representation. Oil paints, which were first used during the early 1400s, made it possible for painters to revise and refine their ideas as they worked.

Listening Links

CHORAL SELECTION

"O Magnum Mysterium" by Tomás Luis de Victoria (c. 1548–1611)

Tomás Luis de Victoria, born in Avila, Spain, was one of the greatest composers of Renaissance polyphony. "O Magnum Mysterium" is a motet that was composed around 1572. The text describes the events surrounding the birth of Christ. The piece features four vocal lines that imitate each other, move together, and weave in and around one another. The texture is quite transparent in the polyphonic sections. Notice how Victoria's use of just a few words during these complex sections makes the text easily understood. Of particular interest is the frequent interplay of major and minor chords. Listen to this piece and see if you can hear the contrasting major and minor tonalities.

INSTRUMENTAL SELECTION

"Canzon XV" by Giovanni Gabrieli (c. 1557–1612)

Giovanni Gabrieli spent most of his life in Venice, Italy, with the exception of the years spent in Munich, where he studied with the great composer Orlando di Lasso (1532–1594). Gabrieli was an organist and resident composer at the Basilica of St. Mark, a huge cathedral right in the center of Venice. "Canzon XV" is written for ten trumpets and trombones. Listen for the contrasts between the contrapuntal writing based on the opening theme and the sounds of big block chords. Tap a steady beat to find where a change in meter takes place in the middle of the selection. As you listen to "Canson XV" again, identify and name the different meters that are used.

Check Your Understanding

1. List three major nonmusical changes that took place during the Renaissance period.

2. Describe polyphony as heard in "O Magnum Mysterium."

3. Describe how music from the Renaissance is different from music of today.

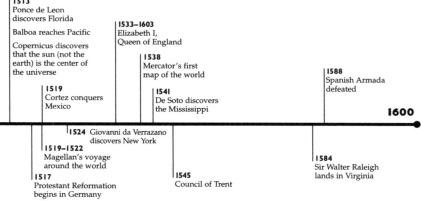

| 1513 Ponce de Leon discovers Florida
| Balboa reaches Pacific
| Copernicus discovers that the sun (not the earth) is the center of the universe
| 1533–1603 Elizabeth I, Queen of England
| 1538 Mercator's first map of the world
| 1588 Spanish Armada defeated
| 1519 Cortez conquers Mexico
| 1541 De Soto discovers the Mississippi
| **1600**
| 1524 Giovanni da Verrazano discovers New York
| 1519–1522 Magellan's voyage around the world
| 1584 Sir Walter Raleigh lands in Virginia
| 1517 Protestant Reformation begins in Germany
| 1545 Council of Trent

Music History *Renaissance* **109**

Answers to Check Your Understanding.

1. Answers will vary. For example, the use of the compass made it possible to explore new continents. The invention of the printing press and mass-produced books helped information spread rapidly. The Protestant Reformation led to the formation of many of the world's present-day Protestant denominations.

2. Polyphony is when two or more melodic lines begin at different places and act independently of each other. In "O Magnum Mysterium" polyphony can be heard throughout the piece, in contrast to the sections sung all together.

3. Answers will vary. Today we use many different instruments to provide interesting accompaniments for songs. During the Renaissance most songs were sung a cappella or with simple instruments that echoed the voice lines. One thing the two styles have in common is a frequent use of dissonance.

ASSESSMENT

Informal Assessment

In this lesson, students showed the ability to:

• Share what they know about the Renaissance period.

• Describe musical characteristics, styles and forms found in Renaissance music.

• Describe some characteristics of Renaissance art.

Student Self-Assessment

Direct students to:

• Review the questions in Check Your Understanding on page 109.

• Write a paragraph answering each of the three questions about music and events during the Renaissance period.

ENRICHMENT

Research Project

Direct students to:

Research the development of musical notation from its beginnings in the Middle Ages through the Renaissance period, where its development was spurred by the invention of the printing press. Include how and when the following became used: one line staff, five line staff, *do* clef, treble clef, bass clef, key signatures, rhythmic stem notation, note heads (diamond, triangle, circular), meter signatures, bar lines, dynamics and markings for tempo.

BAROQUE

OVERVIEW

Objectives

After completing this lesson, students will be able to:

• Describe the Baroque period, including important developments.

• Describe characteristics of Baroque music.

VOCABULARY

Have students review vocabulary in student lesson. A complete glossary of terms is found on page 260 of the student book.

Introduce the Baroque period through visual art. Analyze the painting *The Scale of Love* by Jean Antoine Watteau on page 110. Show Fine Art Transparency 9, *The Scale of Love,* (from the Teacher Resource Binder) and direct students to discuss the use of a focal point in this painting. Review the background information about Baroque art as found on teacher page 112.

 French painter Jean-Antoine Watteau (1684–1721) became the court painter to King Louis XV. He is best known for paintings of characters of scenes from the theater as well as for paintings that show the French aristocracy at play. *The Scale of Love* depicts a guitar player in a brightly colored theatrical costume with a girl seated at his feet as the main focal point. A marble bust of a bearded philosopher appears above the musician, turned to the right where secondary figures, engaged in their own pursuits, pay no attention to the two main actors.

Jean-Antoine Watteau. *The Scale of Love.* c. 1715-18. Oil on canvas. 50.8 x 59.7 cm (19 15/16 x 23 1/2"). National Gallery, London, United Kingdom.

110 Proficient Mixed

RESOURCES

Teacher Resource Binder

Music and History 6, *Baroque Music*

Music and History 8, *Johann Sebastian Bach*

Fine Art Transparency 2, *The Scale of Love,* Jean-Antoine Watteau

Music and History 9, *Fine Art Teaching Strategy—Baroque*

For additional resources, see Music and History section.

Listening Selections CD

(found in the Teacher Resource Binder)

Track 3: *Te Deum*

Track 4: "Spring" from *The Four Seasons,* First Movement

Focus

- Describe the Baroque period, including important developments of the time.
- Describe characteristics of Baroque music.

The Baroque Period— A Time of Elaboration

The **Baroque period** *(1600–1750)* began in Italy as a result of the Catholic Counter Reformation. This movement was in reaction to the Protestant Reformation of the Renaissance period. The Church and its wealthy followers sought to impress the world and reestablish the Catholic Church's influence in political and everyday life. The movement soon spread to all of Europe.

The period is characterized by grandeur and opulence, especially among royalty and the upper classes. Elaborate decoration was used in music, art, architecture and fashion. The term *baroque* has its origins in the French word for "imperfect or irregular pearls." These pearls were often used as decorations on clothing of the period.

Exploration of the world continued and colonies were established in new worlds, thus creating European empires. As goods were brought to Europe from faraway lands, a new wealthy merchant class was created.

Support for the arts was high during this time. The nobility sought to have artists, musicians, playwrights and actors in residence, a form of patronage previously seen only in the church and among royalty. However, the public still had little access to the arts, even though the first concerts for which admission was charged occurred during this time. Music and art remained in the church and in the homes of the powerful and wealthy ruling class.

Important scientific discoveries and theories came from this time. Galileo continued his work in astronomy and physics, and Sir Isaac Newton published *Mathematica Principia*, in which he stated the fundamental laws of gravity and motion. Many consider Newton's book to be among the most important scientific books ever written.

COMPOSERS

Johann Pachelbel
(1653–1706)

Henry Purcell
(1659–1695)

Antonio Vivaldi
(1678–1741)

Johann Sebastian Bach
(1685–1750)

George Frideric Handel
(1685–1759)

ARTISTS

Peter Paul Rubens
(1577–1640)

Anthony van Dyck
(1599–1641)

Rembrandt van Rijn
(1606–1669)

Jan Vermeer
(1632–1675)

Jean-Antoine Watteau
(1684–1721)

AUTHORS

John Milton
(1608–1674)

Molière
(1622–1673)

Daniel Defoe
(1660–1731)

Jonathan Swift
(1667–1745)

Samuel Johnson
(1709–1784)

VOCABULARY

Baroque period

homophony

recitatives

figured bass

concerto grosso

opera

oratorio

program music

Music History *Baroque*   **111**

National Standards

6. Listening to, analyzing, and describing music. **(a, b, c, e, f)**

8. Understanding relationships between music, the other arts, and disciplines outside the arts. **(a, b, c, d, e)**

9. Understanding music in relation to history and culture. **(a, c, d, e)**

LESSON PLAN

Suggested Teaching Sequence

1. **Examine the Baroque period in a historical perspective.**

Direct students to:

- Read and discuss the information found on student page 111.
- Share what they know about the composers, artists and authors listed on this page.
- Turn to the time line on pages 112–113 and read the citations.
- Discuss why these are considered important dates during the Baroque period.
- Identify specific accomplishments that were made during the Baroque period and the people associated with those accomplishments.
- Compare each of these events to what occurred before and after the Baroque period.

2. **Define the musical aspects of Baroque music.**

Direct students to:

- Read and discuss information on Baroque music found on student page 122.
- Discuss developments in music that occurred during this period.
- Define *homophony, recitatives, figured bass, oratorio, opera* and *concerto grosso.*

3. **Discuss the performance guidelines of Baroque music.**

Direct students to:

- Read the Performance Links found on student page 112.
- Discuss the performance guidelines.

LISTENING LESSONS

This feature is designed to expand students' appreciation of choral and instrumental music of the Baroque period.

Choral Selection:
Te Deum **by Henry Purcell**

Direct students to:

• Read the information on student page 113 to learn more Henry Purcell and *Te Deum.*

• Listen to the recorded performance and listen for ways in which Purcell dramatized the words through the music.

• While listening again, chart the organization of the piece. Identify sections by instrumentation and voicing; for example—instruments only, chorus and accompaniment, duet, quartet, solo and so forth.

Instrumental Selection:
"Spring" from *The Four Seasons,* **First Movement by Antonio Vivaldi**

Direct students to:

• Read the information on student page 113 to learn more about Antonio Vivaldi and "Spring," First Movement, from *The Four Seasons.*

• Review the meaning of program music.

• Listen to the recorded performance to identify the elements of spring that Vivaldi chose to portray (birds chirping and singing, streams swiftly moving, sudden and brief thunderstorms, a joyful dance and so forth).

Baroque Music

Music of the Baroque period had a dramatic flair and a strong sense of movement. The quiet a cappella style of the Renaissance gave way to large-scale productions and overall grandeur. Independent instrumental styles evolved, leading to the development of formalized orchestras.

Homophony, *a type of music in which there are two or more parts with similar or identical rhythms being sung or played at the same time,* was very popular during the Baroque period as composers revolted against the polyphony of earlier times.

Other important distinguishing developments in music during the Baroque period were:

• The performance of dramatic **recitatives,** or *vocal solos where the natural inflections of speech are imitated.*

• The singing of solo songs that were homophonic vocal compositions with accompaniment.

• The use of **figured bass,** which is *a set of numbers that are written below the bass line of a piece of music.* These numbers indicate the intirvallic distance between a given bass note and the other chord members, thus denoting choral inversions.

An important form of music in the period was the **concerto grosso,** *a multi-movement composition for a group of solo instruments and orchestra.* Other large works that were developed during this time included the **opera,** *a combination of singing, instrumental music, dancing and drama that tells a story,* and the **oratorio,** *a composition for solo voices, chorus and orchestra that was an extended dramatic work on a literary or religious theme presented without theatrical action.*

Performance Links

When performing music of the Baroque period, it is important to apply the following guidelines:

• Sing with pitch accuracy, especially in chromatic sections.

• Be conscious of who has the dominant theme, and make sure any accompanying parts do not overshadow the theme.

• Keep a steady, unrelenting pulse in most pieces. Precision of dotted rhythms is especially important.

• When dynamic level changes occur, all vocal lines need to change together.

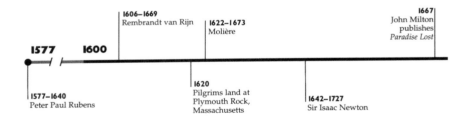

MORE ABOUT

Art in the Baroque Period

The Baroque period was a time of opulence and ornamentation. Using similar forms as the Renaissance, Baroque artists decorated each element. The distinction between the aristocracy and the common people was highly defined during this period, with the wealthy involved in the arts for their own pleasure and in an effort to represent their status in society. In *The Scale of Love,* the wealthy are represented in their finery.

Listening Links

CHORAL SELECTION

Te Deum (excerpt) by Henry Purcell (1659–1695)

English composer Henry Purcell (1659–1695) came from a family of musicians and as a child was a boy chorister at the Chapel Royal. In 1679, he became organist of Westminster Abbey—a position he held for sixteen years. In his later years, Purcell was increasingly prolific, composing some of his greatest church music, including *Te Deum* (1694). In this work, Purcell added an orchestra and a pair of trumpets, never previously used in English church music. The performance was a sensation. Purcell dramatized the words through the music. For example, *heaven* is sung high by the Sopranos, followed by a very low Bass singing the word *earth*. To stress important words, Purcell often used an extended melisma (heard on the words *glorious, goodly, praise*). Find other examples of the interplay between the text and music.

INSTRUMENTAL SELECTION

Spring, First Movement from *The Four Seasons* by Antonio Vivaldi (1878–1741)

Antonio Vivaldi was an Italian composer. He is best known as the master of concertos, having written over 500, half of them for solo violin and orchestra. His most well-known work is *The Four Seasons*. It is a set of four solo concertos for violin, string orchestra and basso continuo. As **program music**, *instrumental music that is composed about a nonmusical subject*, each concerto portrays one of the seasons of the year, corresponding with sonnets that preface each concerto. What elements of spring has Vivaldi chosen to portray in his music?

Check Your Understanding

1. Identify three important nonmusical developments that took place during the Baroque period.

2. Compare and contrast *oratorio* and *opera*.

3. Analyze characteristics of choral music during the Baroque period as heard in *Te Deum* by Henry Purcell.

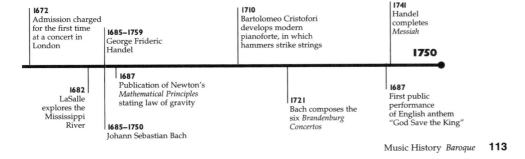

1672
Admission charged for the first time at a concert in London

1685–1759
George Frideric Handel

1710
Bartolomeo Cristofori develops modern pianoforte, in which hammers strike strings

1741
Handel completes *Messiah*

1750

1682
LaSalle explores the Mississippi River

1687
Publication of Newton's *Mathematical Principles* stating law of gravity

1685–1750
Johann Sebastian Bach

1721
Bach composes the six *Brandenburg Concertos*

1687
First public performance of English anthem "God Save the King"

Music History *Baroque* **113**

Answers to Check Your Understanding.

1. Answers will vary. For example, invention of the telescope, discovery of the law of gravity, exploration and colonization, Pilgrims land at Plymouth Rock.

2. Opera and oratorios are both written for solo voices, chorus and orchestra. They both tell a story. Operas, however, are performed on stage with dancing, costuming and scenery. Oratorios are performed in a church or concert setting.

3. Characteristics of choral music during the Baroque period found in *Te Deum* include dramatic flair, large-scale production and overall grandeur, the words dramatized by the music, the use of melismas, terraced dynamics created by sudden changes in instrumentation or voicings.

ASSESSMENT

Informal Assessment

In this lesson, students showed the ability to:

• Share what they know about the Baroque period.

• Describe musical characteristics, styles and forms found in Baroque music.

• Describe some characteristics of Baroque art.

Student Self-Assessment

Direct students to:

• Review the questions in Check Your Understanding on page 113.

• Write a paragraph answering each of the three questions about the Baroque period.

ENRICHMENT

Research Project

As a small group activity, assign each group one of the following questions to discover what was happening musically in North America during the Baroque period:

• Research music found in North America during the Baroque period (1600–1750). What type of music was being sung or played, and who was creating it?

• What influence did the relationship between Europe and North America have on American music during this period?

• Did the Baroque spirit foster any new musical inventions in North America?

• What types of Native American music were prevalent in North America at this time?

• Present findings to the rest of the class.

CLASSICAL

OVERVIEW

Objectives

After completing this lesson, students will be able to:

• Describe the Classical period, including important developments of the time.

• Describe characteristics of Classical music.

MUSIC&ART

Introduce the Classical period through art. Analyze the photograph of *Grand Piano* created by Joseph Böhm on page 114. Direct students to discuss the piano's history, range and decorations. Review background information of art during the Classical period as found on teacher page 116.

MUSIC&ART

The second wife of Napoléon Bonaparte (1769–1821) is believed to have owned this piano. A six-octave range on the piano was customary during the early 1800s. Notice the imperial eagles that crown the legs and nameplate. Joseph Böhm, the builder of this magnificent piano, lived and worked in Vienna, Austria.

Joseph Böhm. *Grand Piano.* c. 1815–20. Wood, various materials. 223.4 cm (87 15/16").
The Metropolitan Museum of Art, New York, New York.

Focus

- Describe the Classical period, including important developments of the time.
- Describe characteristics of Classical music.

The Classical Period— The Age of Enlightenment

The **Classical period** *(1750–1820)* was a time when, as a result of archeological findings, society began looking to the ancient Greeks and Romans for examples of order and ways of looking at life. The calm beauty and simplicity of this ancient art inspired artists, architects and musicians to move away from the overly decorated standards of the Baroque period. The elegant symmetry of Greek architecture in particular was re-created in thousands of buildings in Europe and the New World.

This time was also called "The Age of Enlightenment." Writers, philosophers and scientists of the eighteenth century sought to break from the past and replace the darkness and ignorance of European thought with the "light" of truth. The spirit of democracy was ignited by the writings of thinkers such as Voltaire and Thomas Jefferson. Their writings suggested that through science and democracy, people could choose their own fate.

These new thoughts and ways of thinking became widespread among many of the people of the day. The desire for change became so strong that citizens in a number of countries rebelled against leaders who did not grant them basic civil and economic rights. For example, the American Revolution, in which the colonists rebelled against the British government, was based on many of the principles of the "Enlightenment." The French Revolution resulted in the elimination of the monarchy and the establishment of a new government and a new societal structure in that country. Monarchies throughout Europe that were not overthrown became less powerful; many of these countries adopted a democratic form of government.

COMPOSERS

Christoph Willibald Gluck
(1714–1787)

Carl Philipp Emanuel Bach
(1714–1788)

Johann Christian Bach
(1735–1762)

Franz Joseph Haydn
(1732–1809)

Wolfgang Amadeus Mozart
(1756–1791)

ARTISTS

Pietro Longhi
(1702–1788)

Thomas Gainsborough
(1727–1788)

Francisco Göya
(1746–1828)

Jacques-Louis David
(1748–1825)

AUTHORS

Voltaire
(1694–1778)

Jean Jacques Rousseau
(1712–1778)

Johann Wolfgang von Goethe
(1749–1832)

William Wordsworth
(1770–1850)

Jane Austen
(1775–1817)

VOCABULARY

Classical period

symphony

concerto

sonata

string quartet

Music History *Classical*   **115**

National Standards

6. Listening to, analyzing, and describing music. **(a, b, c, e, f)**
8. Understanding relationships between music, the other arts, and disciplines outside the arts. **(a, b, c, d, e)**
9. Understanding music in relation to history and culture. **(a, c, d, e)**

LESSON PLAN

Suggested Teaching Sequence

1. Examine the Classical period in a historical perspective.

Direct students to:

- Read and discuss the information found on student page 115.
- Share what they know about the composers, artists and authors listed on this page.
- Turn to the time line on pages 116–117 and read the citations.
- Discuss why these are considered important dates during the Classical period.
- Identify specific accomplishments that were made during the Classical period and the people associated with those accomplishments.
- Compare each of these events to what occurred before and after the Classical period.

2. Define the musical aspects of Classical music.

Direct students to:

- Read and discuss information on Classical music found on student page 116.
- Define *symphony, concerto, sonata* and *string quartet.*
- Discuss instruments used in the Classical period.

3. Discuss the performance guidelines of Classical music.

Direct students to:

- Read the Performance Links found on student page 116.
- Discuss the performance guidelines.

This feature is designed to expand students' appreciation of choral and instrumental music of the Classical period.

Choral Selection:
"Gloria" from the *Coronation Mass* by Wolfgang Amadeus Mozart

Direct students to:

- Read the information on student page 117 to learn more about Wolfgang Amadeus Mozart and "Gloria" from the *Coronation Mass.*

- Listen to the recorded performance to identify the sections sung by the full chorus and those sung by the soloists.

- While listening again, identify and list the different ways that the soloists sing together *(a quartet, Soprano and Tenor duet, Soprano and Alto duet, overlapping entries on the word "Amen" in a fugal treatment).*

Instrumental Selection:
Symphony #100 in G Major, Second Movement by Franz Joseph Haydn

Direct students to:

- Read the information on student page 117 to learn more about Franz Joseph Haydn and *Symphony #100 in G Major,* Second Movement.

- Listen to the recorded performance to identify the three large sections and the coda.

- While listening again, write down instruments that are featured in each section.

Music of the Classical Period

Musicians moved away from the heavily ornate styles of the Baroque period and embraced the clean, uncluttered style of the early Greeks and Romans. Instead of many melodies occurring simultaneously, as in the Baroque period, Classical composers wrote clearer music in which one melody sings out while the other parts provide a simple harmonic accompaniment.

The Classical period has been called the "golden age of music." Many forms of music—the **symphony**, *a large-scale work for orchestra;* the **concerto**, *a multi-movement piece for solo instrument and orchestra;* the **sonata**, *a multi-movement piece for solo instrument;* and the **string quartet**, *a form of chamber music that uses two violins, a viola and a cello—* were fully developed during this period. The growing popularity of these forms of music led to the establishment of the string, woodwind, brass and percussion sections of today's orchestras. The piano, with its greater sonority than Baroque keyboard instruments, began to become an important instrument in Classical compositions.

Performance Links

When performing music of the Classical period, it is important to apply the following guidelines:

- Listen for the melody line so the accompaniment parts do not overshadow it.
- Sing chords in tune.
- Make dynamic level changes that move smoothly.
- Keep phrases flowing and connected.

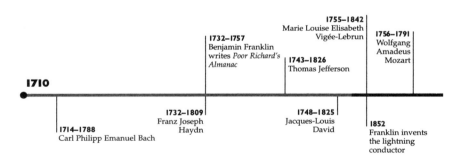

MORE ABOUT...

Art in the Classical Period

The Classical period was highlighted by a return to the ideal of Greek and Roman simplicity and balance. Likewise, social development seemed to swing like a pendulum along a continuum from excess to control. When the Baroque period was at its most opulent, there began to be an upsurge of indignant rebellion from the common people, leading to a return to more sensible, clean, and symmetrical artistic representations. The *Grand Piano* is a beautiful, symmetrical, balanced and uncluttered example of Classical art.

Listening Links

CHORAL SELECTION

"Gloria" from *Coronation Mass* by Wolfgang Amadeus Mozart (1756–1791)

Mozart wrote the *Coronation Mass* for the coronation of Emperor Leopold II of Frankfurt, Germany, in 1790. The piece was written for choir, soloists and full orchestra. "Gloria," the second part of the Mass, can be broken into three sections: a beginning, a middle or development, and an ending. Notice that this ending is much like the beginning. The piece ends with a dramatic coda. One melody sings out while the other parts provide a simple accompaniment. As you listen to this piece, pay attention to the innovative interplay between the soloists. List at least three different ways that the soloists sing together.

INSTRUMENTAL SELECTION

Symphony #100 in G Major, Second Movement by Franz Joseph Haydn (1732–1809)

Haydn's *Symphony #100 in G Major* is also known as the "Military Symphony." It is one of two sets of London symphonies written late in Haydn's career in 1794. It calls for a large orchestra for the time, adding instruments from the Turkish military influence— triangle, cymbals, bass drum and bell tree. Listen to this piece of music, paying attention to the contrasting sections.

Check Your Understanding

1. Identify three important nonmusical developments that took place during the Classical period.

2. What aspects of Mozart's "Gloria" characterize it as being from the Classical period?

3. Describe how music from the Classical period is different from music of the Baroque period.

4. Why do you think this symphony is called the "Military Symphony"?

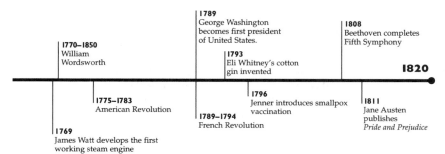

Music History *Classical* **117**

Answers to Check Your Understanding.

1. Answers will vary. Revolutions in the American colonies and in France that produced new governments and new social structures; oxygen was discovered; the first submarine was produced.

2. Mozart's "Gloria" includes music that is based on balance, clarity, and simplicity, uses of homophonic texture most of the time and uses of interesting dynamic contrast.

3. Answers will vary. The music of the Classical period left the exaggerated embellishments and the use of improvisation behind; it emphasized precision and balance.

4. Instruments from the Turkish military bands such as the triangle and cymbals were added to the orchestra for the first time and featured in this piece. Parts of this piece also sound very march-like.

[(A—strings and woodwinds (oboe, bassoon) and French horn; B—triangle, cymbals, woodwinds, strings, trumpet; A'—strings, woodwinds (oboe, flute, bassoon, clarinet), French horn, cymbals, triangle, trumpet; coda—trumpet, tympani, strings, woodwinds, triangle, cymbals)]

ASSESSMENT

Informal Assessment

In this lesson, students showed the ability to:

• Share what they know about the Classical period.

• Describe musical characteristics, styles and forms found in Classical music.

• Describe some characteristics of Classical art.

Student Self-Assessment

Direct students to:

• Review the questions in Check Your Understanding on page 117.

• Write a paragraph answering each of the four questions about the Classical period.

ENRICHMENT

Research Project

As a small group activity, assign each group one of the following leading figures of the Classical period as listed in the sidebar on student page 115. Have each group do research on the contributions of each, and then present findings to the rest of the class.

ROMANTIC

OVERVIEW

Objectives

After completing this lesson, students will be able to:

- Describe the Romantic period, including important developments of the time.
- Describe characteristics of Romantic music.

MUSIC&ART

Introduce the Romantic period through visual art. Analyze the painting by Mary Cassatt on page 118. Direct students to discuss the details in *The Loge*. Why was painter Edgar Degas important to Mary Cassatt? Is there a story in the picture? Review background information on *The Loge* by Cassatt as found on teacher page 120.

MUSIC&ART

American artist Mary Cassatt (1844–1926) is known for her perceptive depictions of women and children. Although born to a prominent Pittsburgh family, Mary Cassatt spent most of her adult life in Paris, France. There, her work attracted the attention of French painter Edgar Degas (1834–1917), who invited her to exhibit with his fellow Impressionist painters. In *The Loge*, two women are at the theater. You can see the rings of theater seats and a massive chandelier behind them, which suggests that they are sitting in luxurious boxes.

Mary Cassatt. *The Loge.* 1882. Oil on canvas. 79.8 x 63.8 cm (31 3/8 x 25 1/8"). National Gallery of Art, Washington, D. C. Chester Dale Collection.

118   Proficient Mixed

RESOURCES

Teacher Resource Binder

Music and History 14, *Romantic Music*

Music and History 17, *Franz Schubert*

Fine Art Transparency 4, *The Loge,* Mary Cassatt

Music and History 18, *Fine Art Teaching Strategy—Romantic*

For additional resources, see Music and History section.

Listening Selections CD

(found in the Teacher Resource Binder)

Track 7: "How Lovely Is Thy Dwelling Place" from the *German Requiem*

Track 8: *Symphony #5 in C Minor,* First Movement

Focus

- Describe the Romantic period, including important developments of the time.
- Describe characteristics of Romantic music.

The Romantic Period— A Time of Drama

The **Romantic Period** *(1820–1900)* was in many ways a reaction against the Classical period, which is often known as the "age of reason." In contrast, the Romantic period could be considered an "age of emotion." A new sense of political and artistic freedom emerged as musicians and artists were no longer employed by the church. The period was characterized by the ideals of liberty and individualism, and of dramatic thought and action.

The Romantic period coincided with the Industrial Revolution. Momentous progress in science and mechanics gave the world the steamboat and rail transportation, as well as the electric light, telephone and telegraph. Cities grew as nonagricultural jobs developed, and members of the middle classes exerted increasing influence. A new sense of patriotism emerged in Europe as well as in the United States.

The Industrial Revolution produced a wealthy middle class. Their new wealth provided music for the masses to a far greater degree than had existed before. Most musicians' incomes were now provided by the sale of concert tickets and published music rather than by the patronage of the church or royalty. This gave musicians larger audiences and more freedom of expression in their compositions.

The painters of the Romantic period took much of their inspiration from nature. The romantic paintings of William Turner and John Constable express the feelings evoked by nature. Later, Impressionist painters, including Edouard Manet, Claude Monet and Pierre-Auguste Renoir, developed new techniques to bring the sense and feeling of nature alive for the viewer.

COMPOSERS

Ludwig van Beethoven (1770–1827)

Franz Schubert (1797–1828)

Frédéric Chopin (1810–1849)

Robert Schumann (1810–1856)

Richard Wagner (1813–1883)

Stephen Foster (1826–1864)

Johannes Brahms (1833–1897)

ARTISTS

James Whistler (1834–1903)

Paul Cezanne (1839–1906)

Claude Monet (1840–1926)

Pierre-Auguste Renoir (1841–1919)

Mary Cassatt (1845–1926)

Vincent van Gogh (1853–1890)

AUTHORS

George Sand (1804–1876)

Henry Wadsworth Longfellow (1807–1882)

Harriet Beecher Stowe (1811–1896)

Charles Dickens (1812–1870)

Leo Tolstoy (1828–1910)

Mark Twain (1835–1910)

VOCABULARY

Romantic period

nationalism

art song

requiem

motive

Music History *Romantic*   **119**

LESSON PLAN
Suggested Teaching Sequence

1. **Examine the Romantic period in a historical perspective.**

Direct students to:

- Read and discuss the information found on student page 119.
- Share what they know about the composers, artists and authors listed on this page.
- Turn to the time line on pages 120–121 and read the citations.
- Discuss why these are considered important dates during the Romantic period.
- Identify specific accomplishments that were made during the Romantic period and the people associated with those accomplishments.
- Compare each of these events to what occurred before and after the Romantic period.

2. **Define the musical aspects of Romantic music.**

Direct students to:

- Read and discuss information on Romantic music found on student page 120.
- Name several important Romantic composers and their contributions.
- Define *nationalism* and *art song*.

3. **Discuss the performance guidelines of Romantic music.**

Direct students to:

- Read the Performance Links found on student page 120.
- Discuss the performance guidelines.

National Standards

6. Listening to, analyzing, and describing music. **(a, b, c, e, f)**
8. Understanding relationships between music, the other arts, and disciplines outside the arts. **(a, b, c, d, e)**
9. Understanding music in relation to history and culture. **(a, c, d, e)**

LISTENING LESSONS

This feature is designed to expand students' appreciation of choral and instrumental music of the Romantic period.

Choral Selection: "How Lovely Is Thy Dwelling Place" from the *German Requiem* by Johannes Brahms

Direct students to:

• Read the information on student page 121 to learn more about Johannes Brahms and "How Lovely Is Thy Dwelling Place" from the *German Requiem*.

• Review the definition of *requiem*.

• Listen to the recorded performance to identify the mood created by this chorus.

• After listening again, describe various ways that Brahms expresses the words of the text through music. (*Answers will vary. An English translation of the words: How lovely is thy dwelling place, O Lord of hosts, for my soul. It longeth, yea fainteth for the courts of the Lord. My soul and body crieth out, yea, for the living God. Blest are they that dwell within Thy house. They praise thy name evermore!*)

Instrumental Selection: *Symphony #5 in C Minor*, First Movement by Ludwig van Beethoven

Direct students to:

• Read the information on student page 121 to learn more about Ludwig van Beethoven and *Symphony #5 in C Minor*.

Romantic Music

Music of the Romantic period focused on both the heights and depths of human emotion. Complexity, exploration and excitement were characteristics of the new compositions. This was in great contrast to the music of the Classical period, which was based on balance, clarity and simplicity.

Many Romantic compositions reflect the period's spirit of **nationalism**, or *pride in a country's history*. Composers used traditional legends, as well as dramas, novels and poems, as the basis for both vocal and instrumental works. There was an increased interest in the traditional folk tunes and folk dances of specific nations or regions. For example, German folk songs can be heard in Robert Schumann's (1810–1856) piano pieces and symphonies. In the United States, the songs composed by Stephen Foster (1826–1864) reflected the culture of the South at that time.

Instrumental music became more elaborate and expressive. The symphonies of Beethoven remain among the most popular and critically acclaimed compositions of Western music. Symphony orchestras increased in size, and percussion instruments held a new place of importance.

As the Romantic period progressed, the most important vocal form became the **art song**, *an expressive song about life, love and human relationships for solo voice and piano*. German art songs are known as lieder, and the most famous composer of lieder was Franz Schubert (1797–1828).

Performance Links

When performing music of the Romantic period, it is important to apply the following guidelines:

• Understand the relation of the text to the melody and harmony.
• Concentrate on phrasing and maintaining a clear, beautiful melodic line.
• Perform accurately the wide range of dynamics and tempos.
• Sing confidently in foreign languages to reflect nationalism in music.

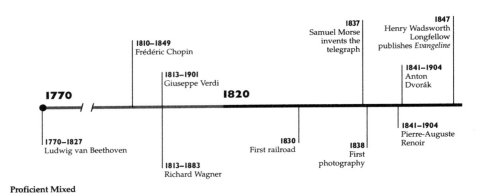

120   Proficient Mixed

MORE ABOUT

Art in the Romantic Period

Visual artists of the Romantic period reflected the era's attitudes with bolder, more colorful works. Point out the details in *The Loge*. An episode in the lives of the middle class is depicted. Ask students to discuss the following question: In which ways does this painter use the elements and principals of art differently than artists of other periods studied?

Listening Links

CHORAL SELECTION

"How Lovely Is Thy Dwelling Place" from *The German Requiem*
by Johannes Brahms (1833–1897)

Johannes Brahms was one of the finest composers of the nineteenth century. A **requiem** *(a mass for the dead)* is a piece containing seven movements combining mixed chorus, solo voices and full orchestra. Brahms intended to portray death as a time of peace and rest. "How Lovely Is Thy Dwelling Place" is a setting of Psalm 84, and is considered to be one of the most beautiful requiem choruses ever written. Toward the end of the piece, the opening melody returns. An unusual use of unison octaves is then heard. Describe the various ways that Brahms expresses the words of the text through his music.

INSTRUMENTAL SELECTION

Symphony #5 in C Minor, First Movement by Ludwig van Beethoven (1770–1827)

Ludwig van Beethoven was one of the greatest composers of all time, particularly noteworthy because he wrote some of his greatest compositions after he had become deaf. His *Symphony #5* has been said to be the musical interpretation of his resolution, "I will grapple with Fate; it shall not overcome me." The first movement has an opening **motive**, *a short rhythmic or melodic idea*, that is immediately recognizable. The development of the motive throughout the piece is a testament to Beethoven's musical genius. Listen to this piece and identify the motive (short, short, short, long). Describe the differences between the first and second themes in this movement.

Check Your Understanding

1. Identify three important nonmusical developments that took place during the Romantic period.

2. Identify characteristics of Romantic music as heard in "How Lovely Is Thy Dwelling Place."

3. Describe how music from the Romantic period is different from music of the Classical period.

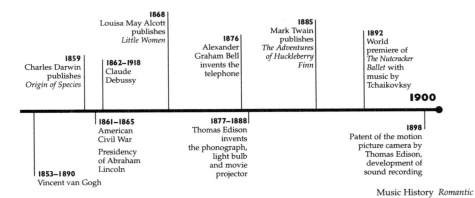

- 1859 Charles Darwin publishes *Origin of Species*
- 1868 Louisa May Alcott publishes *Little Women*
- 1862–1918 Claude Debussy
- 1876 Alexander Graham Bell invents the telephone
- 1885 Mark Twain publishes *The Adventures of Huckleberry Finn*
- 1892 World premiere of *The Nutcracker Ballet* with music by Tchaikovksy
- **1900**
- 1853–1890 Vincent van Gogh
- 1861–1865 American Civil War / Presidency of Abraham Lincoln
- 1877–1888 Thomas Edison invents the phonograph, light bulb and movie projector
- 1898 Patent of the motion picture camera by Thomas Edison, development of sound recording

Music History *Romantic*   **121**

Answers to Check Your Understanding.

1. Answers will vary. For example, Industrial Revolution, development of railroads, steamboats, the telegraph and telephone, photography and sound recordings are few choices they might use.

2. "How Lovely Is Thy Dwelling Place" reflects several characteristics of Romantic music including complexity; melodies that are long and lyrical; a wide range of dynamics; and so forth.

3. Answers will vary. For example, music of the Classical period was structured, less emotional. It emphasized clarity, repose and balance. Music of the Romantic period was full of emotion and less structured than music of the Classical period. Nationalism was an important element in Romantic music.

- Review the definition of motive.
- Listen to the recorded performance to identify the opening motive as well as the first and second themes.
- While listening again to the first section, write descriptions of the first and second themes. Discuss the differences between them *(louder/softer; short, disconnected notes/long, flowing phrases; and so forth)*.

ASSESSMENT

Informal Assessment

In this lesson, students showed the ability to:

- Share what they know about the Romantic period.
- Describe musical characteristics, styles and forms found in Romantic music.
- Describe some characteristics of Romantic art.

Student Self-Assessment

Direct students to:

- Review the questions in Check Your Understanding on page 121.
- Write a paragraph answering each of the three questions about the Romantic period.

ENRICHMENT

Research Project

Symphony #5 in C Minor, First Movement, is written in sonata-allegro form. Have students work with a partner to write a story in sonata-allegro form. Share them with the class.

CONTEMPORARY

OVERVIEW

Objectives

After completing this lesson, students will be able to:

- Describe the Contemporary period, including important developments of the time.
- Describe characteristics of Contemporary music.

Introduce the Contemporary period through visual art. Analyze the painting by Mark Chagall on page 122. Direct students to discuss the use of color and form in *Green Violinist*. Review background information on Chagall's Green Violinist as found on page 124.

MUSIC&ART

Marc Chagall (1887–1985) was a Russian-born French painter and designer. Chagall's distinctive use of color and form is derived from the influence of Russian expressionism and French cubism. In *Green Violinist*, Chagall reflects on his Russian homeland by depicting the figure of the violinist dancing in a rustic village.

Marc Chagall. *Green Violinist*. 1923–24. Oil on canvas, 198 x 108.6 cm (78 x 42 3/4").
Solomon Guggenheim Museum, New York, New York. Gift, Solomon R. Guggenheim, 1937.

122 Proficient Mixed

Focus
- Describe the Contemporary period, including important developments of the time.
- Describe characteristics of Contemporary music.

The Contemporary Period— The End of Isolation

The **Contemporary period** *(1900–present)* has been a period of rapid change spurred by tremendous technological advances. In less than sixty years, aviation progressed from the first airplane to space exploration and man walking on the moon. Technology brought the emergence of the automobile, television, computer and cellular telephone. The recording of music developed and grew. Recorded sound moved from vinyl LPs and audiocassettes to CDs, DVDs and MP3s. Can you imagine a lifestyle without these modern conveniences?

The world has changed from one of many isolated nations to a world where nations come together to attempt to solve worldwide problems such as war, famines, health epidemics and environmental problems such as global warming. People are also less isolated. Rather than staying in one place all their lives, as was most common in other periods, many people move from place to place. Some even move to other countries as well. Satellites orbiting the earth allow people to instantly observe what is going on in other parts of the world. One of the most important developments of the Contemporary period is the creation of the World Wide Web, which allows individual computers to instantly connect to other computers around the globe. School students in the United States taking classes in French, for example, can communicate directly in real time with students in France during a normal class period.

Some of the Contemporary period leaders in the arts include:

- Composers—Duke Ellington (1899–1974), George Gershwin (1898–1937), Leonard Bernstein (1918–1990), Libby Larson (b. 1950)
- Artists—Romare Bearden (1911–1988), Ansel Adams (1902–1984), Alexander Calder (1898–1976), Andy Warhol (1930–1987)
- Dancers—Martha Graham (1894–1991), Twyla Tharp (b. 1941), Bella Zewinsky (b. 1917)

Music History *Contemporary* **123**

COMPOSERS
Ralph Vaughan Williams (1872–1958)
Béla Bartók (1881–1945)
Igor Stravinsky (1882–1971)
Heitor Villa-Lobos (1887–1959)
William Grant Still (1895–1978)
Francis Poulenc (1899–1963)
Aaron Copland (1900–1990)

ARTISTS
Pablo Picasso (1881–1973)
Diego Rivera (1886–1957)
Marc Chagall (1887–1985)
Georgia O'Keeffe (1887–1986)
Jacob Lawrence (1917–2000)
Andrew Wyeth (b. 1917)

AUTHORS
Robert Frost (1874–1963)
Virginia Woolf (1882–1941)
Thorton Wilder (1897–1975)
Ernest Hemingway (1899–1961)
Arther Miller (b. 1915)
James Baldwin (1924–1997)
Gabriel García Márquez (b. 1928)
Lillian Hillman (1905–1984)

VOCABULARY
Contemporary period
dissonance
minimalism
fusion
polyrhythms

LESSON PLAN
Suggested Teaching Sequence

1. Examine the Contemporary period in a historical perspective.
Direct students to:
- Read and discuss the information found on student page 123.
- Share what they know about the composers, artists and authors listed on this page.
- Turn to the time line on pages 124–125 and read the citations.
- Discuss why these are considered important dates during the Contemporary period.
- Identify specific accomplishments that were made during the Contemporary period and the people associated with those accomplishments.

2. Define the musical aspects of Contemporary music.
Direct students to:
- Read and discuss information on Contemporary music found on student page 124.
- Name several important Contemporary composers.
- Discuss three major elements that are often heard in Contemporary music.
- Define *dissonance, minimalism, musical theater, jazz, rock, reggae* and *tejano.*

3. Discuss the performance guidelines of Contemporary music.
Direct students to:
- Read the Performance Links found on student page 124.
- Discuss the performance guidelines.

National Standards
6. Listening to, analyzing, and describing music. **(a, b, c, e, f)**
8. Understanding relationships between music, the other arts, and disciplines outside the arts. **(a, b, c, d, e)**
9. Understanding music in relation to history and culture. **(a, c, d, e)**

LISTENING LESSONS

This feature is designed to expand students' appreciation of choral and instrumental music of the Contemporary period.

Choral Selection:
"Laudamus Te" from *Gloria* by Francis Poulenc

Direct students to:

- Read the information on student page 125 to learn more about Francis Poulenc and "Laudamus Te" from his *Gloria.*

- Listen to the recorded performance to identify sudden changes, accents in the wrong places and beautiful melodies.

- Discuss the different treatments of the repeated phrase "Laudamus Te." *(Usually, the full choir in unison sings this phrase, with accent on "da" and "te." At two places, one part of the choir echoes another on the phrase. It is also sung in big chords with accents on each syllable. The ending adds a new rhythmic emphasis to the phrase.)*

Instrumental Selection:
"Street in a Frontier Town" from *Billy the Kid*, Scene I, by Aaron Copland

Direct students to:

- Read the information on student page 125 to learn more about Aaron Copland and "Street in a Frontier Town" from *Billy the Kid,* Scene I.

- Define *polyrhythms.*

- Listen to the recorded performance to enjoy the energy and drama of this ballet selection.

Music of the Contemporary Period

By the turn of the twentieth century, musicians of all nationalities were searching for original forms of expression. During the first half of the century, nationalism continued to have a large influence. The study of folk songs in their countries enhanced the music of many composers, like Ralph Vaughan Williams (England), Aaron Copland (United States), Béla Bartók (Hungary), and Heitor Villa-Lobos (Brazil).

Three major elements that are often heard in Contemporary music include (1) harmonies that emphasize **dissonance**, *a combination of tones that sounds harsh and unstable,* (2) melodies with angular contours, and (3) rhythms featuring irregular patterns and shifting meters.

During the mid-twentieth century, there was a shift in classical music. Composer Philip Glass (b. 1937) was searching for a new way of writing. He began to compose music that explored the repetition of simple rhythms and minimal melodies. This new form of writing is called **minimalism**. It is *tonal music that stresses the element of repetition with changes that are dictated by a rule or system.*

Also during this period, many different popular music styles emerged. The list below identifies some of the more important ones.

- Musical Theater—centered on Broadway and Hollywood musicals
- Jazz—strong rhythmic and harmonic structures supporting solo and ensemble improvisation
- Rock—music with strongly accented or emphasized beats
- Reggae—a **fusion** *(a combination or blending of different genres of music)* of rock and Jamaican rhythms, instruments and language
- Tejano—a fusion of Mexican and country music

Performance Links

When performing music of the Contemporary period, it is important to apply the following guidelines:

- Sing on pitch, even in extreme parts of your range.
- Tune intervals carefully in the skips found in many melodic lines.
- Sing changing meters and unusual rhythm patterns precisely.
- Perform accurately the wide range in dynamics and tempos.

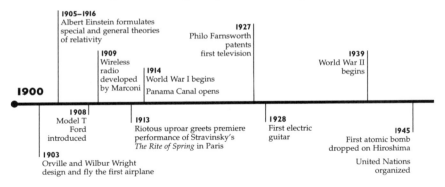

124   Proficient Mixed

MORE ABOUT...

Art from the Contemporary Period

The word that best describes the art of the Contemporary period is *diversity*. It is indeed a period with a style for everyone, where form, function and art are sometimes inextricably bound together. Old ideas are often used, but are many times abandoned for a new way of looking at the world. Today's artists make use of new materials and techniques to express their ideas, beliefs and feelings. Many of these artists are moving away from traditional styles of art. Art movements of the past have given way to an astonishing array of individual art styles. Some of these styles reflect the influence of earlier artists while others reject entirely any reference to historical models.

Listening Links

CHORAL SELECTION

"Laudamus te" from *Gloria* by Francis Poulenc (1899–1963)

Francis Poulenc was one of France's most colorful twentieth-century composers. His style was greatly influenced by Stravinsky, Vivaldi, Palestrina and Victoria. Poulenc's writing is fundamentally tonal, but his music is full of sudden changes in key signatures, dynamics, rhythms and harmonies. He often worked in short musical phrases, repeating them with subtle variations. *Gloria*, written in 1959, is one of his most popular works. He deliberately contrasts text and musical accents. Combinations of different musical styles, accents in all the wrong places, and beautiful melodies make the *Gloria* a Poulenc masterpiece. Discuss how the repeated phrase "Laudamus te" is treated differently on each repetition.

INSTRUMENTAL SELECTION

"Street in a Frontier Town" from *Billy the Kid* by Aaron Copland (1900–1990)

Aaron Copland is one of the most famous composers of the twentieth century. Copland was born in Brooklyn, New York, and was famous for adapting American folk themes into his orchestral works. *Billy the Kid* is one such example. Written as a ballet to tell the story of the outlaw Billy the Kid, Copland divides the saga into six parts: "The Open Prairie," "Street in a Frontier Town," "Prairie Night," "Gun Battle," "Celebration," and "Billy's Death." In "Street in a Frontier Town," many American folk songs are used. Copland adapts these folk songs and uses interesting **polyrhythms**, *a technique in which several different rhythms are performed at the same time*. Listen to this selection. What folk songs and melodies do you recognize?

Check Your Understanding

1. Identify three important nonmusical developments that took place during the Contemporary period.

2. Describe musical characteristics of the Contemporary period as heard in *Gloria*: "Laudamus te" by Francis Poulenc.

3. Describe how music from the Contemporary period is different from music of the Romantic period.

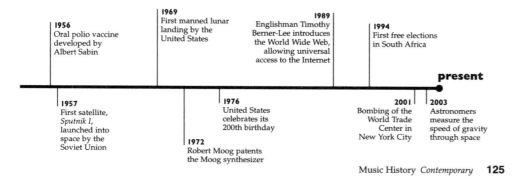

Music History Contemporary 125

- Listen again to identify the folk songs and familiar melodies used by Copland. (*American folk songs—Great Granddad, The Old Chisholm Trail, Goodbye Old Paint—and a Mexican Jarabe dance tune*)

ASSESSMENT

Informal Assessment

In this lesson, students showed the ability to:

- Share what they know about the Contemporary period.

- Describe musical characteristics, styles and forms found in Contemporary music.

- Describe some characteristics of Contemporary art.

Student Self-Assessment

Direct students to:

- Review the questions in Check Your Understanding on page 125.

- Write a paragraph answering each of the three questions about the Contemporary period.

ENRICHMENT

Creative Project

Abstract art can be represented in sound or dance. Have students choose a piece of abstract art and create a sound composition and dance that reflects the elements of the artwork. Perform the sound composition and dance as the art is exhibited on a large screen behind the performers.

Answers to Check Your Understanding.

1. Answers will vary. Examples might include the Space Age/Sputnik; developments in travel and communication; WWI and WWII; theory of relativity.

2. Some characteristics of Contemporary music that are heard in "Laudamus Te" from Poulenc's *Gloria* include dissonant chords, shifts in meter, a wide variation in dynamic levels, a combination of several different musical styles, and so forth.

3. Answers will vary. For example, music of the Romantic period focuses on the heights and depths of human emotion. Nationalism is reflected in many musical works. Music of the Contemporary period is marked by change and experimentation—new forms, new instruments, music written with no tonal center, music featuring a fusion of musical styles, and so forth.

Objectives

- Relate music to history.
- Identify the relationships between the content of the other fine arts and those of music.
- Describe music-related career options including performance.

Suggested Teaching Sequence

Direct students to:

- Read the Spotlight On Musical Theater on student page 126 and define musical theater.
- Discuss the history of American musical theater.
- Identify important musical theater composers and popular shows.
- Make a list of musical theater shows that they have seen live, on a video or DVD.
- Discuss the advantages of participating in a school musical. In small groups, brainstorm about the different types of performers and behind-the-scenes people it takes to put on a school production.

Progress Checkpoints

Observe students' progress in:

✓ Understanding musical theater and its background.

✓ Identifying the different types of people it takes to put on a musical theater production.

✓ Their ability to actively participate in a school musical.

SPOTLIGHT

Musical Theater

Tim McDonald, current Creative Director of Music Theatre International in New York City was asked to share his ideas on musical theater in today's schools. This is what he has to say:

"Musical theater (sometimes spelled "theatre") is a uniquely American art form like jazz and rock-and-roll that has become popular all over the world. Recently, musicals have been in the spotlight with major motion picture releases and television specials. Also, performers like Tom Cruise, Britney Spears and Tom Hanks as well as directors Baz Luhrmann and Tim Burton have credited their success to participating in their high school's musical.

"An annual student musical has become a regular part of the school calendar. In fact, it is estimated that 50,000 productions are presented in school auditoriums and over 2.5 million young people participate in their school musical each year. Most everyone can participate in a student musical on some level. Each person's contribution adds to the success of the production. For those who enjoy singing, dancing or acting, there's probably a role for you, or a place in the ensemble. For those who like to be behind the scenes, there's directing, stage managing, choreography and the technical crew. If your interests lean more towards visual art, there are sets to be designed and painted, props to be imagined, and costumes to be crafted.

"The best part of participating in a musical is that it's a lot of fun! So the next time you see an audition notice, take a chance and audition, or talk to the director about working behind the scenes. Who knows, one day you may credit your school musical with the success of your career."

In 1952, Frank Loesser transformed a fledgling business into what is now known throughout the world as "MTI." Music Theatre International is a theatrical licensing company specializing in Broadway musicals. It has been instrumental in extending the production life of the great American musicals such as, Guys and Dolls, West Side Story, Fiddler On The Roof, Les Misérables, Annie, Of Thee I Sing, Ain't Misbehavin', Damn Yankees, The Music Man, Godspell, Little Shop Of Horrors and the musical theater collaboration of composer/lyricist Stephen Sondheim, among others.

RESOURCES

Teacher Resource Binder

Reference 10, *Career: Comparing Vocal Performance Opportunities*

National Standards

7. Evaluating music and music performances. **(b)**
8. Understanding relationships between music, the other arts, and disciplines outside the arts. **(a)**
9. Understanding music in relation to history and culture. **(b)**

Choral Library

Fiddler Man

OVERVIEW

Composer: John Rutter
(b. 1945)
Text: John Rutter
Voicing: SATB
Key: G major/C major/G major
Meter: Mixed
Form: Strophic variation
Style: American Folk Style
Accompaniment: Piano
Programming: Concert,
Festival

Vocal Ranges:

Soprano

Alto

Tenor

Bass

OBJECTIVES

After completing this lesson, students will be able to:

• Define music form using standard terminology.

• Read music that incorporates rhythmic patterns in simple meter.

• Demonstrate basic performance techniques.

VOCABULARY

Have students review vocabulary in student lesson. Introduce terms found in the music. A complete glossary of terms is found on page 260 of the student book.

Fiddler Man

Composer: John Rutter (b. 1945)
Text: John Rutter
Voicing: SATB

VOCABULARY

variation form
interlude
$\frac{2}{4}$ meter
timbre

🔺 **SPOTLIGHT**

To learn more about timbre and the physiology of singing, see page 69.

Focus

• Analyze the form of a composition.

• Read and perform rhythmic patterns in simple meter.

• Define *timbre*. Use the voice to imitate the sounds of musical instruments.

Getting Started

"It has a good beat and you can dance to it." The famous Television show *American Bandstand* had a segment called "Rate a Record." Teenagers would listen to a new song and tell what would make the song a hit or a miss. In your opinion, what are the musical elements that make a piece of music interesting to the performer and to the listener? Text, melody, harmony and rhythm are just a few characteristics that make music interesting. As for "Fiddler Man," it is the drama that builds with every verse, the driving rhythms, and the vocal lines that perform as musical instruments that make this song a hit.

◆ History and Culture

"Fiddler Man" is the first piece in a set of songs entitled *Three American Lyrics*, written by British composer John Rutter (b. 1945). It is written in **variation form,** *a modification of a musical idea, usually after its initial appearance in a piece.* Although the melody remains virtually the same, it moves from voice to voice, and the supportive parts use a variety of harmonies and accompaniment techniques. If you were to analyze the form of "Fiddler Man," you would discover this organization: introduction, verse 1, verse 2, verse 3, **interlude** *(inserted music used to bridge the verses of a song),* verse 4 and verse 5. As you learn this delightful song, you will discover how each verse is treated differently.

128   Proficient Mixed

RESOURCES

Proficient Sight-Singing
Reading in G Major, pages 71–73
Reading in C Major, pages 13, 26–27, 34–35
Reading in 2/4 Meter, page 66

Teacher Resource Binder
Teaching Master 22, *Exploring Vocal Sounds*
Skill Builder 26, *Rhythm Challenge in Duple Meter*
Vocal Development 17, *Warm-up: Intonation and Choral Blend*
Kodaly 6, *Music Reading: Rhythm*
Dalcroze 11, *Developing Rhythm Skills*

Links to Learning

◆ Vocal

Use the opening section of "Fiddler Man" (measures 1–5) as a vocal warm-up. Treat the first note of each measure as a long tone. Using solfège syllables, Basses sing and hold the first note *(do)*, then the Tenors enter and hold their note *(sol)*, then the Altos *(fa)*, and finally the Sopranos *(do)*. All sing the chord in measure 4 until it is in tune, then move to the chord change in measure 5. Practice until you can sing the entire warm-up in tune and with confidence.

◆ Theory

Read and perform the following rhythmic patterns in $\frac{2}{4}$ **meter,** *a time signature in which there are two beats per measure and the quarter note receives the beat.*

◆ Artistic Expression

Timbre, or "tone color," is *the quality of a person's voice or musical instrument.* An interesting feature of this piece occurs when the voices imitate the instrumental sounds of a fiddle, a banjo and a string bass. Find an example of each in the music. Word stress, diction and articulation play an important part in capturing these instrumental timbres.

Evaluation

Demonstrate how well you have learned the skills and concepts featured in the lesson "Fiddler Man" by completing the following:

• Using measure numbers, identify each of the following sections: introduction, verse 1, verse 2, verse 3, interlude, verse 4 and verse 5. Even though the melody stays the same, describe how each verse is treated differently to create variation. For each verse, which voice part has the melody? Which voice parts have harmony?

• With a partner, select one verse of "Fiddler Man" to perform to demonstrate your ability to read rhythms correctly in $\frac{2}{4}$ meter. Evaluate your performance on the following scale: (1) I was able to perform all rhythms correctly, (2) I was able to perform most of the rhythms correctly, (3) I was able to perform only a few of the rhythms correctly. Work together to identify rhythms that were done incorrectly and discover ways to correct them.

Choral Library *Fiddler Man* **129**

LINKS TO LEARNING

Vocal

The Vocal section is designed to prepare students to sing the opening section of "Fiddler Man."

Have students:

• Use solfège syllables for each part's entrance and hold the chord in measure 4 until it is fully in tune.

• Move to the chord in measure 5 once the previous chord is mastered.

Theory

The Theory section is designed to prepare students to read syncopated rhythmic patterns in 2/4 meter.

Have students:

• Tap or clap the quarter note pulse.

• Speak the exercise while tapping the quarter note pulse.

• Speak the exercise while feeling the quarter note pulse inside.

Artistic Expression

The Artistic Expression section is designed to prepare students to learn about the different timbres they can create with their voices.

Have students:

- Locate in the music examples of various instruments they will imitate with their voices when they sing this piece. *(Answer: Basses—string bass, measure 45; Altos/Tenors—banjo, measure 61; Sopranos—fiddle, measure 78)*

- Be mindful that a combination of proper word stress, clear diction and clean articulation will help them achieve the various timbres of these instruments.

LESSON PLAN

Suggested Teaching Sequence and Performance Tips

1. Introduce

Direct students to:

- Read and discuss the information found in the Getting Started section on student page 128.

- Practice singing the opening section of the song until it is sung in tune and with confidence.

- Practice performing the rhythmic patterns in 2/4 meter as shown in the Theory section on page 129.

For the 1985 ACDA Junior High Honors and Demonstration Choir

Fiddler Man

For SATB and Piano

Words and Music by
JOHN RUTTER

130   Proficient Mixed

TEACHER2TEACHER

Use "Fiddler Man" to focus on diction and intonation, especially in places where extended harmonies are found. Also, the strophic variations present the melodic material in different vocal parts throughout the score. Therefore, close attention must be given to dynamic levels and ensemble balance.

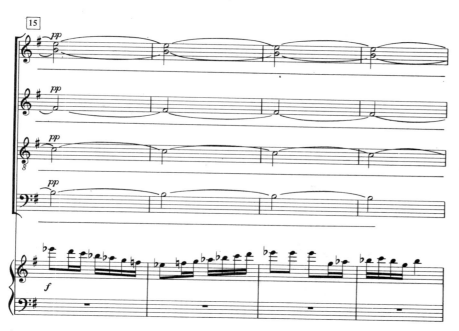

Progress Checkpoints

Observe students' progress in:

✓ Their ability to sing the opening section correctly and in tune.

✓ Their ability to clap the syncopated rhythmic patterns in 2/4 meter.

TEACHING STRATEGY

Performance Techniques

Have students:

1. Identify appropriate performance techniques to be used in the performance of this song.
2. Either in small ensembles or with the entire choir (large ensemble), perform the song exhibiting these performance techniques.
3. Describe the performance techniques experienced during the performance.
4. Critique the performance based on the observed performance techniques.
5. Repeat this process often in both informal and formal concert settings.

2. Rehearse

Direct students to:

- Review the rhythms, pitches and expressive markings in measures 1–9.
- Rehearse the Bass part in measures 10–19, focusing on pitches, rhythms and text. Notice that this passage begins in 3/8 meter at measure 10 and shifts to 2/4 meter at measure 14.
- Rehearse the Tenor, Alto and Soprano parts in the same manner.
- Combine all four parts when all pitches and rhythms are secure.

* If preferred, the introductory section may be omitted and the piece started here.

MORE ABOUT...

Careers in Music: Performance

Many people make a living through professions associated with music. Some are teachers, composers, conductors, managers, salespersons, technicians and more. One of the more visible careers in music is that of a professional performer. As a performer, one may become a solo artist, a member of an ensemble (band, orchestra or vocal group), or a member of a troupe (opera, Broadway). There are many career opportunities in the field of music performance.

- Sight-sing the Bass part in measures 19–27. As the Basses continue to rehearse this section, add the Tenor part at measure 20. When the two parts are secure, add the Alto part at measure 22. When the three parts are secure, add the Soprano part at measure 23.

- Review and perform all parts singing measures 1–27.

- Chant the rhythms in each part in measures 31–43. (You may want to use your preferred rhythm reading method during this exercise.)

- Add text and pitches when all rhythms are accurate. (Consider having all parts learn this main melody, as it will shift to other voice parts throughout the piece.)

- Rehearse the Bass part in measures 45–60. (Meanwhile, allow the Tenors to sight-read and chant their part, the melody, in their heads in measures 47–59).

MORE ABOUT...

John Rutter

John Rutter was born in London, England in 1945. At an early age he began to study music as a chorister. During his undergraduate years at Clare College in Cambridge, he was already composing and publishing scores. From 1975 to 1979 Rutter served as Director of Music at Clare College, where he directed and recorded with the choir. After leaving his post at Clare College, he formed his own group, the Cambridge Singers, a professional level chamber choir. Today, Rutter devotes his time to composing, conducting and recording his choir. His compositional career has included both large and small scale choral works, various orchestra and instrumental and piano pieces, two children's operas and music for television.

- Combine the Tenor and Bass parts with pitches and text once the rhythms are secure.
- Rehearse measures 61–77, by having the Altos and Tenors slowly sight-sing their parts, separately and then together, with assistance from the piano. Notice the tight major second interval that is occurs on beat 2 of measures 64 and 70. (Meanwhile, allow the Sopranos to sight-read and chant the text in their heads in measures 63–75).
- Rehearse the Soprano part in the same section; then add the Bass section. Rehearse the Bass and Soprano parts together. (Notice that the Bass part for this section is the same as that of the previous section.)
- Combine all four parts when all pitches and rhythms are secure.

* like a plucked bass

134 Proficient Mixed

TEACHING STRATEGY

Performing from Memory

Have students:

1. Memorize this piece by learning shorter phrases at a time.
2. Perform it from memory on a program or in competition.
3. Further develop memorization skills by memorizing other songs and solos to perform for the class informally or at formal concerts.

- Sight-sing the Soprano part in measures 79–86. Rehearse the Bass part in measures 79–86. When the part is secure, rehearse the Soprano and Bass parts together.
- Go back to measure 79 and clap the rhythms in the Alto and Tenor parts. When rhythms are secure, add pitches and text.
- Combine the Alto, Tenor and Bass parts in the section. When the three parts are accurate, add the Soprano line.
- Sight-sing, with the support of the piano, the Tenor and Bass lines in measures 87–94. (Notice the similarities of this passage to the Soprano part in measures 79–86.)
- Sight-sing, with the support of the piano, the Soprano and Alto parts together in this section.

TEACHING STRATEGY
Sight-Singing

Have students identify strategies they can use to become better sight-singers:

- At first read only the rhythm, then add the pitch, then text.
- Read simple melodies and two parts before trying four.
- Practice a little every day, using new materials.
- Don't worry about making mistakes. When a mistake is disastrous, analyze what happened so it can be addressed, practiced, and improved.
- Challenge each other with support and good humor.
- Remember that sight-singing, like any skill, needs to be practiced to improve.

- Combine all four parts when all pitches and rhythms are secure.
- Slowly sight-sing the Bass part in measures 95–107. Add the Tenor part when the Bass part is secure.
- Chant the text in rhythm in the Soprano and Alto in measures 97–98 and measures 101–102. When rhythms are secure, add pitches and text. Rehearse the entire section in four parts.
- Sight-sing all four parts on a neutral syllable simultaneously in measures 109 to the end of the piece. (Notice that this section draws from previous material, namely measures 61–77). Use the piano for support as needed. When all pitches are accurate, add text.

TEACHING STRATEGY

Solo and Small Ensemble Performances

Have students:

1. Prepare solos and small ensembles for performance or competition.
2. Interpret music symbols and terms referring to dynamics, tempo and articulation during the performance.
3. Critique and analyze the quality of the performance using standard terminology.

Progress Checkpoints

Observe student's progress in:

✓ Their ability to sing the independent lines in the piece correctly and in tune.

✓ Their ability to perform all rhythms in 3/8 and 2/4 meter with accuracy.

Choral Library *Fiddler Man* **137**

MORE ABOUT...

The Variation Form of Fiddler Man

The musical idea is presented in Verse 1 with Soprano and Altos. In the first variation, the Tenors sing the melody while the Basses sing an imitative string bass line. For the second variation (Verse 3), Sopranos sing the melody while all other voice parts sing in an instrumental style. In the transition, all voice parts are instrumental in style, imitating the fiddler. In the third variation, the Tenor and Basses harmonize the melody while the Soprano and Altos add embellishments. The final variation the melody moves from part to part. Encourage students to listen to each other as they sing, so not to drown out the melody as it moves from part to part.

3. Refine

Direct students to:

- Go back and discuss all the dynamic markings in the score. Decide as a class what the levels will be for *pp, mp, mf,* and so forth. Since balance will be an important factor in the piece, rehearse the piece in such a way that the melody is always prominent.

- Sing the various instrumental parts adjusting the timbre of their voices to match the sound of each instrument. (For example, string bass timbre beginning at measure 45, banjo timbre in measure 61, and fiddle timbre at measure 78.)

- Address any remaining pitch issues. Check and reinforce parts in areas where the following occur: divisi, dissonances of a major second, and transitions between verses.

* If preferred, A.T.B. may tacet for these eight measures, in which case piano should play.

TEACHING STRATEGY

Concert Etiquette

Have students:

1. Identify appropriate concert etiquette in a variety of settings (formal concerts, informal concerts, large concert halls, small concert halls, and so forth).

2. Attend a variety of live performances.

3. Discuss the appropriate and inappropriate concert behaviors observed.

4. Write a short analysis of appropriate concert etiquette for each setting.

Progress Checkpoints

Observe student's progress in:

✓ Their ability to perform the piece, observing all dynamic and expression markings.

✓ Their ability to not overpower the other lines when they do not have the melody.

✓ Their ability to adjust the timbre of their voices throughout the piece.

Encourage your students to expore **music.glencoe.com**, the Web site for *Experiencing Choral Music.* You may wish to preview the rich content before directing your students online. Options available on the Web site include:

- Web Link Exercises
- Interactive Projects
- Audio Samples

ASSESSMENT

Informal Assessment

In this lesson, students showed the ability to:

- Define and apply their knowledge of variation form.
- Read and perform rhythmic patterns in simple meter.
- Define timbre and to adjust the timbre of their voices to imitate various instruments.

TEACHING STRATEGY

Maintaining a Steady Tempo

This may seem like an obvious requirement for advanced ensembles, but it is sometimes overlooked as more sophisticated concepts are addressed. If you notice your choir seems to be pushing the tempo in this song, consider having your students do the following:

- Pat the beat almost inaudibly as they sing.
- Sing with the metronome.

Also, help your students understand that those who are struggling with tempo cannot hold back the choir alone; they will only split the ensemble. Keeping a steady tempo is something all must feel and do together.

Student Self-Assessment

Have students evaluate their individual performances based on the following:

- Diction
- Expressive Singing
- Posture
- Accurate Rhythms
- Intonation

Have each student rate his/her performance of this song in the areas above on a scale of 1–5, 5 being the best.

ASSESSMENT

Evaluating the Quality of a Performance

Have students:

1. Watch a video or listen to an audio recording of this piece as performed by the choir.
2. Compare this performance to exemplary models such as other recordings or other live performances of the piece.
3. Develop constructive suggestions for improvement based on the comparison.

Individual and Group Performance Evaluation

To further measure growth of musical skills presented in this lesson, direct students to complete the Evaluation section on page 129.

- Have students get into small groups and identify by measure number where each section of the piece is. Guide them in determining which part(s) has the melody and harmony in each section. [*Answers: Introduction: measures 1–27 (no melody); Verse 1: measures 30–43 (melody Soprano/Alto); Verse 2: measures 46–59 (melody Tenor); Verse 3: measures 62–75 (melody Soprano); Interlude: measures 79–94 (melody shifts); Verse 4: measures 98–107 (melody Tenor/Bass); Verse 5: measures 110 to the end (melody Soprano)]*

- Have students find partners and select a section of the song to perform, focusing on correct rhythms. Help them rate their performance as indicated and to find ways to improve where needed.

142 Proficient Mixed

TEACHING STRATEGY

Creative Expression

Direct students to write music that incorporates complex rhythmic patterns. Have students:

1. Select a meter:
- simple meter (2/4, 2/4, 4/4)
- compound meter (6/9, 9/8, 3/8)
- asymmetric meter (5/8, 7/8)
2. Write a four-measure complex rhythmic pattern using the selected meter.
3. Perform their compositions for the class.

EXTENSION

Be A Composer

The verses of "Fiddler Man" depict a story in sequence. With each verse, the story becomes increasingly dramatic. Verse 5 concludes the story in which the banjo's strings break, the bass falls asleep, and the fiddler man continues to play until he vanishes from sight. In small groups, have students devise a new scenario the gives this story another ending. Encourage them to think about introducing new characters, or simply change what happens to the existing characters. Once they decide upon a scenario, have them write a verse that fits the melody and rhythm of the existing verses. Allow them perform their verses for the class.

ASSESSMENT
Creating an Assessment Rubric

Have students:

1. Discuss the characteristics of a desirable performance of this piece, using all their knowledge of performance techniques.
2. Identify the criteria by which they think an adjudicator might assess the performance of this piece.
3. For each criterion, decide what characteristics will comprise an adequate, good, very good and excellent performance.
4. Create a rubric chart.
5. Use the rubric to assess quartets or small ensembles performing all or part of this song.

ENRICHMENT

Arranging Musical Melodies

Direct students to:

1. Select one phrase from this song that they know and enjoy singing.

2. Think of creative ways to perform this phrase differently, for example, by using different dynamics, altering the word stress, changing the articulation, and so forth.

3. Create an arrangement of the phrase by adding a descant, adding a simple accompaniment, re-voicing the phrase, adding instruments, writing a new text, changing the meter, and so forth.

4. Have students take turns performing their arrangements for the class.

EXTENSION

Compare and Contrast Form

The form used in "Fiddler Man" and "The Little Beggarman" (page 10) is strophic—a form in which the melody repeats while the words change from verse to verse. Listen to a recording of both songs. Have students:

• Identify the form of "Fiddler Man" and "The Little Beggarman" as strophic.

• Compare and contrast the strophic form used in both songs. How are they similar? How are they different? Compare and contrast the treatment of texture, harmony, placement of melody, dynamics, tempo and so forth.

144   Proficient Mixed

Additional National Standards

The following National Standards are addressed through the Assessment, Extension, Enrichment and bottom-page activities:

4. Composing and arranging music within specified guidelines. **(a)**

7. Evaluate music and music performances. **(a, b)**

9. Understanding music in relation to history and culture. **(c)**

144

SPOTLIGHT

Arranging

When asked how he approaches choral arranging, composer and arranger Roger Emerson had this to say:

"Generally, an arranger takes the basic melody and accompaniment of a song and prepares it (arranges it) so that it may be performed by a group of instruments or voices. These are things that I take into consideration.

Key

Specifically, as a choral arranger, I begin by finding the best key for the melody. That means finding the scale to use that makes the song the most comfortable to sing. I look for the highest and lowest note of the song, and what ranges would work best for my group of singers.

Melody and Harmony

I then determine the best places for the singers to sing unison or where harmony would be most effective. Using the basic chord symbols as a guide, I like to make the song more interesting by substituting expanded or more colorful chords throughout the song. Depending on the group who will perform the song, I will then write out parts for soprano, alto, tenor and baritone or bass singers, using the melody and new chords that I have chosen.

Accompaniment

The next step is to create a piano accompaniment that supports and hopefully enhances the vocal parts. Particularly in 'pop' style arrangements, the left hand carries a bass line while the right hand plays chords.

Finishing the Arrangement

The final step is to add lyrics, dynamic and style markings.

There are books that provide guidelines for arranging such as chord voicings and comfortable ranges for each instrument or voice, but most 'arrangers' will tell you (like the commercial says) JUST DO IT! Then listen to the outcome and see if you like the way it sounds. We all began somewhere. Good luck!"

Contemporary composer Roger Emerson has over 500 titles in print and 15 million copies in circulation. He is one of the most widely performed choral composers in America today. After a twelve-year teaching career, he now devotes himself full-time to composing, arranging and consulting.

Spotlight *Arranging* **145**

ARRANGING

Objectives

• Create and arrange music within specified guidelines.

Suggested Teaching Sequence

Direct students to:

• Read the Spotlight On Arranging on student page 145 and discuss the definition of an arrangement.

• Discuss the four elements of arranging presented by arranger Roger Emerson.

• What decisions must be made in creating an arrangement?

• Using the guidelines presented on this page, write a simple vocal arrangement to a familiar song.

• Perform the arrangement for the class.

• Find other familiar songs and write arrangements for those as well.

Progress Checkpoints

Observe students' progress in:

✓ Their ability to identify the techniques used in arranging.

✓ Their ability to write a simple arrangement of a familiar song.

Finale from *The Gondoliers*

OVERVIEW

Composer: Sir Arthur Sullivan (1842–1900), arranged by John Leavitt

Text: William S. Gilbert (1836–1911)

Voicing: SATB

Key: F major

Meter: 3/8

Form: Through-composed

Style: Romantic British Operetta

Accompaniment: Piano

Programming: Concert Closer, Honor Chorus, Thematic Programming

Vocal Ranges:

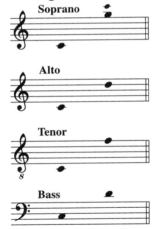

OBJECTIVES

After completing this lesson, students will be able to:

- Demonstrate fundamental skills (crisp articulation) while performing.
- Perform expressively music representing the Victorian operetta.

VOCABULARY

Have students review vocabulary in student lesson. Introduce terms found in the music. A complete glossary of terms is found on page 260 of the student book.

Finale from *The Gondoliers*

Composer: Sir Arthur Seymour Sullivan (1842–1900), arranged by John Leavitt

Text: William S. Gilbert (1836–1911)

Voicing: SATB

VOCABULARY

operettas

lyrics

score

diction

accidental

Focus

- Sing music using clean and crisp articulation.
- Perform music representing the Victorian operetta.

Getting Started

Rodgers and Hammerstein…
Lewis and Clark…
Simon and Garfunkel…
Ben and Jerry's…

These partnerships confirm the old adage that two heads are better than one. Gilbert and Sullivan, responsible for creating the most celebrated English language **operettas** *(light operas)* ever produced, are just such a team. Their operettas convey a sense of the Victorian period and are important as a source of insight into middle-class entertainment of the period and the use of political and social satire. Gilbert's witty **lyrics** *(the words of a song)* and Sullivan's magical **score** *(a notation showing all parts of an ensemble)* have found their way into the hearts of audiences around the world. *The Gondoliers* (1889) was the last great sensation for the duo after such masterpieces as *H.M.S. Pinafore* (1878) and *The Pirates of Penzance* (1879).

◆ History and Culture

The Gondoliers is a story of two brothers, Marco and Giuseppe Palmieri, who jointly rule the kingdom of Barataria until it is determined which one of them is the rightful heir. This chorus, sung near the beginning of Act II, returns as a celebratory finale. Locate places in the score where Sullivan skillfully connects the music to the lyrics. In measures 27–42, "clitter clatter" and "pitter patter"—sung rapidly and repeatedly— create a musical onomatopoeia (the naming of a thing or action by a vocal imitation of the sound associated with it). Look for other examples of clever partnerships.

SPOTLIGHT

To learn more about diction, see page 31.

RESOURCES

Proficient Sight-Singing

Reading in F Major, pages 45–46

Reading Accidentals, pages 30–31

Teacher Resource Binder

Evaluation Master 6, *Diction Check-up*

Evaluation Master 9, *Evaluating Rhythmic Accuracy*

Skill Builder 21, *Pitch and Kodály*

Vocal Development 8, *Articulation*

Interdisciplinary 24-25, *Theatre*

For additional resources, see TRB Table of Contents.

Links to Learning

◆ **Vocal**

Diction is *the pronunciation of words while singing.* To develop skill in singing with clear diction and intonation, sing measures 27–42 in a comfortable octave. Start with a slow, steady tempo and gradually increase the speed. Perform the following example for practice.

◆ **Theory**

Although this arrangement is written in the key of F major, it uses **accidentals** (*symbols used in music to change or alter pitches*) to change the pitch of some notes. The pitch *fa* is sometimes raised to *fi*, *sol* to *si*, and *do* to *di*. Perform the following example to practice singing music containing accidentals.

Evaluation

Demonstrate how well you have learned the skills and concepts featured in the lesson "Finale from *The Gondoliers*" by completing the following:

* Work with a partner and give each other different tempos to sing measures 27–42 using clean articulation, accurate intonation and a steady beat. How well were you able to sing with clean articulation and accurate intonation while maintaining a steady beat?

* Sing measures 85–92 to show your ability to sing pitches altered with accidentals. Evaluate how well you were able to sing all pitches in tune.

RESOURCES

Proficient Mixed Rehearsal/Performance CD

CD 2:4 Voices

CD 2:5 Accompaniment Only

CD 3:15 Vocal Practice Track—Soprano

CD 4:14 Vocal Practice Track—Alto

CD 5:14 Vocal Practice Track—Tenor

CD 6:14 Vocal Practice Track—Bass

National Standards

1. Singing, alone and with others, a varied repertoire of music. **(a, b, c)**

5. Reading and notating music. **(a)**

6. Listening to, analyzing and describing music. **(b)**

9. Understanding music in relation to history and culture. **(a)**

LINKS TO LEARNING

Vocal

The Vocal section is designed to prepare students to sing fast, technical phrases with clear diction and accurate intonation.

Have students:

* Sing the example at a slow and comfortable speed.

* Guard against rushing and make sure they do not take the example any faster than they are able.

* Sing measures 27–42 (in a comfortable octave) to reinforce the exercise.

Theory

The Theory section is designed to prepare students to sing accidentals in the key of F major.

Have students:

* Sing each part individually and combine parts only when all notes are secure.

* Pay special attention to the accidentals, making sure all pitches are in tune.

LESSON PLAN

Suggested Teaching Sequence and Performance Tips

1. Introduce

Direct students to:

- Read and discuss the information found in the Getting Started section on student page 146.
- Listen to a recording or watch a video excerpt of this chorus and discuss the differences between operetta, musical theater and choral ensemble singing.
- Practice measures 27–42 as outlined in the Vocal section. Practice these phrases in small groups so students can sing and assist each other.
- Find a partner (a Tenor with a Bass, and a Soprano with an Alto) and sing measures 11–26 using solfège syllables. Then have an Soprano/Alto group combine with a Tenor/Bass group and sing measures 11–26 using solfège syllables as a quartet. Repeat the process with measure 43–60.

Finale from *The Gondoliers*
(Dance A Cachucha))

For SATB and Piano

Arranged by
JOHN LEAVITT

WILLIAM S. GILBERT
and SIR ARTHUR SULLIVAN

148   Proficient Mixed

TEACHER 2 TEACHER

There seems to be a universal attraction between Gilbert and Sullivan and high school students. The combination of witty lyrics, engaging melodies and over-the-top characters are timelessly irresistible to young singers. Take a look at the complete score for *The Gondoliers* for solos and ensembles to program with this chorus. In addition, a high school choir could successfully perform *Trial By Jury* or *The Sorcerer*, two of the shorter Gilbert and Sullivan operettas.

Xe - res we'll drink Man - za - nil - la, Mon - te - ro.

*Love, when it runs in a - bun - dance, en - hanc - es The

reck - less de - light of that wild - est of danc - es! To the

*original text "Wine"

- Find a partner and decide on a rhythmic sequence using snapping, clapping, or patsch that emphasizes the "heavy-light-light" feel of the 3/8 meter. Sing measures 61–78 while performing the rhythmic sequence.

- Decide (as a class) on one rhythmic sequence that is comfortable and natural for the majority. Have the Sopranos, Altos and Tenors recite their solfège syllables in rhythm while the basses perform the rhythmic sequence. Repeat with the Basses reciting their solfège syllables for the same measures while the Sopranos, Altos and Tenors perform the rhythmic sequence.

Progress Checkpoints

Observe students' progress in:

✓ Their ability to sing using accurate solfège syllables.

✓ Their ability to internalize the pulse in 3/8 meter and to perform all rhythms correctly.

CONNECTING THE ARTS

Drama and Music

To learn more about *The Gondoliers*, have student write program notes, identifying the characters and explaining the dramatic circumstances surrounding this chorus. Or consider having students divide into groups, find a scene from *The Gondoliers*, learn the dialogue, add blocking and present the scene for the class.

2. Rehearse

Direct students to:

- Group themselves into SATB quartets. Depending on the number of quartets in the class, assign each quartet a 4, 8, or 16 measure phrase to sing with the text. Allow quartets to perform for and critique each other.

- Stand together as quartets, but in a large circle with the entire class. Choose one quartet to sing their phrase(s), and without inserting extra beats, move clockwise to the next quartet. They will sing their phrase(s), regardless of score order. After going all the way around the circle, have quartets mix-up and sing again, producing a new arrangement of the phrases. Repeat with several quartets adding the rhythmic sequence from above to the performance.

- Sing the entire piece in the correct order with the text.

TEACHING STRATEGY

Creative Evaluation

Have each student imagine he/she is a musical director who is auditioning singers for the chorus for an upcoming performance of *The Gondoliers*. Direct each student to create an audition checklist, including vocal and performance skills. Have them use their lists to assess a performance of this song by your choir.

*orignal text: "Wine"

TEACHING STRATEGY

Musical Elements of Style

The combination of musical elements determines the style of a piece. Have students:

1. Compile a list of musical elements that might affect style.

2. Share the lists to compile one master list.

3. Sing known songs, trying out different styles, and then try to describe the musical elements that are characteristic of that style. (For example, try salsa, opera, Broadway, rock, military, lullaby, and so forth.)

4. Select appropriate literature for a particular style.

3. Refine

Direct students to:

- Divide into SATB sectionals and sing each respective voice part with attention to dynamic markings and syllabic stress. Return to SATB quartets and sing originally assigned phrases with syllabic stress and dynamics. Allow quartets to sing for each other and demonstrate the stylistic choices.

- Discuss operetta chorus blocking. *(the singing is always dominant, gestures are small and compliment the meaning of the words)*

- Remain in SATB quartets and block their original phrase as two sets of partners with gestures that enhance the meaning and the style. Allow quartets to perform for and critique each other.

- Sing the entire song as a blocked operetta number and then as a conventional choral piece.

152   Proficient Mixed

CAREERS IN MUSIC

Music as an Avocation

One school activity that helps develop students' stage presence is participation in musical theater. If your school periodically stages plays or musicals (or if there is a community theater that accepts volunteers), this might be an avocation of interest to some students. Explain that a role in the musical theatre or a play can be varied. It can be as simple as being a member of the background chorus or "crowd scene" to playing the lead role and learning numerous lines and solo numbers. Have students compare and contrast this avocations opportunity with other they might have already pursued.

MORE ABOUT...

A Gondoliers Glossary

As students learn this piece, use the following list to help them learn the meaning of the text.

- Cachucha, fandango, bolero—various Spanish dances
- Xeres and Mazanilla—sherry wines
- Montero—Gilbert invented this name of sherry to rhyme with bolero.
- quandary—predicament or state of perplexity
- premé, stali (PRAY-may, stah-LEE)—shouts of communication between gondoliers. Premé means veer to the left and stali means veer to the right when boats need to pass each other.

ASSESSMENT

Informal Assessment

In this lesson, students showed the ability to:

- Perform music with excellent articulation.
- Learn about and perform music the represents the Victorian operetta.

CULTURAL CONNECTIONS

18th Century Italy

To learn more about the culture of Italy when the story from *The Gondoliers* takes place, have students research popular dress of eighteenth-century Italy. Have them design and sketch costumes for two characters in *The Gondoliers.*

Lyrics under music:
lie - ri, Both skill - ful and war - y,___ Free___ from this___ quan -

da - ry,___ Con - tent - ed___ are___ we.___ Ah!___

Ah!

Student Self-Assessment

Have students evaluate their individual performances based on the following:

- Diction
- Breath Management
- Accurate Pitches
- Accurate Rhythms
- Intonation

Have each student rate his/her performance of this song in the areas above on a scale of 1–5, 5 being the best.

TEACHING STRATEGY

Performance Techniques

Have students:

1. Identify appropriate performance techniques to be used in the performance of this song.
2. Either in small ensembles or with the entire choir (large ensemble), perform the song exhibiting these performance techniques.
3. Describe the performance techniques experienced during the performance.
4. Critique the performance based on the observed performance techniques.
5. Repeat this process often in both informal and formal concert settings.

Individual and Group Performance Evaluation

To further measure growth of musical skills presented in this lesson, direct students to complete the Evaluation section on page 147.

- Have students find a partner and sing the measures indicated at various tempos. Help them evaluate how well they were able to sing the passage.

- Have students sing measures 85–92 to show their ability to sing passages with accidentals. Assist them in evaluating their performance in relation to correct pitches and overall intonation.

Encourage your students to expore **music.glencoe.com**, the Web site for *Experiencing Choral Music*. You may wish to preview the rich content before directing your students online. Options available on the Web site include:

- Web Link Exercises
- Interactive Projects
- Audio Samples

goodbye, ca - chu - ca, fan - dan - go, bo - le - ro We'll

dance a fare - well to that mea - sure. Old

Xe - res, a - dieu, Man - za - nil - la, Mon - te - ro, We

MUSIC AND HISTORY

"Great Partnerships"

Organize a "Great Partnerships" day for the choir. Working in pairs, have students develop a presentation about a famous duo in history that includes dialogue, costumes and music.

leave you with feel - ings of plea - sure, with feel - ings of

pleas - ure!

Additional National Standards

The following National Standards are addressed through the Assessment, Extension, Enrichment and bottom-page activities:

7. Evaluate music and music performances. **(a, b)**

8. Understanding relationships between music, the other arts, and disciplines outside the arts. **(a, b, c)**

SPOTLIGHT

Vocal Jazz

Vocal jazz expert Stephen Zegree was asked to share his ideas on vocal jazz. This is what he had to say:

"Vocal jazz is probably the newest and most dynamic trend in choral music education. Traditional classical concert choir literature has been sung for over 500 years, but jazz choir literature has been available to students like you for only the past thirty years. It can be quite challenging to learn, but it almost always is FUN to study and perform.

Why should vocal jazz be an important part of your music education?

- Jazz music was born and raised in the United States. It is our unique musical contribution to the world. It is important to celebrate and embrace the music that comes from our own history and cultural experience.

- The source of much of our vocal jazz repertoire is the songs written by the great American songwriters. Composers such as George Gershwin, Duke Ellington, Richard Rodgers, Irving Berlin, Cole Porter, Jerome Kern and Harold Arlen (and their lyricists) are responsible for the art songs of our country and of the twentieth century.

- Through the study of vocal jazz you have the opportunity to develop your aural skills, creativity and overall musicianship through better understanding of rhythm, harmony and improvisation.

There are many excellent professional vocal groups who have made recordings that I would highly recommend listening to for a better understanding and appreciation for this excellent art form. These groups include The Manhattan Transfer, The Real Group, New York Voices, The Singers Unlimited and Take Six. Some of the greatest solo jazz singers whose recordings and videos you can find include Ella Fitzgerald, Sarah Vaughan, Billie Holiday, Carmen McRae, Mel Torme, Mark Murphy, Bobby McFerrin, Kurt Elling and Nat 'King' Cole.

By all means, make vocal jazz an important part of your musical life."

Stephen Zegree is a professor of music at Western Michigan University, where he teaches piano and jazz, performs with the Western Jazz Quartet, and conducts Gold Company, an internationally recognized jazz-show vocal ensemble. The winner of numerous competitions, awards and honors, Dr. Zegree is in demand as a guest conductor, pianist, clinician and adjudicator around the world.

Spotlight *Vocal Jazz*   **159**

VOCAL JAZZ

Objectives

- Perform expressively repertoire representing diverse cultures and styles.
- Classify by style representative examples of music.

Suggested Teaching Sequence

Direct students to:

- Read the Spotlight On Vocal Jazz on student page 159 and define share what they learned.
- Compare the elements of vocal jazz singing to classical singing.
- Direct the class to make a list of vocal jazz singers they know and identify characteristics of their singing. What about their singing classifies them as vocal jazz artists?
- Apply the techniques presented on this page to the performance of "New York State of Mind" on page 191.

Progress Checkpoints

Observe students' progress in:

✓ Their ability to define and describe the concept of vocal jazz.

✓ Their ability perform various vocal jazz techniques.

✓ Their ability to apply vocal jazz techniques in the performance of a song.

RESOURCES

Teacher Resource Binder

Vocal Development 1–6, *Keep the Joy in Singing!*
Vocal Development 11, *Flexibility And Range*

National Standards

1. Singing, alone and with other, a varied repertoire of music. **(a, b, c)**

Holy, Holy, Holy

OVERVIEW

Composer: A. Jeffrey LaValley, edited by Henry Leck

Text: A. Jeffrey LaValley

Voicing: SATB

Key: Db major/D major/ Eb major

Meter: 4/4

Form: Strophic

Style: Gospel

Accompaniment: Piano

Programming: Festival, Concert, Multicultural

Vocal Ranges:

OBJECTIVES

After completing this lesson, students will be able to:

• Read music that incorporates rhythmic patterns (syncopation) in simple meter.

• Perform expressively music representing the gospel style.

VOCABULARY

Have students review vocabulary in student lesson. Introduce terms found in the music. A complete glossary of terms is found on page 260 of the student book.

Holy, Holy, Holy

Composer: A. Jeffrey LaValley, edited by Henry Leck

Text: A. Jeffrey LaValley

Voicing: SATB

VOCABULARY

gospel music

tessitura

falsetto

tenuto

Focus

• Perform rhythmic patterns that contain syncopation.

• Describe and perform music representing gospel style.

SPOTLIGHT

To learn more about gospel music, see page 39.

Getting Started

Can you think of a chorus or a verse of a song that you like singing over and over? When you sing it over and over, do you change the tempo, the volume, or even the key? In the gospel music tradition, favorite choruses or verses can be repeated many times during a performance. This allows the opportunity to vary the musical elements, such as rhythm, melody, harmony, instrumentation (tone color) and dynamics. As you practice and perform "Holy, Holy, Holy," find ways in which the composer uses repetition to develop a powerful and exciting gospel-style composition!

◆ History and Culture

"Holy, Holy, Holy" is written in the style of **gospel music,** which is *religious music that originated in the African American churches of the South.* It contains rhythmically syncopated passages and improvisation, as well as repetition of phrases. Another common characteristic found in gospel music is the use of three parts (Soprano, Alto and "Men") rather than the more traditional four parts (SATB). Overall, the **tessitura** *(the average highness or lowness in pitch of a vocal piece)* for the men's part in "Holy, Holy, Holy" is very high. Because of this, the Basses sometimes have to sing in **falsetto,** or *the register in the male voice that is far above the natural voice.*

RESOURCES

Proficient Sight-Singing

Sight-Singing in D Major, pages 104–106

Sight-Singing in Eb Major, pages 115–116

Reading Syncopated Rhythms, page 85

Teacher Resource Binder

Evaluation Master 3, *Assessing Performance of Syncopated Rhythms*

Evaluation Master 8, *Evaluating Musical Expression*

Vocal Development 11, *Flexibility and Range*

Vocal Development 17, *Warm-up: Intonation and Choral Blend*

For additional resources, see TRB Table of Contents.

Links to Learning

◆ **Vocal**

An important aspect of this song is to maintain a consistency of tone while changing the vowel sound. Perform the following example by singing on "loo" and then again on the vowels indicated.

◆ **Theory**

To practice syncopated rhythms, divide the class into two groups. Group 1 claps the sixteenth note patterns, while group 2 claps the accents. Start at a very slow tempo, gradually increasing the speed. Chant the text after you have mastered performing the accented rhythms.

◆ **Artistic Expression**

To perform "Holy, Holy, Holy" in authentic gospel style, observe the **tenuto** (*hold a note for its full value*) markings found in measures 8–12. Add a sudden somewhat breathy crescendo and diminuendo to these notes while maintaining a steady tempo.

Evaluation

Demonstrate how well you have learned the skills and concepts featured in the lesson "Holy, Holy, Holy" by completing the following:

- With a partner, perform the example in the Theory section above. Evaluate how well you were able to clap the accented rhythms. Switch roles.

- Sing measures 8–15 using elements of gospel-style singing, including application of tenuto markings, accented syncopated rhythms, and contrast in repeated sections. Evaluate how well you were able to demonstrate all three.

Vocal

The Vocal section is designed to prepare students to:
- Sing chord progressions found in the song.
- Maintain a consistency of tone between vowels sounds.

Have students:
- Sing each part of the example separately on *loo*.
- Sing parts together once all pitches are secure and in tune.
- Sing the example again, using the vowel sounds indicated.

Theory

The Theory section is designed to prepare students to read syncopated rhythms like the ones found in "Holy, Holy, Holy."

Have students:
- Divide into two groups, with one group clapping the steady sixteenth note pulse and the other group claps the notes, while observing the accents.
- Begin at a slow tempo and increase to the performance tempo as they are able.
- Reverse roles.

RESOURCES

Proficient Mixed Rehearsal/Performance CD

CD 2:6 Voices

CD 2:7 Accompaniment Only

CD 3:16 Vocal Practice Track—Soprano

CD 4:15 Vocal Practice Track—Alto

CD 5:15 Vocal Practice Track—Tenor

CD 6:15 Vocal Practice Track—Bass

National Standards

1. Singing alone and with others, a varied repertoire of music. **(a, b, c, d)**

5. Reading and notating music. **(a, b)**

6. Listening to, analyzing and describing music. **(b, c)**

9. Understanding music in relation to history and culture. **(a)**

Artistic Expression

The Artistic Expression section is designed to prepare students to observe *tenuto* markings while performing.

Have students:

• Locate the *tenuto* markings in measures 8–11.

• Sing these notes with a breathy *crescendo* and *diminuendo,* while maintaining the steady tempo of the piece.

LESSON PLAN

Suggested Teaching Sequence and Performance Tips

1. Introduce

Direct students to:

• Read and discuss the information found in the Getting Started section on student page 160.

• Practice singing the harmonic progressions as shown in the Vocal section. Remind students to observe each fermata in the example.

• Practice reading the rhythm patterns in the Theory section.

• Practice measures 8–11 of the piece, closely observing the *tenuto* markings.

Holy, Holy, Holy

For SATB and Piano

Edited by HENRY LECK

Words and Music by
A. JEFFREY LAVALLEY

162   Proficient Mixed

TEACHER2TEACHER

"Holy, Holy, Holy" is a good example of a contemporary gospel-style praise chorus. The words are simple, yet powerful, the close harmony is written in just three parts, and repetition is an important compositional feature.

In order for repetition to be effective in gospel-style singing, it must be varied through dynamics, articulation, rhythm or key signature. Use the expression markings and modulations as a guide for bringing about a dramatic effect during your choir's performance.

-ly   is   the Lord __ of   hosts. ___

-ly   is   the Lord __ of   hosts.

-ly   is   the Lord __ of   hosts. ___

Wor - thy,   wor - thy of __ the hon - or,   wor - thy of __ the glo -

Wor - thy,   wor - thy of __ the hon - or,   wor - thy of __ the glo -

Wor - thy,   wor - thy of __ the hon - or,   wor - thy of __ the glo -

-ry   is   the Lord __ of   hosts. ___

-ry   is   the Lord __ of   hosts. ___

-ry   is   the Lord __ of   hosts. ___

Choral Library *Holy, Holy, Holy* **163**

MUSIC AND MOVEMENT

Gospel-Style Movement

It is almost impossible to sing music in the gospel style without feeling the urge to move! Encourage memorization of this song and practice a simple "rock and clap" exercise with your students and incorporate it into your performance. Decide as a class the point in the score where it might be appropriate to add this movement.

2. Rehearse

Direct students to:

- Review measures 8–11 and fix any problem pitches or rhythms. When all is secure, sing the passage with the text.

- As a class, analyze measures 12–15. Notice that the pitches and rhythms are exactly the same as measures 8–11. Chant the text in rhythm, then sing the pitches of the section.

- Chant the text of measures 16–22 while tapping a steady quarter note pulse. Notice that the phrases are somewhat imitative. Repeat until the rhythms are secure. Next, with the support of the piano, add pitches, allowing each part to sight-sing the phrases. Rehearse until secure.

MORE ABOUT...

A. Jeffrey LaValley

A. Jeffrey LaValley, gospel songwriter, keyboardist, producer and arranger, has written and produced for a number of gospel artists and choirs across the country. Born in Milwaukee, Wisconsin, Mr. LaValley has served as choral director of the Gospel Music Workshop of America, an organization founded by the legendary James Cleveland. The primary goal of this organization is to keep the gospel music tradition alive through education and performance.

Ho - ly, ho - ly, ho - ly, ho -

Ho - ly, ho - ly, ho - ly, ho -

Ho - ly, ho - ly, ho -

Ho - ly, ho - ly, ho - ly, ho -

- ly, ho - ly, ho - ly, ho - ly is the Lord __ of hosts.

- ly, ho - ly, ho - ly, ho - ly is the Lord __ of hosts.

- ly, ho - ly, ho - ly, ho - ly is the Lord __ of hosts.

Wor - thy, wor - thy of __ the hon -

Wor - thy, wor - thy of __ the hon -

Wor - thy, wor - thy of __ the hon -

- Go back to the beginning of the piece and rehearse through measure 22.
- Notice that the remainder of the piece involves a repetition of the material presented in measures 8–22.

Progress Checkpoints

Observe students' progress in:

✓ Their ability to sing all rhythmic patterns, especially syncopated ones, with accuracy.

✓ Their ability to sing in three-part, gospel-style harmony.

Choral Library *Holy, Holy, Holy* **165**

TEACHING STRATEGY

Concert Etiquette

Have students:

1. Identify appropriate concert etiquette in a variety of settings (formal concerts, informal concerts, large concert halls, small concert halls, and so forth).

2. Attend a variety of live performances.

3. Discuss the appropriate and inappropriate concert behaviors observed.

4. Write a short analysis of appropriate concert etiquette for each setting.

3. Refine

Direct students to:

- Analyze the score and discuss how it is constructed. (Questions to consider: How is the material repeated? How does it change in terms of key signature and text?)
- Discuss how dynamics can play a role in creating a dramatic effect during performance.
- Sing the entire piece, once they are more aware of how repetition is presented, observing all dynamics and expressive markings.

CURRICULUM CONNECTIONS

Technology in Music

Have students:

1. Identify technology used in music (computer, midi, mp3, CD, audio/video recordings, synthesizer, sound equipment, electronic sounds, and so forth).
2. Discuss what effect technology has on music.
3. Create a musical composition using a form of technology.
4. Perform a solo or small ensemble for the class incorporating technology.

Progress Checkpoints

Observe students' progress in:
- ✓ The use of audible contrasting dynamics.
- ✓ Their understanding of how repetition is used in this piece.
- ✓ Their ability to perform the repetition is a way that is dramatic and expressive.

CULTURAL CONNECTIONS

History of Gospel Music

Gospel music is a genre of the twentieth century, originating with the sacred songs of the African-American churches of South. Gospel singers have been known to take simple melodies and vocally embellish them, such as using full falsetto voices, shouting, humming, growling, moaning, whispering, crying or screaming. Fancy melismas, syncopated rhythms, blue notes and repeated fragments of the text are musical ways of improvising a gospel song. Much of the blues and soul styles found in today's pop music can be traced to the gospel style.

ASSESSMENT

Informal Assessment

In this lesson, students showed the ability to:

- Perform rhythms with syncopation.
- Observe and perform all tenuto markings.
- Describe and perform music in the gospel style.

VOCAL DEVELOPMENT

Singing in the Falsetto Register

The word *falsetto* comes from the Latin word *falsus,* meaning "false." The falsetto voice is the fourth register of the male voice that extends far above the natural high voice. "Holy, Holy, Holy" features a Tenor and Bass part that can be sung mostly using the falsetto register. To help the young men in your choir develop their falsetto register, use warm-up exercises that have a range of an octave or a tenth. Encourage them to sing with good breath support and with a free, relaxed throat.

Thank you, thank you, thank you, thank __ you, thank you, thank __ you, thank __

Thank you, thank you, thank __ you, thank ____ you, thank you, thank __ you, thank __

Thank you, thank you, thank __ you, thank ____ you, thank you, thank __ you, thank __

__ you to the Lord __ of hosts. __

__ you to the Lord __ of hosts. __

__ you to the Lord __ of hosts.

He shall reign __ for-ev __ er. __

He shall reign __ for-ev __ er. __

He shall reign.

Choral Library Holy, Holy, Holy **169**

TEACHING STRATEGY

Musical Elements of Style

The combination of musical elements determines the style of a piece. Have students:

1. Compile a list of musical elements that might affect style.

2. Share the lists to compile one master list.

3. Sing known songs, trying out different styles, and then try to describe the musical elements that are characteristic of that style. (For example, try salsa, opera, Broadway, rock, military, lullaby, and so forth.)

4. Select appropriate literature for a particular style.

Individual and Group Performance Evaluation

To further measure growth of musical skills presented in this lesson, direct students to complete the Evaluation section on page 161.

- Have students find a partner and perform the rhythm in the Theory section for each other. Assist them as they evaluate how well they were able to clap the accents while maintaining a steady pulse.

- With the same partner, have students sing measure 8–15, using the elements of gospel-style singing presented in the lesson. Aid them in their self-evaluation of their performance.

ENRICHMENT

Improvisation

Encourage students to improvise musical melodies while performing. Select an eight-bar phrase from "Holy, Holy, Holy." Ask volunteers to improvise a melodic descant above the melody as the choir sings the written notation. Have students take turns improvising.

170 Proficient Mixed

Additional National Standards

The following National Standards are addressed through the Assessment, Extension, Enrichment and bottom page activities:

7. Evaluate music and music performances. **(a)**

In Flanders Fields

Composer: John Jacobson and Roger Emerson, arranged by Roger Emerson
Text: Dr. John McCrae
Voicing: SATB

In Flanders Fields
OVERVIEW

Composers: John Jacobson and Roger Emerson, arranged by Roger Emerson
Text: Dr. John McCrae
Voicing: SATB
Key: F major
Meter: 3/4 meter
Form: Strophic
Style: Contemporary American Song
Accompaniment: Piano
Programming: Concert, Contest, or Festival. Appropriate for patriotic events.

Vocal Ranges:

VOCABULARY

phrase
suspension
resolution

Focus

• Demonstrate musical artistry through musical phrasing.

• Use standard terminology to describe a suspension.

• Relate music to poetry.

🔺 **SPOTLIGHT**

To learn more about vowels, see page 57.

Getting Started

What images come to mind when you hear the word *patriotism*? For some, it is the image of the American flag or the Capitol building in Washington, D.C. For others, it is the image of the rows of white crosses at Arlington National Cemetery, honoring those who have given their lives defending their country. Singing "In Flanders Fields" can help you tell a story of true heroism and patriotism.

◆ History and Culture

Dr. John McCrae (1872–1918) was a surgeon assigned to the First Field Artillery Brigade in World War I. During a battle that lasted seventeen days, he experienced firsthand the horror of war. The death of a young friend and former student particularly affected Dr. McCrae. The doctor performed the funeral ceremony for the young soldier in the absence of a chaplain.

Sitting in the back of an ambulance, watching the poppies blow in the wind across the newly dug graves, McCrae wrote the poem "In Flanders Fields" in twenty minutes. Disgusted by the situation, he threw the poem away. As fate would have it, another officer found it and sent it to newspapers in England, where it was published in December of 1915. Over the years, there have been several settings of this poem to music.

Choral Library *In Flanders Fields* **171**

OBJECTIVES

After completing this lesson, students will be able to:

• Demonstrate fundamental skills while performing.

• Identify harmonic elements of music (suspension).

• Define the relationships between other subjects and music.

VOCABULARY

Have students review vocabulary in student lesson. Introduce terms found in the music. A complete glossary of terms is found on page 260 of the student book.

RESOURCES

Proficient Sight-Singing

Sight-Singing in F Major, pages 45–46, 54
Reading Rhythms in 3/4 Meter, page 14

Teacher Resource Binder

Teaching Master 23, *Beyond the Words— "In Flanders Fields"*
Evaluation Master 4, *Checking Out Phrasing*
Vocal Development 15, *Vowels*
Dalcroze 16, *Musical Style*
Reference 16, *Expanding a Musical Vocabulary*

LINKS TO LEARNING

Vocal

The Vocal section is designed to prepare students to sing musical phrases correctly.

Have students:

- Sing the example on one breath.
- Shape the phrase so there is an audible dynamic contrast between the beginning and end of the phrase in contrast to the peak of the phrase.

Theory

The Theory section is designed to prepare students to define and perform a suspension.

Have students:

- Sight-sing each example, paying attention to intonation.
- Listen to one another and allow the suspended note to be heard over the others.

Links to Learning

◆ Vocal

Perform the following example as a continuous **phrase** *(a musical sentence containing a beginning, middle and end)*. Plan your breathing so that you can sing the phrase in one breath. Begin and end the phrase softly and determine where the peak or loudest part of the phrase should be. It is also important to sing with tall, uniform vowels.

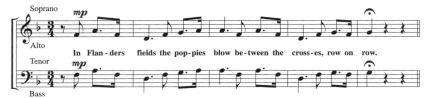

◆ Theory

A **suspension** is *a technique in which one or more musical tones in a chord are held over into the following chord, producing a momentary discord.* In the following example, the Alto part holds the F from beat 2 to beat 3, thus creating a suspension on the downbeat of beat 3. In performance, stress the suspended pitch and sing it louder than the following note of **resolution** *(a technique in which a dissonant chord resolves to a consonant chord or a point of rest)*. Sing on a neutral syllable such as "loo."

Evaluation

Demonstrate how well you have learned the skills and concepts featured in the lesson "In Flanders Fields" by completing the following:

- Select one person from each section of the choir to serve as a listener. As the choir performs "In Flanders Fields," have the listeners answer these questions:
    - Did the choir sing each phrase with a beginning, middle, and an ending?
    - Could the resolution of the suspensions be clearly heard?
- In your own words, write a summary of the meaning of the poem "In Flanders Fields." In what ways can a careful analysis of the text improve your performance?

RESOURCES

Proficient Mixed Rehearsal/Performance CD

CD 2:8 Voices

CD 2:9 Accompaniment Only

CD 3:17 Vocal Practice Track—Soprano

CD 4:16 Vocal Practice Track—Alto

CD 5:16 Vocal Practice Track—Tenor

CD 6:16 Vocal Practice Track—Bass

National Standards

1. Singing alone and with others, a varied repertoire of music. **(a, b, c, d)**
5. Reading and notating music. **(a, b)**
6. Listening to, analyzing and describing music. **(b, c)**
8. Understanding relationships between music, the other arts and disciplines outside the arts. **(c)**

In Flanders Fields

For SATB and Piano

Arranged by
ROGER EMERSON

Words by Dr. JOHN McCRAE
Music by JOHN JACOBSON and ROGER EMERSON

Choral Library *In Flanders Fields*   **173**

LESSON PLAN

Suggested Teaching Sequence and Performance Tips

1. Introduce

Direct students to:

- Read and discuss the information found in the Getting Started section on student page 171.
- Practice singing the musical phrase in the Vocal section.
- Practice singing the passages with suspensions in the Theory section.

Progress Checkpoints

Observe student's progress in:

- ✓ Their ability to sing phrases musically and correctly.
- ✓ Their ability to sing harmonic progressions with suspensions in tune.

TEACHER 2 TEACHER

"In Flanders Fields" offers many opportunities for students to express their feelings and ideas about events happening in the world today. Allow time for discussion and interaction.

2. Rehearse

Direct students to:

- Sing the measures 5–14 on a blended and unified oo vowel. Add words when pitch, rhythm and phrasing are secure.
- Follow the same sequence to learn the next section, measures 14–27. (Since the Soprano part is the same as the first verse, place emphasis on Alto, Tenor and Bass parts.)
- Follow the same sequence to learn the next section, measures 27–44. Pay particular attention to the suspensions in the Alto part as noted in the Vocal section. (Add piano accompaniment only when all parts are secure. Note that the accompaniment does not always double the vocal parts.)

Progress Checkpoints

Observe students' progress in:

✓ Their ability to sing in four parts.

✓ Their ability to sing phrases correctly.

*Opt.-Tenors only to m.27

174   Proficient Mixed

MORE ABOUT...

Meaning of Text

Flanders is the name of the whole western part of Belgium. It is flat country where people speak Flemish, a kind of Dutch. Flanders Fields is the name of an American War Cemetery in Belgium, where 368 Americans are buried. This ancient battleground is situated near the village of Waregem, quite a distance from the place where McCrae actually wrote his poem. The bronze foot of the flagstaff in the cemetery is decorated with daisies and poppies.

3. Refine

Direct students to:
- Pay attention to the dynamic and expressive markings in the score. The dynamics and phrasing indicated in the score are essential for a successful performance of this piece.
- Work to blend choral tone with unified round and tall vowel sounds.
- Keep the tone spinning with energy across each long note. It takes more energy and breath to sing *piano* than *forte*.
- Make each section as intense as possible with sensitive use of rubato and phrasing.

Progress Checkpoints

Observe students' progress in:
- ✓ The use of contrasting dynamics.
- ✓ Their ability sing the piece expressively.
- ✓ Creating a blended choral tone with unified vowel sounds.

CURRICULAR CONNECTIONS

Music and Poetry

For centuries, poets have written about war. Find a poem about war to read to the class and discuss the various characteristics given to war in each poem. How are the poems similar and how are they different?

ASSESSMENT

Informal Assessment

In this lesson, students showed the ability to:

- Sing phrases expressively.
- Describe and perform suspensions.
- Relate music to poetry.

Student Self-Assessment

Have students evaluate their individual performances based on the following:

- Vowels
- Expressive Singing
- Phrasing
- Posture
- Correct Part-Singing

Have each student rate his/her performance of this song in the areas above on a scale of 1–5, 5 being the best.

Individual and Group Performance Evaluation

To further measure growth of musical skills presented in this lesson, direct students to complete the Evaluation section on page 172.

- Select a student to serve as a listener while the choir sings "In Flanders Fields." Assist the listener in giving an evaluation of the choir's performance.
- Have students summarize the poem "In Flanders Fields" in their own words. Discuss with them how a good understanding of a song's text can help them improve their performance.

176   Proficient Mixed

MORE ABOUT...

"In Flanders Fields"

Composers John Jacobson and Roger Emerson offer the following description of the text: "In 1919 Dr. John McCrae wrote the stirring poem entitled *In Flanders Fields*. In fifteen short lines, McRae captures the courage, valor, awe and stark reality of war. The images he invokes of young people's lives, once so full of hope and beauty, vanquished by the ravages of warfare, are some of the most moving ever penned. To this day, it continues to be an emotional salute to the young men and women who have given their lives in warfare protecting the lands, the people and the dreams we cherish most. His challenge to take up the torch of fallen warriors is as desperate a challenge to remember as any we will find in the English language."

in Flan - ders fields, in Flan - ders fields. We shall not

sleep, though pop - pies grow in Flan - ders fields, in Flan - ders

fields.

EXTENSION

Music and Other Subjects

To help your students connect music with the other subjects they are studying, consider the following activities:

After choir members have memorized the text, ask a poet or literature teacher to come talk with the students about the poem. Discuss not only the images and themes in the poem, but the poem's structure and poetic devices.

Have students locate Belgium on a map of the world.

ENRICHMENT

Patriotism

In his poem, "In Flanders Fields," John McCrae spoke of the horrors of war. He was so moved that he called his countrymen to arms. Ask students what events in their lifetime have made them feel patriotic.

Additional National Standards

The following National Standards are addressed through the Assessment, Extension, Enrichment and bottom-page activities:

7. Evaluate music and music performances. **(a)**

9. Understanding music in relation to history and culture. **(a)**

Jabula Jesu

OVERVIEW

Composer: Zulu Folk Song, arranged by Stephen Hatfield
Text: Zulu Folk Song
Voicing: SSATB
Key: F major
Meter: 4/4
Form: ABABAB Coda
Style: Zulu Folk Song
Accompaniment: A cappella
Programming: Festival, Multicultural

Vocal ranges:

OBJECTIVES

After completing this lesson, students will be able to:

- Read music that incorporates polyrhythms.
- Define the relationship between music and movement.
- Expressively perform music representing the Zulu culture.

VOCABULARY

Have students review vocabulary in student lesson. Introduce terms found in the music. A complete glossary of terms is found on page 260 of the student book.

178

Jabula Jesu

Composer: Zulu Folk Song, arranged by Stephen Hatfield
Text: Zulu Folk Song
Voicing: SSATB

VOCABULARY

polyrhythms
ostinato
syllabic stress

Focus

- Perform ostinato and polyrhythm patterns accurately.
- Respond to music by creating movement.
- Perform music representing the Zulu culture.

Getting Started

How would you describe a perfect day in your life—one of those days when you revel in the simple joy of being alive? On such a day, the rhythm of your life seems to flow with great ease. While you have many tasks to do on this perfect day, you find yourself multi-tasking with ease! As a singer, you may express your joy for the day by singing, humming or whistling. "Jabula Jesu" is a piece that expresses the joy of life and a perfect day. The many layers of musical ideas flow together with ease, creating an exciting sense of joy and well-being.

SKILL BUILDERS

To learn more about the key of F major, see Proficient Sight-Singing, *page 45.*

◆ History and Culture

"Jabula Jesu" is a folk song from the Zulu tribe of South Africa. African folk songs often employ **polyrhythms** (*a technique in which several different rhythms are performed at the same time*). The combination of various rhythms creates an intriguing, driving beat. For the Zulu people, music is the "food of life," and if the music does not contain polyrhythms, it has no rhythm! The harmonies of Zulu music are often an intertwining of parts. The English translation of the Zulu text is as follows:

Sithi jabula (no) Jesu	We say, be joyful (with) Jesus
Sithi thandanza, Solly thandanza	We say, play Solly, have a good time
Weh Solly thandanza Solly	Hey, Solly, have a good time
Lalela	Listen

178 Proficient Mixed

RESOURCES

Proficient Sight-Singing

Sight-Singing in F Major, pages 45–46, 54
Reading Syncopated Rhythms, page 85

Teacher Resource Binder

Teaching Master 24, *Pronunciation Guide for "Jabula Jesu"*
Evaluation Master 15, *Diction Check-up*
Vocal Development 9, *Diction*
Dalcroze 11, *Developing Rhythm Skills*
Reference 26, *IPA Vowels*
For additional resources, see TRB Table of Contents.

Links to Learning

◆ Vocal

Perform the following example containing polyrhythms to develop rhythmic precision and accurate pitch. Practice one line at a time and then practice two lines together in different combinations. Then, perform all parts at the same time.

◆ Theory

The following example is an **ostinato** pattern, or *a repeated musical figure, rhythmic pattern or phrase.* When this syncopated pattern is divided into eight notes, the note grouping is 1-2-3, 1-2-3, 1-2. Perform the following example to develop rhythmic precision. Observe the articulation markings for proper **syllabic stress** (*the stressing of one syllable over another*), but do not overemphasize them.

Evaluation

Demonstrate how well you have learned the skills and concepts featured in the lesson "Jabula Jesu" by completing the following:

- Identify measures in the music that use the same rhythmic pattern as the ostinato pattern found in the Theory section above. Are you able to read and perform the rhythms accurately?

- In an SATB quartet with one singer on a part, perform measures 1–22. Evaluate your vocal independence. Evaluate how well the small ensemble was able to sing polyrhythms.

Vocal

The Vocal section is designed to prepare students to sing polyrhythms accurately.

Have students:

- Sing each part separately, paying attention to intonation and correct rhythms.

- Combine parts when all pitches and rhythms are secure.

Theory

The Theory section is designed to prepare students to:

- Learn the ostinato pattern found in "Jabula Jesu."

- Sing with proper syllabic stress.

Have students:

- Clap or chant with text the rhythm of the ostinato.

- Follow the articulation markings to help them use correct syllabic stress.

Choral Library *Jabula Jesu* **179**

RESOURCES

Proficient Mixed Rehearsal/Performance CD

CD 2:10 Voices

CD 2:11 Accompaniment Only

CD 3:18 Vocal Practice Track—Soprano

CD 4:17 Vocal Practice Track—Alto

CD 5:17 Vocal Practice Track—Tenor

CD 6:17 Vocal Practice Track—Bass

National Standards

1. Singing alone and with others, a varied repertoire of music. **(a, b, c, d)**

5. Reading and notating music. **(a, b)**

8. Understanding relationships between music, the other arts and disciplines outside the arts. **(b)**

9. Understanding music in relation to history and culture. **(a)**

LESSON PLAN

Suggested Teaching Sequence and Performance Tips

1. Introduce

Direct students to:

- Read and discuss the information found in the Getting Started section on student page 178.
- Practice the example in the Vocal section.
- Practice the example in the Theory section.

Progress Checkpoints

Observe students' progress in:

✓ Their ability to sing music with polyrhythms correctly.

✓ Their correct use of syllabic stress by observing articulation markings, such as accent and staccato.

For "Fanfare" at Mayfield Secondary School, Brampton, Ontario

Jabula Jesu

For SSATB a cappella

Arranged by
STEPHEN HATFIELD

Zulu Folk Song

180 Proficient Mixed

TEACHER 2 TEACHER

This setting of a Zulu folk song is an energetic and joyful expression of praise. The arrangement is strong and musically solid, yet it retains the rhythmic vitality of the original folk song. For the most part, the tessitura falls well within each section's midrange. The rhythmic component is by far the most compelling aspect of the whole piece. There are many occurrences of the typical African rhythmic practice of layering ostinati and polyrhythms one on top of the other. "Jabula Jesu" provides a marvelous opportunity for your choir to vocally project the joy of life.

2. Rehearse

Direct students to:

- Analyze the musical score by identifying measures containing the rhythms identical or similar to those given in the Vocal and Theory sections.
- Clap and/or step each of the measures in the above sections. It is vital at this time that the rhythm become eurhythmic, that is, flowing and expressive in movement. You can facilitate this by accompanying the first rhythm on a hand drum. First play the rhythm literally. When the students seem to be "getting it," play only the basic pulse. This will create interesting syncopations which the students will then internalize.

TEACHING STRATEGY

Performance Techniques

Have students:

1. Identify appropriate performance techniques to be used in the performance of this song.
2. Either in small ensembles or with the entire choir (large 185

- Start with a very slow tempo and clap and/or step each rhythm. Accelerate gradually until the performance tempo is reached. When the faster tempos are achieved the steps should become lighter and buoyant. Repeat this over and over until students have internalized each rhythm.

TEACHING STRATEGY

Composing in Asymmetric Meter

After students are proficient in performing polyrhythms as found in "Jabu Jesu," challenge them to create a two-part polyrhythmic composition in 7/8 or 5/8 meter. These meters are examples of asymmetric meter, a meter in which the strong beats create combinations of groups of two and three. Direct students to select a partner and take turns performing their compositions for the class.

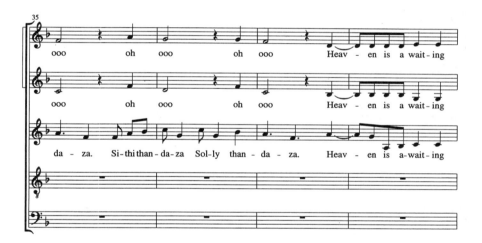

Progress Checkpoints

Observe students' progress in:

✓ Accurate and expressive clapping, tapping and stepping. In order for the dance-like energy of this to be captured it is essential that the students movements be free and uninhibited. Help them with this by making this activity challenging and fun. Be sure to praise often. Bring attention to those students who possess a natural grace and have them model for the rest of the class.

Encourage your students to expore **music.glencoe.com**, the Web site for *Experiencing Choral Music.* You may wish to preview the rich content before directing your students online. Options available on the Web site include:

• Web Link Exercises

• Interactive Projects

• Audio Samples

3. Refine

Direct students to:

- Sing entire song one part at a time while moving rhythmically in a flowing manner. Try singing the entire piece while:
    1) Stepping the underlying quarter note pulse.
    2) Stepping the rhythm.
    3) Doing the first step as ♩ ♩ ♩ where appropriate.
- Orbit a central point in a fairly disciplined manner. Your chorus will benefit from the hearing each other and the other parts as they move. Be sure there is enough room so there aren't any collisions!
- Do the above movement as they accompany themselves with small percussion instruments.

CURRICULUM CONNECTIONS

Multicultural Dances

Have students research African dances using books and recordings or resources in the community. Direct them to learn some of the dances and compare the movements and musical characteristics to those found in "Jabula Jesu."

Observe students' progress in:

✓ Their ability to maintain perfect focus and concentration in the midst of the other parts.

✓ Their ability to experience the rhythmically ecstatic mood of the music while stepping the rhythm.

✓ Perfect spatial relations – the quarter note step should be twice as big as the eighth note. The dotted quarter should be three times as big as the eighth.

ASSESSMENT

Creating an Assessment Rubric

Have students:

1. Discuss the characteristics of a desirable performance of this piece, using all their knowledge of performance techniques.
2. Identify the criteria by which they think an adjudicator might assess the performance of this piece.
3. For each criterion, decide what characteristics will comprise an adequate, good, very good and excellent performance.
4. Create a rubric chart.
5. Use the rubric to assess quartets or small ensembles performing all or part of this song.

ASSESSMENT

Informal Assessment

In this lesson, students showed the ability to:

- Perform ostinato and polyrhythms patterns accurately.
- Create movement appropriate to the music being performed.
- Perform music representing the Zulu culture.

TEACHING STRATEGY

Performing from Memory

Have students:

1. Memorize this piece by learning shorter phrases at a time.
2. Perform it from memory on a program or in competition.
3. Further develop memorization skills by memorizing other songs and solos to perform for the class informally or at formal concerts.

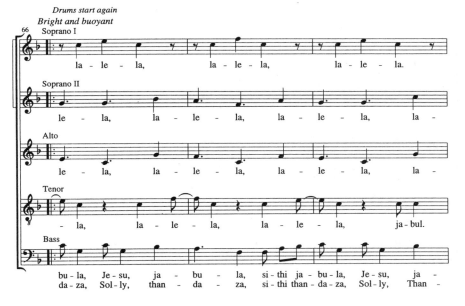

TEACHING STRATEGY

Moving Through Shared Space

If your students are not used to moving in class, they may feel awkward or conspicuous in this situation. Give them guidelines to provide structure to the experience. Begin with one person moving through the rehearsal space without bumping into anyone or anything. Then add one person, then two more, and so on, until everyone is up and moving. This type of movement will become a real challenge when they are singing in four parts independently, moving randomly in the room, and hearing the other parts around them.

Student Self-Assessment

Have students evaluate their individual performances based on the following:

- Accurate Rhythms
- Expressive Singing
- Phrasing
- Accurate Pitches
- Correct Part-Singing

Have each student rate his/her performance of this song in the areas above on a scale of 1–5, 5 being the best.

Individual and Group Performance Evaluation

To further measure growth of musical skills presented in this lesson, direct students to complete the Evaluation section on page 179.

- After students are able to perform the ostinato pattern on page 179, have them find similar patterns in the music. *(measures 1–5, 9–13, 17–21, 25–29, 33–37, 41–45, 65–69)* Evaluate the performance by asking, "How accuate were the rhythms? Which voice parts need more work?"

- In SATB quartets with one singer on a part, have students sing measures 1–22. Have each student evaluate how well he/she was able to sing independently within the group. Then ask the students how well the quartet was able to sing polyrhythms accurately.

EXTENSION

Music and Movement

The rhythmic drive of "Jabula Jesu" compels one to move with the music. Have your students improvise and create sequences of stepping and clapping to enhance their musical performance. Or, encourage them to create choreography for measures 1–9 using a stepping and clapping sequence, and allow them to share their choreography with the class.

ENRICHMENT

Improvisation

Some student may be reluctant to try improvisation. As a teacher, it is important to set up guidelines and to create a safe environment. Remind students that any effort is a worthy effort. Praise students often. Follow these steps to lead students to successful improvisation.

1. Play on a keyboard, guitar or some other instrument the I-IV-V-I chord progression. Play it several times until students become familiar with it.

2. Ask for volunteers to improvise a musical melody above the chord progression. Singers may use nonsense or scat syllables.

3. Have students analyze ways in which they can improve their skills in improvisation.

188   Proficient Mixed

Additional National Standards

The following National Standards are addressed through the Assessment, Extension, Enrichment and bottom-page activities:

3. Improvising melodies, variations and accompaniments. **(b)**

6. Listening to, analyzing and describing music. **(b, c)**

New York State Of Mind

Composer: Billy Joel, arranged by Steve Zegree
Text: Billy Joel
Voicing: SATB

VOCABULARY

scat singing

upbeat

improvisation

Focus

- Perform music that contains close harmony.
- Use musical terminology to describe *scat singing* and *upbeat.*
- Perform music representing vocal jazz style.

Getting Started

Have you ever forgotten the words to a song while you were singing it? Did you find yourself making up words or singing syllables that fit into the style of the music? If so, then you were scat singing. **Scat singing,** *improvisational singing that uses nonsense syllables instead of words,* was first made popular by jazz legends Louis Armstrong (1901–1971) and Ella Fitzgerald (1917–1996). Louis used it to imitate the sounds of the instruments in his band. In this arrangement of "New York State Of Mind," you will have the opportunity to scat sing.

SPOTLIGHT

To learn more about vocal jazz and improvisation, see pages 159 and 247.

◆ History and Culture

"New York State Of Mind" is a vocal jazz arrangement of the popular Billy Joel ballad. The composer and arranger have used several devices to create a relaxed style. One element is the frequent use of expanded chords: chords that use more than the root, third and fifth degree of the scale. These expanded chords may include the seventh or ninth degree of the scale. The end result is close harmony. Another melodic device is the use of the **upbeat,** or *one or several notes of a melody that occur before the first barline or fall on a weak beat that leans toward the strong beat.* These harmonic and stylistic elements contribute to the relaxed style of this piece.

Choral Library *New York State Of Mind* **189**

New York State of Mind

OVERVIEW

Composer: Billy Joel, arranged by Steve Zegree
Text: Billy Joel
Voicing: SATB
Key: F major/G major
Meter: 4/4
Form: Intro AA'BA'A''B'A'' Coda
Style: American Pop
Accompaniment: Piano
Programming: Pops Concert, Salute to America, Solo Opportunities

Vocal Ranges:

OBJECTIVES

After completing this lesson, students will be able to:

- Demonstrate independently, accurate intonation while performing moderately difficult literature.
- Define concepts of musical performances using standard terminology.

VOCABULARY

Have students review vocabulary in student lesson. Introduce terms found in the music. A complete glossary of terms is found on page 260 of the student book.

RESOURCES

Proficient Sight-Singing

Sight-Singing in F Major, pages 45–46

Sight-Singing in G Major, pages 71–73, 77

Reading Rhythms in 4/4 Meter, pages 2, 6

Reading Tied Notes, pages 42, 50

Teacher Resource Binder

Evaluation Master 8, *Evaluating Musical Expression*

Evaluation Master 16, *Performance Evaluation: Part-Singing*

Skill Builder 14, *Improvising Melodies*

Dalcroze 16, *Musical Style*

For additional resources, see TRB Table of Contents.

- Perform expressively from notation a varied repertoire of music representing diverse styles.

LINKS TO LEARNING

Vocal

The Vocal section is designed to prepare students to sing a section of music in a scat style.

Have students:

- Sing measures 77–92 at a slow tempo using the syllables written below the staves.
- Sing measures 77–92 at a faster tempo using the syllables written below the staves.
- Improvise a new melody with different syllables as the accompaniment is played in measures 77–92.

Artistic Expression

The Artistic Expression section is designed to prepare students to identify strong and weak beats in the measure.

Have students:

- Sing the Artistic Expression exercises putting a slight stress on the notes that are on the first and third beats.
- Sing the exercises with less stress on the notes that are on the second and fourth beats.
- Sing exercises in a conversational tone where the lyrics are sung as if spoken to a friend.

Links to Learning

◆ **Vocal**

To practice scat singing, sing measures 77–92 at a very slow tempo. Then, gradually increase the tempo. Finally, sing the passage by improvising the syllables and/or the melody. **Improvisation** is *the art of singing or playing music, making it up as you go.*

◆ **Artistic Expression**

In $\frac{4}{4}$ meter, the strong beats are most often beats 1 and 3, while the weak beats are 2 and 4. Perform the following examples by putting more stress on the words that fall on the strong beats, and putting less stress on words that fall on the weak beats (upbeat) while moving forward to the strong beat. Sing in your appropriate range.

Hop a flight to Mi - am - i Beach or to Hol - ly - wood.

I'm in a New York___ state of mind.

Evaluation

Demonstrate how well you have learned the skills and concepts featured in the lesson "New York State Of Mind" by completing the following:

- In a quartet with one singer on a part, sing measures 23–26 to demonstrate your ability to sing chords in close harmony.
- Locate in the music three examples using the element of upbeat.

New York State Of Mind

For SATB and Piano

Arranged by
STEVE ZEGREE

Words and Music by
BILLY JOEL

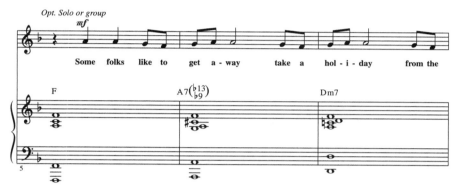

Choral Library *New York State Of Mind*   **191**

LESSON PLAN

Suggested Teaching Sequence and Performance Tips

1. Introduce

Direct students to:

- Read and discuss the information found in the Getting Started section on page 189.

- Practice singing the measures that include scat syllables as described in the Vocal section on page 190. Relate to those measures in the song.

- Practice singing the melodies that have notes on strong and weak beats in the Theory section on page 190. Note that these melodies are from measures 9–11 and 17–19, respectively.

TEACHER 2 TEACHER

Popular vocal music permeates our society. Many popular works utilize seventh chords in the accompaniment and vocal parts. This element can contribute to a relaxed style that is characteristic of some pop-style music.

Observe students' progress in:

✓ Singing scat syllables and corresponding pitches.

✓ Putting the correct emphasis on words on strong and weak beats.

TEACHING STRATEGY

Maintaining a Steady Tempo

This may seem an obvious requirement for advanced ensembles, but is sometimes overlooked as more sophisticated concepts are addressed. Have students:

• Pat the beat almost inaudibly as they sing.

• Sing with a metronome on occasion.

• Listen to recorded performances when they are inclined to rush, describe the problem, and suggest solutions.

• Understand that students who are struggling with tempo cannot hold back the group alone; they will only split the ensemble. It must be something the group feels together.

2. Rehearse

Direct students to:

- Sight-sing the melody in measures 5–19. Notice the use of pitches on strong and weak beats. The singing should have a relaxed, conversational feel to it.
- Sight-sing the parts in measures 23–38.
- Sight-sing parts in measures 41–74. Notice the balance between singing in unison and parts with each style being the same volume.
- Chant the scat syllables in rhythm for measures 77–92. This section should have a sound as if the choir is improvising as a whole. Then add pitches.
- Sight-sing the parts in measures 95–110.

ASSESSMENT

Evaluating the Quality of a Performance

Have students:

1. Watch a video or listen to an audio recording of this piece as performed by the choir.
2. Compare this performance to exemplary models such as other recordings or other live performances of the piece.
3. Develop constructive suggestions for improvement based on the comparison.

- Establish a new key at measure 113 (G major) and sight-sing the parts in measures 113–134.
- Practice measures 135–end at a slow tempo. Then practice measures 135–136 with a flexible beat. The a tempo is observed beginning at measure 137.

Progress Checkpoints

Observe students' progress in:
- ✓ Singing the correct pitches and rhythms.
- ✓ Sight-singing in various styles including scat syllables.
- ✓ A balance of volume when singing in parts and unison.
- ✓ Performing with a free tempo and then a tempo.

TEACHING STRATEGY

Performing a Solo

Direct students to locate the solo found in measures 5–19 of "New York State of Mind." Have them identify the musical terms and symbols for dynamics such as *mp and f (forte)*. Have students take turns performing the solo, interpreting the musical terms and symbols for dynamics as they perform.

3. Refine

Direct students to:

- Sing the entire song in parts. Identify if the first section (measures 5–19) is to be song by a soloist or small group.
- Sing measures 77–92 as a solo or ensemble. Work towards an improvisatory feel to this section. These measures could be an improvised solo by a vocalist or pianist.
- Observe the *ritardando,* free tempo and a tempo in measures 133–137.
- Retain a balanced sound whether singing on strong or weak beats and parts or unison.

MORE ABOUT...

Arranger Steve Zegree

Stephen Zegree is Professor of Music at Western Michigan University, where he teaches piano and jazz, performs with the Western Jazz Quartet, and conducts Gold Company, an internationally recognized jazz-show vocal ensemble. Dr. Zegree is a cum laude graduate of Miami University, where he earned the Bachelor of Music degree in piano performance. He earned the Master of Music degree at Indiana University in piano and jazz, and completed doctoral studies in conducting at the University of Missouri-Kansas City Conservatory of Music, which included a tenure as conducting assistant to Dr. Eph Ehly.

Observe students' progress in:

✓ Singing solo sections with confidence using the correct rhythms and pitches.

✓ Balance of ensemble sound in various choral textures.

✓ Flexibility of tempos as indicated by the arranger.

196   Proficient Mixed

CONNECTING THE ARTS
Phrasing in the Arts

Have students:

• Discuss how the phrase is represented in arts other than music—dance, drama, visual art, or poetry.

• Watch, look at, listen to, or read in language or visual arts to experience how the phrase is managed.

• Discuss the artist how they do or do not use the concept of phrasing.

• Discuss with performers whether and how they consider phrasing in their work.

• Share the information collected and construct a presentation of demonstration based on their finding entitled "Phrasing in the Arts," or a title of their own choosing.

al - i - ty____ and it's fine with me, 'cause I've let it slide.____

Asus A Dm7 Cm7 F7

60

div.
Don't care if it's Chi-na-town or on Ri-ver-side.

B♭ D7 Gm7

63

Unis. *mp*
I don't have an - y rea - sons I've
Unis. *mp*

D♭/E♭ E♭/E F(add9) A7/E Dm7 Dm7/C

66

ASSESSMENT

Informal Assessment

In this lesson, the students showed the ability to:

- Sing solos and small ensemble sections in tune.
- Sight-sing in the keys of F major and G major.
- Observe various tempos and rhythmic feels.

Choral Library *New York State Of Mind* **197**

Student Self-Assessment

Have students evaluate their individual performances based on the following:

- Phrasing
- Expressive Singing
- Intonation
- Accurate Rhythms
- Correct Part-Singing

Have each student rate his/her performance of this song in the areas above on a scale of 1–5, 5 being the best.

TEACHING STRATEGY

Solo and Small Ensemble Performances

Have students:

1. Prepare solos and small ensembles for performance or competition.
2. Interpret music symbols and terms referring to dynamics, tempo and articulation during the performance.
3. Critique and analyze the quality of the performance using standard terminology.

To further measure growth of musical skills presented in this lesson, direct students to complete the Evaluation section on page 190.

- After singing measures 23–26 as a quartet with one person on a part, review each performance by asking, "How in tune were the chords? Which person(s) needs to sing more in tune and how does he/she accomplish this?"

MUSIC LITERACY

Harmonic Sequences

To help students expand their music literacy, have them:

- Use what they know about melodic sequences to predict the definition of harmonic sequence.
- Identify harmonic sequence as a harmonic progression repeated at least twice in sequence.
- Find places in "New York State of Mind" where there are harmonic sequences, for example, measure 41–48 (ii–V–I).
- Discuss any musical characteristics helpful in identifying harmonic sequences, such as similar melodic shapes, and the presence of accidentals.

EXTENSION

Programming

Have students locate other songs and arrangements about cities in the United States. Open the choral library for possible choices or research songs at a local music store or on the Internet. Organize soloists or small groups to sing the songs for the choir, other classes, the administration or at your next concert.

CURRICULUM CONNECTIONS

Journalism

Have students:

- Discuss the role of a music critic.
- Review some of the critiques found in the local paper.
- Write a critique of their taped performance or the recorded performance of "New York State of Mind," identifying the good characteristics and making suggestions for improvement.
- Send the best critiques to the school newspaper for publication.

Encourage your students to expore **music.glencoe.com**, the Web site for *Experiencing Choral Music.* You may wish to preview the rich content before directing your students online. Options available on the Web site include:

- Web Link Exercises
- Interactive Projects
- Audio Samples

MORE ABOUT...

Billy Joel

Born in the Bronx, New York, on May 9, 1949, Billy Joel studied classical piano as a child. According to Billy Joel, his early influences were Ray Charles, Otis Redding, The Rolling Stones, The Beatles, Dave Brubeck and Sam Cooke. "New York State of Mind" has become a classic in the world of popular music. "New York State of Mind" was nominated for a Grammy in 2002 as Best Pop Collaboration with Vocals.

Don't care if it's Chi-na-town or on Ri-ver-side.

I don't have an-y rea-sons I've

left them all___ be - hind.   I'm in a

TEACHING STRATEGY

Phrasing

Have students:

- Review the staccato and legato articulation decided upon for performance of the piece.
- Look at the piece and determine where the phrases begin and end.
- Discuss how to combine the articulation and shaping of phrases. (The articulation should not stop students from building energy toward the peak of each phrase, then releasing energy to the end of the phrase.)
- Sing with articulation and shaping of phrases.

ENRICHMENT
Performing Solos

Solo performance is an important element of vocal development. Encourage students to perform solos whenever possible. When preparing to sing a solo, have students first identify all musical symbols and terms for dynamics, tempo and articulation found in the music. Have them make decisions about how they should interpret those markings. As students perform their solos for the class, evaluate their performance based on the following criteria:

- Did they sing with expression?
- Were all pitches and rhythms accurate?
- Was the solo memorized?
- Did they interpret in an appropriate manner the musical symbols and terms found in the music?

Below is a suggested list of solos that may be used for solo performances.

Treble Voices—Moderate
"Nymphs and Shepherds" by Purcell
"Du bist wie eine Blume" by Shumann
"The Daises" by Barber
"Sebben, crudele" by Caldara
Tenor Bass Voices—Moderate
"Caro, mio ben" by Giordani
"Tu lo sai" by Torelli
"Bist du bei mir" by Bach
"Heavenly Grass" by Bowles

Additional National Standards

The following National Standards are addressed through the Assessment, Extension, Enrichment and bottom-page activities:

1. Singing, alone and with others, a varied repertoire of music. **(b)**

5. Reading and notating music. **(b)**

7. Evaluating music and music performances. **(a)**

8. Understanding relationships between music, the other arts, and disciplines outside the arts. **(a)**

Lyrics under the vocal lines: I'm in a New York state of mind.

Ah

Oh

Oo

CURRICULUM CONNECTIONS
Technology in Music

Have students:

1. Identify technology used in music (computer, midi, mp3, CD, audio/video recordings, synthesizer, sound equipment, electronic sounds, and so forth).

2. Discuss what effect technology has on music.

3. Create a musical composition using a form of technology.

4. Perform a solo or small ensemble for the class incorporating technology.

O My Luve's Like A Red, Red Rose

OVERVIEW

Composer: René Clausen
Text: Robert Burns (1759–1796)
Voicing: SATB
Key: G major
Meter: 3/4
Form: Through-composed
Style: Contemporary American Song
Accompaniment: Piano, Violin, Cello
Programming: Festival, Contest

Vocal Ranges:

OBJECTIVES

After completing this lesson, students will be able to:

- Perform expressively from notation a varied repertoire of music representing styles from diverse cultures.
- Identify harmonic parts.
- Relate music to history and culture.

VOCABULARY

Have students review vocabulary in student lesson. Introduce terms found in the music. A complete glossary of terms is found on page 260 of the student book.

O My Luve's Like A Red, Red Rose

Composer: René Clausen
Text: Robert Burns (1759–1796)
Voicing: SATB

VOCABULARY

phrasing
nuance
dissonance
consonance

Focus

- Demonstrate musical artistry through expressive phrasing.
- Use standard terminology to describe *dissonance* and *consonance*.
- Relate music to history and culture.

Getting Started

You have heard the quote "It's not *what* you say, but *how* you say it." We find ourselves at the greeting-card counter looking for something to help us say the things we cannot express and hope these words will convey our thoughts and wishes. The poet Robert Burns (1759–1796), known as Scotland's "best-loved bard," certainly had no trouble expressing his thoughts. The text of his poem "O My Luve's Like A Red, Red Rose" has inspired many composers and performers. The intense level of emotion found in this poem expressing undying love enables us to embody feelings for which we may have no words. The exquisite setting of this poem will challenge you to perform with equally exquisite musical **phrasing** (*a method of expressing a musical idea, comparable to a line or sentence in poetry*).

◆ **History and Culture**

Robert Burns is probably best known for his songs "Auld Lang Syne" and "Comin' Thro' the Rye." He collected about 300 original and traditional Scottish songs for books compiled in his day. He also wrote many poems to be sung to Scottish folk tunes. Robert Burns died in 1796 at the age of thirty-seven. While he was popular in his own lifetime, his popularity was nothing compared to the heights it has reached since his death.

As you continue singing, it is important to know how the voice works. Turn to page 25 to learn more about how the human voice functions.

SPOTLIGHT

To learn more about physiology of the voice, see page 25.

RESOURCES

Proficient Sight-Singing

Teacher Resource Binder

Teaching Master 25, *Robert Burns, a Scottish Poet*

Evaluation Master 4, *Checking Out Phrasing*

Evaluation Master 8, *Evaluating Musical Expression*

Skill Builder 1, *Building Harmony*

For additional resources, see TRB Table of Contents.

Links to Learning

◆ **Vocal**

Locate measures 73–79 in the music. Sing this passage to develop breath control and **nuance** *(subtle variations in tempo, phrasing and dynamics to enhance a musical peformance)*. Observe all tempo and dynamic markings.

◆ **Theory**

Read and perform the following example to practice **dissonance** *(a combination of pitches or tones that clash)* and **consonance** *(harmonies in chords or music that are pleasing to the ear)*. The dissonance pitches have been circled.

Evaluation

Demonstrate how well you have learned the skills and concepts featured in the lesson "O My Luve's Like A Red, Red Rose" by completing the following:

• Listen to a class recording of "O My Luve's Like A Red, Red Rose." Evaluate the performance based on (1) musical phrasing, (2) subtle changes in tempo and dynamics (nuances), and (3) expressive singing. How well did you do?

• Locate in the music one example of *dissonance* and *consonance*.

Choral Library *O My Luve's Like A Red, Red Rose* **207**

Vocal

The Vocal section is designed to prepare students to sing with musical nuance and good breath control.

Have students:

• Sing measures 73–79 at a slow tempo with no changes in volume.

• Sing measures 73–79 observing the dynamic markings and adjust the volume accordingly.

• Sing measures 73–79 observing the tempo markings and adjusting the speed of the beat accordingly.

Theory

The Theory section is designed to prepare students to recognize the difference between dissonant and consonant harmonies.

Have students:

• Sing their parts using solfège syllables.

• Sing their parts using the text.

• Sing their parts emphasizing the dissonant pitches which have been circled and then sing the resolved harmony softer.

RESOURCES

Proficient Mixed Rehearsal/Performance CD

CD 2:14 Voices

CD 2:15 Accompaniment Only

CD 3:20 Vocal Practice Track—Soprano

CD 4:19 Vocal Practice Track—Alto

CD 5:19 Vocal Practice Track—Tenor

CD 6:19 Vocal Practice Track—Bass

National Standards

1. Singing, alone and with others, a varied repertoire of music. **(a)**

6. Listening to, analyzing, and describing music. **(b)**

8. Understanding relationships between music, the other arts, and disciplines outside the arts. **(b)**

LESSON PLAN

Suggested Teaching Sequence and Performance Tips

1. Introduce

Direct students to:

- Read and discuss the information found in the Getting Started section on page 206.
- Practice singing measures 73–79 as described in the Vocal section on page 207 on a neutral vowel to practice breath control.
- Practice singing the four-part exercise in the Theory section on page 207 that illustrates consonance and dissonance.

For Frankie

O My Luve's Like A Red, Red Rose

For SATB and Piano, Violin and Cello

Words by
ROBERT BURNS

Music by
RENÉ CLAUSEN

208   Proficient Mixed

TEACHER 2 TEACHER

Through this lesson the performance of musical ideas is achieved through the knowledge of the shapes of its subdivisions and phrases. Also, how those units relate and contribute to the musical ideas (shapes) as a whole will be explored.

Progress Checkpoints

Observe students' progress in:

✓ Singing a section of music with good breath control while observing musical nuances.

✓ Singing an exercise that includes consonance and dissonance.

MORE ABOUT...

Composer René Clausen

René Clausen, composer and conductor of the Concordia Choir, Concordia College, Moorhead Minnesota, is a graduate of St. Olaf College, Northfied, Minnesota. He holds a master's degree in conducting performance from the University of Illinois, and is currently pursuing the degree of Doctor of Musical Arts in Choral Conducting from the University of Illinois.

Prior to his appointment as conductor of the Concordia Choir in 1986, he served as the Director of Choral Activities at West Texas State University and as an assistant professor of choral music at Wichita State University. He is known throughout the United States for his compositions and choral clinics.

2. Rehearse

Direct students to:

- Sight-sing the parts in measures 5–24 using solfège syllables. Then sing using the text. Practice staggered breathing, give musical shape to notes and phrases. Tenors should bring out their dissonant note in measure 23 which resolves in measure 24.
- Sight-sing the parts in measures 25–42 using solfège syllables and then with the text. Relate dissonant pitches in measures 33 and 34 to the exercise in the Theory section on page 207.

MORE ABOUT
Dissonance in the Twenty-first Century

Have students:

- Listen to and write down the sounds around them for three minutes.
- Share lists, and categorize the sounds as environmental of human-made, consonant or dissonant.
- Discuss sound pollution as one aspect of environmental concern.
- Invite an ear specialist to discuss any immediate dangers to people's hearing within the community.
- Research and find music that uses or explores environmental sound, such as "An American in Paris" by Gershwin, "Doot, Doot" by Mannheim Steamroller, "And God Created Great Whales" by Hovhaness, and so on.

- Sight-sing the parts in measures 50–60 using solfège syllables and then with the text.
- Sight-sing the parts in measures 61–end using solfège syllables and then with the text. Soprano II's should bring out the dissonant pitch and its resolution in measure 70.

Progress Checkpoints

Observe students' progress in:

✓ Singing the correct pitches and rhythms.

✓ Sight-singing melodies and harmonies.

✓ Singing dissonant and consonant pitches.

✓ Their ability to use staggered breathing to help shape phrases.

CONNECTING THE ARTS

Processes in the Arts

Have students:

1. Find examples of artwork or art forms from the Baroque period, describing how they exhibit the characteristics of the period. (Choose from visual art, architecture, dance, drama, poetry or literature.)

2. Discuss how the processes used in the other areas are the same and different from music, taking into consideration the roles of artists, performers and audience.

3. Find other examples from the same art category, but from a different style, period or culture.

4. Discuss similarities and differences between the examples.

3. Refine

Direct students to:

- Sing the entire song using solfège syllables and correct rhythms.

- Sing measures 5–24 *legato*, connecting each pitch to the next so as to create a sustained line through the phrase.

- Sing with tall, lifted vowels, particularly on longer note values. Sustain vowels and do not allow consonants to enter too early.

212   Proficient Mixed

Encourage your students to expore **music.glencoe.com**, the Web site for *Experiencing Choral Music*. You may wish to preview the rich content before directing your students online. Options available on the Web site include:

- Web Link Exercises
- Interactive Projects
- Audio Samples

- Observe dynamic markings throughout. Perform *crescendos* and *decrescendos* as an ensemble.
- Perform parts with *ritardandos* and a tempos observed.

Progress Checkpoints

Observe students' progress in:

✓ Their ability to stagger the breathing, give musical shape to notes and phrases.

✓ Performance of correct dynamics and tempos as indicated by the composer.

MORE ABOUT...

Poet Robert Burns

Robert Burns lived from 1759 to 1796. His poetic text has ideas that we can understand, but in Scotland during the historical period in which he lived, the idiom was quite different from today. To help students understand the poem, write the text of the song on the board, eliminating any repetitions, and discuss the meaning of the poem. Have students write a similar message using contemporary language, but keeping the feeling of Burn's poem. They may share their work or keep it in a journal, and share it only with you.

ASSESSMENT

Informal Assessment

In this lesson, the students showed the ability to:

- Sing dissonant and consonant harmonies.
- Sight-sing in the key of G major.
- Create a smooth, *legato* line within phrases.
- Fluctuate the tempo by slowing down and then resuming the original speed of the beat.

214 Proficient Mixed

TEACHING STRATEGY

Guiding Composition

Guiding student composition is a delicate balance. On one hand, you want to build self-esteem through praise and encouragement. On the other hand, you want to encourage growth and push students beyond the obvious to the interesting and creative. The writing process used in Language Arts offers a series of steps that can become a process for musical composition as well. The first step is planning; then a first draft. Next is a peer consultation and a first revision. This process continues until students feel they are close to a finished work. At this point, a conference is scheduled with you. There is more revision until a final product is achieved, which is written and performed.

Student Self-Assessment

Have students evaluate their individual performances based on the following:

- Breath Management
- Phrasing
- Tall Vowels
- Expressive Singing
- Intonation

Have each student rate his/her performance of this song in the areas above on a scale of 1–5, 5 being the best.

Choral Library *O My Luve's Like A Red, Red Rose* **215**

Individual and Group Performance Evaluation

To further measure growth of musical skills presented in the lesson, direct students to complete the Evaluation section on page 207.

- After listening to a recording of the choir's performance on "O My Luve's Like A Red, Red Rose," evaluate the performance by asking, "How did the phrases sound? Did they sound like a complete musical thought? Were the tempo and dynamics observed correctly? How expressive was the singing?"

- After locating one example of dissonance and one example of consonance, have students compare their findings with a friend.

216   Proficient Mixed

EXTENSION

Composing

Have students locate examples of poetry that could be set to music. Individually or in small groups have the students begin the process of writing melodies that could be sung with the poems as the text. For more advanced classes, have the students write harmonic accompaniments for the melodies. Perform the new pieces for the choir or select a few to be sung at your next concert.

Additional National Standards

The following National Standards are addressed through the Assessment, Extension, Enrichment and bottom-page activities:

2. Performing, alone and with others, a varied repertoire of music. **(b)**

4. Composing and arranging music within specific guidelines. **(a)**

5. Reading and notating music. **(a)**

7. Evaluating music and music performances. **(a)**

8. Understanding relationships between music, the other arts, and disciplines outside the arts. **(a)**

Plaisir d'amour

OVERVIEW

Composer: Johann Paul Martini (1741–1816), arranged by Goff Richards

Text: Jean Pierre Claris de Florian

Voicing: SATB

Key: A major/A minor

Meter: 6/8

Form: ABA'

Style: Classical Italian Aria

Accompaniment: A capella

Programming: Festival, Concert

Vocal Ranges:

OBJECTIVES

After completing this lesson, students will be able to:

- Demonstrate in ensembles accurate intonation and rhythm while performing moderately easy to moderately difficult literature.
- Identify harmonic parts when performing music.
- Sing in groups a varied repertoire of music.

VOCABULARY

Have students review vocabulary in student lesson. Introduce terms found in the music. A complete glossary of terms is found on page 260 of the student book.

Plaisir d'amour

Composer: Johann Paul Martini (1741–1816), arranged by Goff Richards
Text: Jean Pierre Claris de Florian
Voicing: SATB

VOCABULARY

avocation

crescendo

diminuendo

modulation

parallel keys

SPOTLIGHT

To learn more about vocal health, see page 91.

Focus

- Sing in a legato style with accurate intonation and rhythm.
- Identify and perform music that contains modulations.
- Perform music representing the Classical period.

Getting Started

Have you ever been in a class where two different people share the same name? When the name is called, two people respond. It can be confusing. "Plaisir d'amour" has been attributed to various composers because the composer's last name, Martini, is a common name. The true composer is Johann Paul Martini (1741–1816). Martini himself went by several different names during his lifetime. For a while he used the pseudonym "Schwarzendorf" (German for "black village"), but later he became known as "Martini il Tedesco." By whatever name he is known, he wrote a lovely melody that has remained a favorite for over 200 years.

◆ History and Culture

This beautiful eighteenth-century love song has been performed and recorded by both classical and popular singers. Elvis Presley recorded it as "Can't Help Falling in Love." Folk singer Joan Baez has recorded it, as has classical singer Charlotte Church. This arrangement was written for the King's Singers, a British choral ensemble of six men who began singing together in 1968 while attending King's College in Cambridge. Today, the King's Singers tour worldwide and have released over seventy-five recordings featuring many different musical styles.

Professional singers must take care of their voices, because the voice is their instrument. Whether you choose a career in singing or continue to sing as a hobby, or **avocation** (*not related to a job or career*), you should treat your voice well at all times.

RESOURCES

Proficient Sight-Singing

Sight-Singing in A Major, pages 138–139

Sight-Singing in A Minor, pages 36–39

Reading Rhythms in 6/8 Meter, pages 114, 117

Teacher Resource Binder

Teaching Master 26, *Pronunciation Guide for "Plaisir d'amour"*

Evaluation Master 4, *Checking Out Phrasing*

Evaluation Master 15, *Diction Check-up*

Evaluation Master 16, *Performance Evaluation: Part-Singing*

For additional resources, see TRB Table of Contents.

Links to Learning

◆ Vocal

Perform the following example to practice singing legato. Connect each pitch to the next by keeping a steady stream of air flowing throughout the phrase. Shape the second phrase using the dynamic markings indicated, with a gentle **crescendo** (*a dynamic marking that indicates to gradually sing louder*) and **diminuendo** (*a dynamic marking that indicates to gradually sing softer*).

Plai - sir d'a - mour___ ne du - re q'un_ mo - ment___ Cha -

cresc.

dim.

grin d'a - mour du - re tou - te la vi - e.___

◆ Theory

Perform the following example on *loo* to practice singing a **modulation** (*a change in the key or tonal center of a piece of music within the same song*). This modulation, much like the one in measures 23–27, is from A major to A minor. These keys are called **parallel keys** (*major and minor keys having the same keynote, or home tone*).

Evaluation

Demonstrate how well you have learned the skills and concepts featured in the lesson "Plaisir d'amour" by completing the following:

- Form a quartet to sing measures 1–12 to reveal your ability to sing in a legato style, with accurate intonation and rhythm. Evaluate how well you did.

- Form a quartet to sing the modulation from measures 21–29. Based on the performance, answer these questions: (1) How well were the Sopranos and Altos able to sing in tune their first pitch in measure 25? (2) Were the Tenors able to sing measure 25 in tune? (3) Was the ensemble able to establish the tonality of the new key immediately?

Choral Library *Plaisir d'amour* **219**

LINKS TO LEARNING

Vocal

The Vocal section is designed to prepare students to:

- Sing the opening phrase of the song.
- Sing *legato* throughout a phrase.
- Sing dynamic marks as indicated.

Have students:

- Sing the melody using solfège syllables.
- Sing using solfège syllables with a *legato* articulation.
- Sing the *crescendo* and *diminuendo* where marked.
- Learn the French pronunciation.
- Sing the French with a *legato* articulation while observing the dynamics.

Theory

The Theory section is designed to prepare students to sing a modulation.

Have students:

- Sing each part in the Theory exercise.
- Identify the Tenor change from C♯ to C♮ as necessary to the success of the modulation.
- Sing the exercise in parts on the syllable "loo."

LESSON PLAN

Suggested Teaching Sequence and Performance Tips

1. Introduce

Direct students to:

- Read and discuss the information found in the Getting Started section on page 218.
- Practice singing the opening phrase *legato* and with the dynamic as marked in the Vocal section on page 219.
- Practice singing the modulation exercise in the Theory section on page 219.

Progress Checkpoints

Observe students' progress in:

- ✓ Singing a phrase using legato articulation.
- ✓ Singing dynamics as marked.
- ✓ Singing a modulation.

© 1995 The K.S. Music Co. Ltd.
International Copyright Secured   All Rights Reserved

220   Proficient Mixed

TEACHER 2 TEACHER

The lyrical melody in "Plaisir d'amour" is a wonderful opportunity to focus on singing *legato,* particularly because this arrangement weaves the melody into parts other than the Soprano line. A creative programming idea is to feature this song adjacent to an arrangement of "Can't Help Falling In Love" made popular by Elvis Presley.

221

2. Rehearse

Direct students to:

- Read the rhythms throughout on counting syllables. Note that the pattern first encountered in the Soprano part at measure 7 recurs elsewhere in the other parts (Alto and Tenor, measure 11; Tenor and Bass, measure 17).
- When rhythms are exact and correct, learn the French lyrics. Chant them using the correct rhythms. Refer to Teacher Resource Binder, Teaching Master 26.
- Assign divisi and sight-sing the piece using solfége, section-by-section. Locate varied repetitions of measures 5–8 at 21–24 and 41–44.
- As needed, review each part to verify correct rhythms and pitches before singing all parts together.
- When pitches are exact and correct, replace solfége syllables for the French lyrics.

Progress Checkpoints

Observe students' progress in:

✓ Chanting correct rhythms.

✓ Pronouncing the French correctly and in rhythm.

✓ Singing correct pitches in tune to create the harmonies.

MORE ABOUT...

The King's Singers

When the history of choral music in the last quarter of the twentieth century is written, The King's Singers will be featured prominently. Since their inception in 1965, The King's Singers have never waned in popularity. Their name comes from the fact that the original members met in college when they were choral scholars at King's College of Cambridge University. Choral scholars are the finest choral musicians, selected by rigorous audition, who provide music for daily chapel services. "Plaisir d'amour" is from one of several collections of arrangements by members of the King's Singers for their own ensemble to perform. Their contributions to choral music—as both performers and arrangers—is significant.

3. Refine

Direct students to:

- Count/sing the entire piece.
- Focus on the indicated tempo changes given at some phrase endings. Refine the transition between the end of one phrase and the beginning of the next.
- Apply the musical shaping as indicated by the dynamic marks.

Progress Checkpoints

Observe students' progress in:

✓ Singing correct pitches and rhythms.

✓ Pronouncing the French correctly.

✓ Performing the indicated tempo changes as an ensemble.

✓ Shaping the dynamics smoothly, rather than rigidly.

222   Proficient Mixed

TEACHING STRATEGY

Basic Rhythms in 6/8 Meter

If students are not familiar with patterns in 6/8 meter, have them:

- Count from 1–6, with each number getting one beat.
- Count this pattern four times.
- Add hand claps on 1 and 4 as they continue to count, feeling the strong pulses in 6/8 meter.
- Change the patterns to new ones they suggest; for example: clap 1, 3, 4, and 6 each time (this creates the quarter-eighth quarter-eighth pattern), and so on.

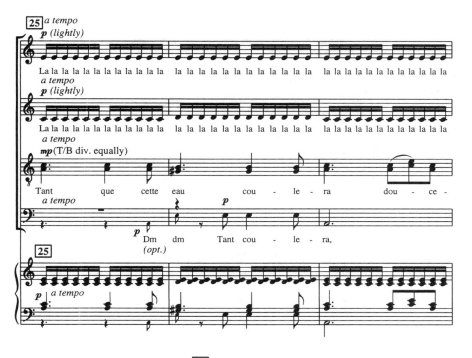

ASSESSMENT

Informal Assessment

In this lesson, students showed the ability to:

- Sing a lyrical melody legato.
- Sing a modulation from A major to A minor.

Student Self-Assessment

Have students evaluate their individual performances based on the following:

- Phrasing
- Diction
- Foreign Language
- Expressive Singing
- Intonation

Have each student rate his/her performance of this song in the areas above on a scale of 1–5, 5 being the best.

TEACHING STRATEGY
Legato Articulation

Have students:

- Glide from vowel to vowel with as little jaw movement as possible.
- Practice shaping the mouth when singing vowels. Feel the sensation and shape of each "pure" vowel, ah (a), eh (ε), ee (i), oh (o), oo (u), when singing.
- Sing from vowel to vowel, listening for uniformity of sound production.
- Sing alternating vowels on a single note, listening for the flow from vowel to vowel, such as *eh-ah-eh*, *oo-oh-ah*, *oo-eh-ee*, and so on.
- Sing alternating vowels as above on changing notes, such as *do-re-do-ti-do*.
- Learn that *legato* singing stems from the uniformity and resonance of vowels when sung correctly.

Individual and Group Performance Assessment

To further measure growth of musical skills presented in this lesson, direct students to complete the Evaluation section on page 219.

- After singing measures 1–12 as a quartet with one on a part, review each performance by asking, "How legato were the phrases? How accurate was the intonation and rhythm?"

- After singing measures 21–29 as a quartet, evaluate the performance by asking, "How accurate was the modulation from A major to A minor? Which section(s) needs more work with singing the correct pitches?"

224   Proficient Mixed

CAREERS IN MUSIC

Music as Avocation

Three areas of music that many students may enjoy outside of the classroom are singing in a community or church choir, singing and acting in a musical theater or singing or playing in a band. Ask students if they already participate in an outside musical group. Ask those that are to share their experiences with others. Music can be a life-long **avocation** *(not related to a job or career)* for those who want to continue studying music. Encourage students to explore ways to use their music skills outside of the classroom.

EXTENSION

Cadential 6/4

Many of the cadences in this arrangement of "Plaisir d'amour" are versions of the cadential 6/4: measures 7–8, 11–12, 15–16, 23–24, 39, and 43–44. Sing each cadence. Notice that the Bass always sings down a perfect fifth (most often, *so–do*). One voice doubles the Bass singing so throughout, or descending *so–fa–mi*. The voice part that begins on mi most often descends *mi–re–do*. And the voice part that begins on *do* most often sings *do–ti–do*. Several of the cadences vary or ornament the above patterns. Analyze each to determine how the cadence is ornamented or varied from the description given above.

Additional National Standards

1. Singing, alone and with others, a varied repertoire of music. **(a)**

5. Reading and notating music. **(b)**

7. Evaluating music and music performances. **(a)**

Salmo 150

OVERVIEW

Composer: Ernani Aguiar
Text: Psalm 150
Voicing: SATB
Key: A minor
Meter: 12/8
Form: Through-composed
Style: Contemporary Brazilian Anthem
Accompaniment: A cappella
Programming: Festival, Concert

Vocal Ranges:

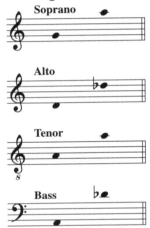

OBJECTIVES

After completing this lesson, students will be able to:

- Read music that incorporates rhythmic patterns in compound meters.
- Create music within specified guidelines.
- Perform expressively from notation a varied repertoire of music representing styles from diverse cultures.

VOCABULARY

Have students review vocabulary in student lesson. Introduce terms found in the music. A complete glossary of terms is found on page 260 of the student book.

Salmo 150

Composer: Ernani Aguiar
Text: Psalm 150
Voicing: SATB

VOCABULARY

articulation
minor tonality
compound meter

SKILL BUILDERS

To learn more about compound meter, see Proficient Sight-Singing, page 130.

Focus

- Read and perform rhythmic patterns in compound meter.
- Write and perform music in minor tonality.
- Perform music representing the Brazilian culture.

Getting Started

In math class you have learned that most numbers can be divided into smaller fractions. Music is also ruled by that theory. The great American choral conductor Robert Shaw (1916–1999) taught that there is a rhythmic feeling in all music—a subdivision of the longer pulse. In "Salmo 150" you must take the time to learn to count the song before you try to sing it. It is the rhythmic awareness that will allow the piece to work. Before singing a note, figure out each rhythmic pattern—just as you have to learn simple arithmetic before you could ever do calculus!

◆ History and Culture

Ernani Aguiar (b. 1949) is one the better-known contemporary Brazilian composers. In addition to his choral music, Aguiar has also written many short instrumental pieces. "Salmo 150" captures the style of this composer with its instrumental sound and rhythmic patterns that require the voice to take on an instrumental style of rapid **articulation** *(the amount of separation or connection between notes).*

The English translation of the Latin text for "Salmo 150" is as follows:
Praise the Lord in His sacred place, praise Him in the firmament of His power.
Praise Him for His mighty acts, praise Him according to His excellent greatness.
Praise Him with the sound of the trumpet, praise Him with the psaltery and harp.
Praise Him with the timbrel and dance, praise Him with strings and pipes.
Praise Him with high-sounding cymbals, praise Him with cymbals of joy.
Let everything that hath breath praise the Lord!

226   Proficient Mixed

RESOURCES

Proficient Sight-Singing

Sight-Singing in A Minor, pages 36–39

Reading Rhythms in Simple Meter and Compound Meter, page 113

Reading Rhythms in 12/8 Meter, pages 118–119

Teacher Resource Binder

Teaching Master 27, *Pronunciation Guide for "Salmo 150"*

Teaching Master 28, *A Minor Melodic Pattern*

Evaluation Master 9, *Evaluating Rhythmic Accuracy*

Evaluation Master 15, *Diction Check-up*

For additional resources, see TRB Table of Contents.

Links to Learning

◆ Vocal

Establish the feeling of the **minor tonality** (*music is based on a minor scale with* la *as its keynote, or home tone*) by singing the following example on solfège syllables. Then, sing on a neutral syllable until you can sing all of the rhythms correctly.

la la la do

◆ Theory

Read and perform the following rhythmic example in **compound meter** (*a time signature in which the division of the beat is based on three eighth notes and the dotted quarter note receives the beat*).

Evaluation

Demonstrate how well you have learned the skills and concepts featured in the lesson "Salmo 150" by completing the following:

- To demonstrate your understanding of compound meter, count or chant the rhythm for your part in measures 1–9. Evaluate how well you were able to perform with accurate rhythm.

- Using the pitches *la, ti, do, re, mi* in the key of A minor, write a two-measure melodic pattern in minor tonality. Begin and end your composition on *la*. You may use a compound meter featured in "Salmo 150." Check your work for melodic and rhythmic accuracy.

LINKS TO LEARNING

Vocal

The Vocal section is designed to prepare students to establish a feeling for minor tonality using solfège syllables.

Have students:

- Sing the melody using solfège syllables.

- Sing the melody on a neutral syllable such as *loo.*

Theory

The Theory section is designed to prepare students to perform a rhythmic pattern in compound meter.

Have students:

- Read the rhythmic pattern using a counting system.

- Clap the rhythmic pattern as they tap the dotted-quarter note pulse.

RESOURCES

Proficient Mixed Rehearsal/Performance CD

CD 2:18 Voices

CD 2:19 Accompaniment Only

CD 3:22 Vocal Practice Track—Soprano

CD 4:21 Vocal Practice Track—Alto

CD 5:21 Vocal Practice Track—Tenor

CD 6:21 Vocal Practice Track—Bass

National Standards

1. Singing, alone and with others, a varied repertoire of music. **(a)**

4. Composing and arranging music within specific guidelines. **(a)**

5. Reading and notating music. **(a)**

Salmo 150
(Psalm 150)

For SATB, a cappella

Liturgical Latin

Music by
ERNANI AGUIAR

LESSON PLAN

Suggested Teaching Sequence and Performance Tips

1. Introduce

Direct students to:

- Read and discuss the information found in the Getting Started section on page 226.
- Practice singing the melody in A minor in the Vocal section on page 227. Relate to the key of the song.
- Practice performing the rhythmic pattern in the Theory section on page 227. Relate rhythms to those used in the song.

Progress Checkpoints

Observe students' progress in:

✓ Singing a melody in a minor key.
✓ Performing rhythms in compound meter.

TEACHER 2 TEACHER

Many times when we start a difficult piece like "Salmo 150," we tend to push too fast to get to words and pitch. Do not attempt to learn this piece in such a manner. Take it slow! Take it slow! Take it slow! Do not start pitches until the rhythmic patterns can be counted correctly by the students, not just a few of your better singers. Gradually work the tempo faster and faster but only after the choir understands the counting.

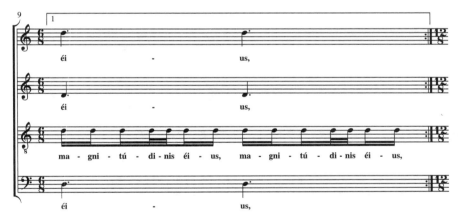

2. Rehearse

Direct students to:

- Practice the text/rhythm in measures 9–10, measures 16–20 and measure 25. Start chanting the text in rhythm with a slow tempo. Allow the pulse to increase as the text and counting become accurate.

- Practice singing measures 16–17, which is in the key of B♭ minor and then shifts back to A minor in measure 18.

Progress Checkpoints

Observe students' progress in:

✓ Their ability to accurately chant the words in rhythm.

✓ Their ability to accurately sing correct pitch, rhythm and text.

TEACHING STRATEGY

Identifying a Key as Minor

Discuss and identify strategies for determining whether a piece is in major or minor. Some possible strategies include:

- Look at the key signature, and determine the possible major key.
- Look at the notation, especially the beginning chord, and the chords at the ends of phrases, identifying the tonal center.
- Determine if the tonal center matches the major key, or is a third below, indicating the relative minor.
- If minor, look for altered tones. If there are none, it is natural minor. If there are altered tones, it is possibly harmonic minor.

3. Refine

Direct students to:

- Isolate voice parts that should be prominent—melodic in nature. Choir members should understand when they have the melody or when they are accompaniment. Adjust their volume accordingly.
- Internalize the sense of stress to the strong beats in order for the music to dance. Singing 12 equal eighth notes in 12/8 meter will not work—nor will singing 24 equally-weighted sixteenth notes.

Progress Checkpoints

Observe students' progress in:

✓ Proper blend and balance in reference to melodic themes and supportive parts.

✓ Their performance of the stress to strong beats through syllabic emphasis and accent of notes.

TEACHING STRATEGY

Sight-Singing Rhythms

When sight-singing is formally assessed, both pitch and rhythm are factors taken into consideration. Have students:

Discuss the following reasons why reading rhythm correctly minimizes sight-singing mistakes: Even if the pitch suffers, the rhythm is correct. Missing the rhythm of a sight-singing exercise in order to resolve a pitch problem maximizes the mistake. If the rhythm is wrong the pitch is automatically wrong because it is in the wrong place in time. Negotiating the correct rhythm increases the singer's chance of recovering the pitch in subsequent measures of the sight-singing material.

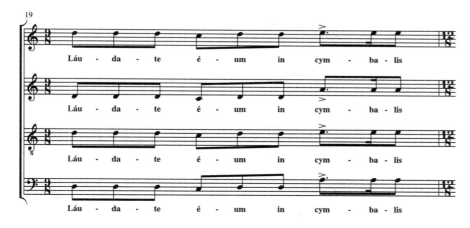

Informal Assessment

In this lesson, students showed the ability to:

- Count and perform rhythmic patterns in compound meter.
- Sing and explore music from various cultures (Brazil).
- Sing appropriate music expressively.

Student Self-Assessment

Have students evaluate their individual performances based on the following:

- Diction
- Foreign Language
- Expressive Singing
- Accurate Rhythms
- Correct Part-Singing

Have each student rate his/her performance of this song in the areas above on a scale of 1–5, 5 being the best.

CONNECTING THE ARTS

Artistic Freedom in the Contemporary Period

Have students:

- Research how artistic freedom has been the focus of controversy during the Contemporary period, using written sources, interviews with art educators and/or practicing artists in the community, and through electronic mail and Internet research sites.
- Identify ways in which the arts have shaped society and been influenced by social, political, and economic pressures.
- Identify any parallels they may find between the arts as a social tool in the Contemporary period, and in other periods of history, or in other cultures.

Individual and Group Performance Evaluation

To further measure growth of musical skills presented in this lesson, direct students to complete the Evaluation section on page 227.

- After counting or chanting measures 1–9 for a friend from another section of the choir, review each performance by asking, "How accurate were the rhythms? Which measures need more work?" Then switch roles.

- After writing a two-measure melodic pattern in A minor, compare it with one written by a friend. Evaluate the compositions by asking, "Were the melodies rhythmically correct? Did they stay within the specified pitches of A minor?"

232 Proficient Mixed

MORE ABOUT...

Expressive Elements of Music

In language, expression is used to communicate mood. The expressive elements of tempo, dynamics, tone color, pitch, articulation and intensity help to convey mood. These same expressive elements are available in performing music, and help the performer to establish and communicate the intended mood. It is up to the performer to understand and interpret the intentions of the composer and arranger. In a large group, the conductor frequently helps the group make these decisions, so they are all interpreting the piece in the same way.

25

Láu - da - te Dó - mi-num, Láu-da - te Dó-mi-num, Láu-da - te Dó - mi-num, Láu-da - te Dó - mi -

Láu - da - te Dó - mi-num, Láu-da - te Dó-mi-num, Láu-da - te Dó - mi-num, Láu-da - te Dó - mi -

Láu - da - te Dó - mi-num, Láu-da - te Dó-mi-num, Láu-da - te Dó - mi-num, Láu-da - te Dó - mi -

Láu - da - te Dó - mi-num, Láu-da - te Dó-mi-num, Láu-da - te Dó - mi-num, Láu-da - te Dó - mi -

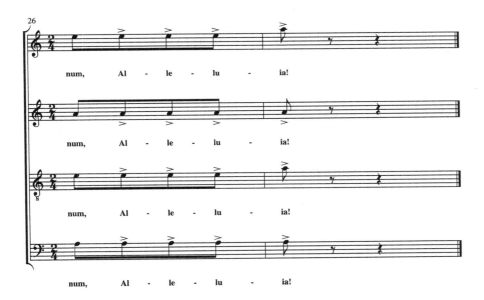

26

num, Al - le - lu - ia!

num, Al - le - lu - ia!

num, Al - le - lu - ia!

num, Al - le - lu - ia!

EXTENSION

Creating a Percussion Accompaniment

Compose a percussion part for "Salmo 150," which could be done in small groups or by sections. Take the best ideas from each group and combine them to create a fuller accompaniment. Play the accompaniment with the singing and perform it at your next concert.

Additional National Standards

The following National Standards are addressed through the Assessment, Extension, Enrichment and bottom-page activities:

1. Singing, alone and with others, a varied repertoire of music. **(c)**

4. Composing and arranging music within specific guidelines. **(a)**

7. Evaluating music and music performances. **(a)**

8. Understanding relationships between music, the other arts, and disciplines outside the arts. **(b)**

Seasons Of Love

OVERVIEW

Composer: Jonathan Larson,
   arranged by Roger Emerson
Text: Jonathan Larson
Voicing: SATB
Key: F major
Meter: 4/4
Form: Intro ABCA'BCA''B'C''
   Coda
Style: Broadway
Accompaniment: Piano
Programming: Concert Closer,
   Broadway Theme

Vocal Ranges:

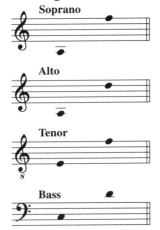

OBJECTIVES

After completing this lesson,
students will be able to:

• Demonstrate in ensembles
   fundamental skills while
   performing moderately
   easy to moderately difficult
   literature.

• Create a variety of
   musical phrases.

VOCABULARY

Have students review
vocabulary in student lesson.
Introduce terms found in the
music. A complete glossary
of terms is found on page
260 of the student book.

Seasons Of Love

Composer: Jonathan Larson, arranged by Roger Emerson
Text: Jonathan Larson
Voicing: SATB

VOCABULARY

melisma

improvisation

Focus

• Read and perform melismatic passages.

• Sing an improvised melodic line.

SPOTLIGHT

*To learn more about
musical theater and
improvisation, see pages
126 and 247.*

Getting Started

   Test your knowledge of musical theatre. The following
analogies have to do with novels, plays or operas that have been
successfully adapted into Broadway musicals. Complete the
following analogies.

   The Princess and the Pea is to *Once Upon a Mattress* as
      Don Quixote is to _____.
   The Matchmaker is to *Hello Dolly!* as *Pygmalion* is to _____.
   Romeo and Juliet is to *West Side Story* as *The Comedy of Errors*
      is to _____.
   And here's one with the answer.
   Madame Butterfly is to *Miss Saigon* as *La Boheme* is to *Rent!*

◆ History and Culture

   Rent opened on Broadway on April 29, 1996. It is loosely
based on Giacomo Puccini's (1858–1924) opera *La Boheme*, the
tragic tale of four impoverished artists living in Paris in the
1890s. In *Rent*, the setting is the Lower East Side of New York
City during the 1990s.

   Act II opens with the company number, "Seasons Of Love."
In a life of feast or famine, it is certainly understandable to ask,
"How do you measure a year in the life?" *Rent* has an additional
tragic chapter. The young and talented Jonathan Larson wrote
the book, music and lyrics, which have won numerous awards,
including a Pulitzer Prize and several Tony awards. He died
unexpectedly at age thirty-five before opening night. Unlike
Puccini, he did not live to see his creation become a triumph.

RESOURCES

Proficient Sight-Singing

Sight-Singing in F Major, pages 45–46

Reading Rhythms in 4/4 Meter,
   pages 2, 6

Reading Tied Notes, page 42

Reading Sixteenth Notes and Eighth
   Notes, pages 62–64

Teacher Resource Binder

Teaching Master 29, *The Show Goes On!*

Skill Builder 14, *Improvising Melodies*

Reference 10, *Career: Comparing
   Performance Opportunities*

Reference 16, *Expanding a Musical
   Vocabulary*

For additional resources, see TRB Table
   of Contents.

Links to Learning

◆ **Vocal**

Read and perform the following example to practice a **melisma** *(a pattern with several notes sung on one syllable)*. Strive for pitch accuracy while singing in a relaxed pop style.

love?

◆ **Artistic Expression**

Practice these steps to explore **improvisation** *(the art of sing or playing music, making it up as you go)*.

1. Memorize the solo passage in the example.
2. Add three to five more pitches per measure to the vocal line.
3. Relax and remember that this is spontaneous music-making!

Five hun - dred twen-ty-five thou - sand   six hun-dred min - utes,

five hun - dred twen-ty-five thou - sand   mo - ments so___ dear.___

Evaluation

Demonstrate how well you have learned the skills and concepts featured in the lesson "Seasons Of Love" by completing the following:

- Identify and perform a melismatic passage in your voice part.
- Practice singing the solo in measures 62–65 with a partner. Work through the steps to improvise and perform your creation for the class.

Vocal

The Vocal section is designed to prepare students to sing a melodic pattern that includes a melisma in a pop style.

Have students:

- Sing the Vocal exercise using the syllable *loo*.
- Sing the Vocal exercise on the word *love*.

Artistic Expression

The Artistic Expression section is designed to prepare students to improvise a new melodic line based on a given melody.

Have students:

- Sing the solo line several times until it is memorized.
- Add several pitches to each measure that keep with the style of the melody.
- Adjust lyrics accordingly.

RESOURCES

Proficient Mixed Rehearsal/Performance CD

CD **2:20** Voices
CD **2:21** Accompaniment Only
CD **3:23** Vocal Practice Track—Soprano
CD **4:22** Vocal Practice Track—Alto
CD **5:22** Vocal Practice Track—Tenor
CD **6:22** Vocal Practice Track—Bass

National Standards

1. Singing, alone and with others, a varied repertoire of music. **(c)**
4. Composing and arranging music within specific guidelines. **(a)**

LESSON PLAN

Suggested Teaching Sequence and Performance Tips

1. Introduce

Direct students to:

- Read and discuss the information found in the Getting Started section on page 234. Answers to the analogies are *Man of La Mancha, My Fair Lady* and *The Boys From Syracuse.* If the students know the story line or characters for any of the analogies, ask them to share the information with the class. Discuss any other adaptations the students know in the musical, film or television genre. Introduce Puccini and *La Boheme.*

- Practice singing the melodic line in the Vocal section on page 235. Relate to the Alto part in measures 23–24.

- Practice singing the melody in the Theory section on page 235. Repeat until it is memorized. Improvise new melodies by adding several pitches to each measure in a relaxed pop style.

From Rent
Seasons Of Love
For SATB and Piano

Arranged by
ROGER EMERSON

Words and Music by
JONATHAN LARSON

236   Proficient Mixed

TEACHER 2 TEACHER

Although *Rent* is loosely based on *La Boheme,* Jonathan Larson paralleled his characters quite closely to those of Puccini.

Both *Rent* and *La Boheme* tell their stories with strength and poignancy.

LA BOHEME	RENT
Rudolfo, the poet	Roger, the musician
Marcello, the artist	Mark, the film maker
Colline, the philosopher	Tom Collins, a friend
Schaunard, the musician	Angel, the street musician
Mimi, the seamstress	Mimi, the dancer
Benoit, the landlord	Benny, the landlord
Musetta, the fun loving girl	Maureen, the activist
Alcindoro, Musetta's old admirer	JoAnne, Maureen's friend

how do you meas-ure, meas-ure a __ year? __ In day-lights, in sun-sets, in

mid-nights, in cups __ of cof-fee; in inch-es, in miles, in laugh-ter, in __ strife? __ In

five hun-dred twen-ty five thou-sand six hun-dred min - utes; how do you meas-ure a

- Listen to the original Broadway recording of "Seasons Of Love." Start a list on the board of similarities and differences between the recording and the choral score. Continue to add to the list as you rehearse. Discuss how the unique qualities of choral singing (i.e., vocal blend, tone quality, rhythmic precision) will give this version a different sound from the Broadway version.

Progress Checkpoints

Observe students' progress in:

✓ Their ability to determine analogies for musical theater questions.

✓ Their ability to maintain a steady beat.

✓ Their ability to discriminate between musical theater vocal sound and choral ensemble vocal quality.

Choral Library *Seasons Of Love* **237**

CONNECTING THE ARTS

From Opera to Musical Theater

Listen to or watch a production of *La Boheme* while following a translation. Then, listen to the original Broadway production of *Rent*. List similarities and contrasts. Share your findings with a drama class.

2. Rehearse

Direct students:

- Chant the solfège syllables for measures 5–12 while tapping a subdivided pulse. Sing measures 5–12 using solfège syllables, keeping a steady beat. Repeat chanting and singing solfège syllables for measures 13–20.

- Rehearse in voice part sectionals measures 21–32 using solfège syllables. Allow sections to sing for the class while the other students tap a steady pulse.

- Divide the class into SATB ensembles. Have each ensemble learn measures 33–56 without the solo lines beginning in measure 33 and measure 41. Allow time for every singer in each ensemble to sing the solo line while the rest of the group sings the accompanying parts.

- Return to SATB ensembles and sing measure 57 to the end using solfège syllables. Ask students to explain what is happening melodically at measure 62 (sections A and B melodies are sung simultaneously).

238   Proficient Mixed

CURRICULUM CONNECTIONS

The Math of Life

What other ways can you "measure a year in the life?" Figure out how many pizza dinners, weekend days, trips to the grocery store, loads of laundry, and so on that are in a year. Write the list on the board and add to it periodically.

- Sing the entire song using solfège syllables, then with words. Have two sections sing at a time (e.g., Sopranos and Basses; Tenors and Altos). As they sing, switch randomly between the two groups, asking students to begin singing in the middle of phrases, measures or even words. Repeat with a different paring of voice parts.

- Give all singers the numbers 1, 2, 3, or 4. Call out a number and have only the students with that number stand and sing. Ask students to continue singing silently in their heads while you randomly switch numbers.

Progress Checkpoints

Observe students' progress in:

✓ Their ability to contribute to small ensemble rehearsals.

✓ Their ability to sing independently in SATB quartets.

✓ Maintaining breath support throughout the phrase.

MORE ABOUT...

The Opera *La Boheme*

Encourage students to familiarize themselves with the story and music of Puccini's opera *La Boheme*.

When Rudolfo first meets Mimi, he tells her about his hopes and dreams in the aria "Che gelida manina." She then tells him about her life in "Si, mi chiamano Mimi." Have the students listen to these two arias while reading the translation, since they are often considered among the most famous arias in the opera world.

3. Refine

Direct students to:

- Sing the piano accompaniment in measures 1–4 as an SA(TB) trio or quartet a cappella with a steady beat. In SATB quartets, sing these four measures and add an original text. Allow time for quartets to sing for and critique each other.

- Discuss musical elements that can be varied in improvisation (i.e., rhythm, melody, text, and so on)

- Working in SATB quartets, allow time for students to experiment with improvisation. Three members of the quartet should sing the original words created for measures 1–4 three times while one singer improvises a solo line for measures 33–44. Repeat and allow all students to have the opportunity to improvise as many times as possible.

240   Proficient Mixed

CURRICULUM CONNECTIONS

Technology in Music

Have students:

1. Identify technology used in music (computer, midi, mp3, CD, audio/video recordings, synthesizer, sound equipment, electronic sounds, and so forth).
2. Discuss what effect technology has on music.
3. Create a musical composition using a form of technology.
4. Perform a solo or small ensemble for the class incorporating technology.

Oo _____

brid - ges ___ he burned or the way that she died. ___

Bb(add9)   Am7   Gm7 C7sus   Dm   C   Dm   Am

43

time now to sing out though the sto - ry nev - er ends. ___ Let's

Bb(add9)   Am7   Gm7 C7sus   F   C   Dm   Am

45

cresc.   div.   Unis.

cel - e - brate, re - mem - ber a year in the life of ___ friends. _ Re-mem-ber the

cresc.   Unis.

Bb(add9)   Am7   Gm7 C7sus   Dm   C   Dm   Am

cresc.

47

Choral Library *Seasons Of Love*   **241**

- As a choir, sing the entire song on words, choosing different students to improvise to the melodic line at measure 62. Discuss ideas for using expressive and dynamic markings to vary each repeated section.

Progress Checkpoints

Observe students' progress in:
- ✓ Their encouragement and support for each soloist.
- ✓ Their ability to sing expressively an accompanying harmonic line.

CONNECTING THE ARTS

Radio Programming

Put together a radio program of improvisation in music. Find examples from classical music and jazz; instrumental and vocal. Record your program and play it for the class. With your teacher's permission, play sections of it for the school on the school's sound system. Ask for feedback from your listeners on their likes and dislikes, recognition of styles and performers, and so forth.

ASSESSMENT

Informal Assessment

In this lesson, students showed the ability to:

- Consistently perform syncopated patterns at a steady, relaxed pace in a pop style.
- Independently learn a short phrase by sequentially addressing rhythm, pitch, and text in a small group setting.

MORE ABOUT...

The Musical *Rent*

Jonathan Larson received the 1996 Pulitzer Prize for Drama for *Rent*. The musical also received four 1996 Tony Awards as well as Best Musical Awards from the New York Drama Critics Circle. Mr. Larson had written music for "Sesame Street" and the children's book and cassettes *An American Tail* and *Land Before Time*. *Rent* premiered on February 13, 1996 at New York Theatre Workshop and opened at the Nederlander Theatre on Broadway on April 29, 1996. Mr. Larson died unexpectedly on January 25, 1996; ten days before his 36th birthday.

Student Self-Assessment

Have students evaluate their individual performances based on the following:

- Phrasing
- Expressive Singing
- Intonation
- Accurate Rhythms
- Correct Part-Singing

Have each student rate his/her performance of this song in the areas above on a scale of 1–5, 5 being the best.

TEACHING STRATEGY

Listening and Classifying

Prepare a listening activity for your choir using the Rehearsal/Performance CDs. Have students listen to the following recordings and then identify/classify them as folk songs or classical songs. Ask students to explain why they classified each listening example as they did.

1. "The Little Beggarman" (page 10—Irish folk song)
2. "Sicut Locutus Est" (page 60—classical—Bach)
3. "Sanctus" (page 86—classical—Mozart)
4. "Jabula Jesu" (page 180—Zulu folk song)
5. "Der Tanz" (page 94—classical—Schumann

Individual and Group Performance Evaluation

To further measure growth of musical skills presented in this lesson, direct students to complete the Evaluation section on page 235.

- After singing a melismatic passage from your part as a solo, evaluate the performance by asking, "Were the pitches and rhythms correct? Did I sing using pop-style phrasing?"

- After singing the solo in measures 62–65 with a partner, improvise a similar melodic line. Select one of the improvised melodies and sing it for the class. Review each performance by asking, "How creative was the solo? Did it capture a similar flavor as the original melody? What could be some areas for improvement?"

244   Proficient Mixed

Encourage your students to expore **music.glencoe.com**, the Web site for *Experiencing Choral Music.* You may wish to preview the rich content before directing your students online. Options available on the Web site include:

- Web Link Exercises
- Interactive Projects
- Audio Samples

EXTENSION

Playing the Piano

Encourage students to learn to play the piano accompaniment to "Seasons of Love." If they don't know how to play the piano very well, have them learn either the right or left hand of the piano accompaniment in measures 1–4 while a classmate plays the other hand. If they do know how to play the piano, learn the accompaniment for the entire song and play it for the class.

MORE ABOUT...

Arranger Roger Emerson

Roger Emerson received his degree in Music Education from Southern Oregon University and served as music specialist for twelve years in the Mt. Shasta Public School system. He concluded his teaching career at the College of the Siskiyous, also in Northern California, and now devotes full time to composing, arranging and consulting. Roger currently resides in Mt. Shasta, California with his wife Mari and daughters Cassie and Kayla.

Additional National Standards

The following National Standards are addressed through the Assessment, Extension, Enrichment and bottom-page activities:

1. Singing, alone and with others, a varied repertoire of music. **(a)**

2. Performing, alone and with others, a varied repertoire of music. **(c)**

3. Improvising melodies, variations and accompaniments. **(c)**

5. Reading and notating music. **(b)**

6. Listening to, analyzing, and describing music. **(a)**

7. Evaluating music and music performances. **(a)**

SPOTLIGHT

Improvisation

Improvisation is *the art of singing or playing music, making it up as you go.* **Scat singing** is *an improvisational style of singing that uses nonsense syllables instead of words.* Sometimes, these nonsense sounds can imitate the sound of an instrument. Scat singing, especially as a solo, can be the scariest part of singing jazz.

According to Dr. Kirby Shaw, one of the top vocal jazz composers and conductors in the world today, here are some suggestions to help build your confidence in this fun and exciting art form.

- Start your scat solo with a short melodic or rhythmic idea from the tune being performed. There is nothing wrong in having a preconceived idea before starting to sing a scat solo! By gradually developing the idea as you sing, you will have an organized solo that sounds completely improvised.

- Start with scat syllables like "doo" when singing swing tunes. Try "bee," "dee," and "dn" for occasional accented eighth notes on the upbeat of beats (1 *and* 2 *and* 3 *and* 4 *and*). Try "doot" or "dit" for short last notes of a musical phrase.

- Be able to imitate any sound you like from the world around you, such as a soft breeze, a car horn or a musical instrument. There might be a place for that sound in one of your solos.

- Listen to and imitate note-for-note the great jazz singers or instrumentalists. Musicians like Ella Fitzgerald, Jon Hendricks, Louis Armstrong or Charlie Parker can be an inspiration to you.

- Learn to sing the blues. You can listen to artists like B.B. King, Stevie Ray Vaughan, Buddy Guy or Luther Allison. There are many recordings from which to choose.

In short, learn as many different kinds of songs as you can. The best scat singers quote from such diverse sources as nursery rhymes, African chant and even opera. Above all, have fun as you develop your skills!

Composer/arranger Kirby Shaw's music has been sung around the world and has sold millions of copies. As a performer, Dr. Shaw has scatted one-on-one with such notables as Bobby McFerrin, Al Jarreau, Jon Hendricks and Mark Murphy. As a member of the ensemble, he enjoys singing vocal jazz with Just 4 Kicks, a zany four-man a cappella vocal jazz ensemble.

Spotlight *Improvisation* **247**

RESOURCES

Teacher Resource Binder

Vocal Development 1–6, *Developing the Voice*
Skill Builders 14, *Improvising Melodies*

National Standards

1. Singing, alone and with other, a varied repertoire of music. **(a, b, c)**
3. Improvising melodies, variations and accompaniments. **(a, b, c)**

IMPROVISATION

Objectives
- Create rhythmic and melodic phrases.
- Improvise musical melodies.

Suggested Teaching Sequence
Direct students to:
- Read the Spotlight On Improvisation on student page 247 and define improvisation and scat singing.
- Identify the steps to follow in learning to scat sing.
- Practice scat singing as described on page 247. Teacher may model, students imitate.
- Apply scat singing techniques to a familiar song.
- Make a list of vocal jazz singers they know and identify characteristics of their singing.
- Apply the techniques presented on this page to the performance of "Seasons of Love" on page 234.

Progress Checkpoints
Observe students' progress in:
- ✓ Their ability to define and describe the concept of improvisation.
- ✓ Their ability to demonstrate scat singing.
- ✓ Their ability to apply improvisation techniques in the performance of a song.

The Star-Spangled Banner

OVERVIEW

Composer: John Stafford Smith (1759–1836), arranged by Barry Talley

Text: Francis Scott Key

Voicing: SATB

Key: C major

Meter: 4/4 and 3/4

Form: Medley

Style: Patriotic

Accompaniment: A cappella

Programming: Concert Opener, Festival, Patriotic Concert

Vocal Ranges:

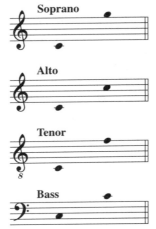

Soprano

Alto

Tenor

Bass

OBJECTIVES

After completing this lesson, students will be able to:

• Define concepts of music notation, including accidentals.

• Demonstrate in ensembles accurate rhythm, including dotted rhythms.

• Relate music to history, society and culture.

VOCABULARY

Have students review vocabulary in student lesson. Introduce terms found in the music. A complete glossary of terms is found on page 260 of the student book.

The Star-Spangled Banner

Composer: John Stafford Smith (1759–1836), arranged by Barry Talley
Text: Francis Scott Key
Voicing: SATB

VOCABULARY

national anthem
accidental

🔺 **SPOTLIGHT**

To learn more about concert etiquette, see page 104.

Focus

• Describe and sing an accidental accurately.

• Read and perform rhythmic patterns that contain dotted rhythms.

• Relate the music to history, to society and to culture.

Getting Started

The flag and the **national anthem** *(a patriotic song adopted by a nation through tradition or decree)* are symbols of national pride and patriotism. What does the phrase "O'er the land of the free and the home of the brave" mean to you? What images do you visualize when you sing "The Star-Spangled Banner?" Write down your thoughts and share them with the class.

◆ History and Culture

You may know who wrote the words to "The Star-Spangled Banner," but do you know who wrote the original music? His name is John Stafford Smith (1750–1836). Smith was an English composer and organist who composed "To Anachreon in Heaven" in 1770 for the London Anacreonic Society, an aristocratic group dedicated to the promotion of the arts. Now, it is the tune to "The Star-Spangled Banner."

During the War of 1812, the British fleet attacked Fort McHenry, which is located outside Baltimore, Maryland. During the attack, Francis Scott Key was aboard a British warship trying to gain the release of an American prisoner. The next morning, the flag was still there. Inspired by this sight, Key wrote the words to "The Star-Spangled Banner" on the back of a letter he had in his pocket. It was printed on flyers and distributed throughout Baltimore. In 1931, the United States Congress officially recognized "The Star-Spangled Banner" as our national anthem. It is proper concert etiquette to stand whenever "The Star-Spangled Banner" is performed.

248 Proficient Mixed

RESOURCES

Proficient Sight-Singing

Sight-Singing in C Major, pages 7, 9, 13, 26–27, 34–35

Reading Rhythms in 4/4 Meter, page 2

Reading Rhythms in 3/4 Meter, page 14

Reading Dotted Eighth/Sixteenth Note Rhythms, page 76

Teacher Resource Binder

Teaching Master 30, *"The Star-Spangled Banner"—My View*

Reference 16, *Expanding a Musical Vocabulary*

For additional resources, see TRB Table of Contents.

Links to Learning

◆ **Vocal**

Although this arrangement is written in the key of C major, it uses **accidentals** (*sharps, flats or naturals that are not included in the key signature of a piece of music*) to change the pitch of some notes. The pitch *fa* is sometimes raised to *fi*, and the pitch *sol* is sometimes raised to *si*. Perform the following C major scale with accidentals. Sing in an appropriate octave.

do re mi fa fi sol si la ti do ti la si sol fi fa mi re do

For more practice singing accidentals, perform the following example.

do re mi fa sol la ti do do   do ti la sol fa mi re do do

do re mi fi sol si la ti do   do ti la si sol fi fa mi re do do

◆ **Theory**

Read and perform the following rhythmic patterns that contain dotted rhythms.

ti ti ti ti ti ti tim ka ta tim ka ta tim ka ta ta–a–a

ti ti ti ti tim ka ta ti ti tim ka ta tim ka ti ti ta–a–a

Evaluation

Demonstrate how well you have learned the skills and concepts featured in the lesson "The Star-Spangled Banner" by completing the following:

- Sing the Vocal examples above to show your ability to sing accidentals in tune. You may do this with a partner, taking turns singing for each other. Critique each other's performance.

- Chant or clap the rhythms in measures 5–13 that contain dotted notes. Evaluate how well you were able to perform the dotted rhythms accurately. Rate your performance as (1) all rhythms were correct, (2) most rhythms were correct, or (3) only a few of the rhythms were correct.

Choral Library *The Star-Spangled Banner* **249**

LESSON PLAN

Suggested Teaching Sequence and Performance Tips

Direct students to:

- Read and discuss the information found in the Getting Started section on page 248.
- Sight-sing the C major scale with accidentals in the Vocal section on page 249.
- Clap and speak the dotted rhythm patterns in the Theory section on page 249.
- Locate and circle the accidentals in the music. Sight-sing measures 1–4 with accurate pitches.
- Locate all dotted rhythms in the music. Sight-sing measures 1–4 again, this time focusing on pitch as well as rhythm.
- Sing through entire piece.
- Sing expressively by singing all dynamic levels as indicated in the score.
- Bring out the melody when it shifts from part to part.

Progress Checkpoints

Observe students' progress in:

- ✓ Singing accidentals with accuracy.
- ✓ The ability to accurately perform dotted rhythms.
- ✓ The ability to successfully transfer altered pitches from the Vocal section to the music itself.
- ✓ Singing with accurate pitch and rhythm.
- ✓ Singing with dynamic contrast throughout the piece.
- ✓ Balancing the melody within the ensemble.

The Star-Spangled Banner

For SATB, a cappella

Arranged by
BARRY TALLEY

Words by FRANCIS SCOTT KEY
Music by JOHN STAFFORD SMITH

250   Proficient Mixed

TEACHER 2 TEACHER

The feeling of our nation's pride and patriotism has never been stronger. Discuss whether "The Star-Spangled Banner" has taken on a more personal meaning since the events of September 11, 2001. Write down or share the images that come to mind when performing this piece.

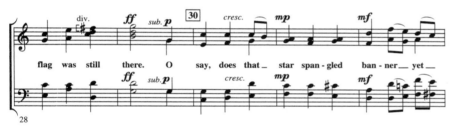

ASSESSMENT

Informal Assessment

In this lesson, the students showed the ability to:

- Identify and successfully sing chromatic lines found in the music.
- Sing with appropriate dynamics and balance.

Student Self-Assessment

Have students evaluate their individual performances based on the following:

- Posture
- Expressive Singing
- Intonation
- Accurate Pitch
- Accurate Rhythms

Have each student rate his/her performance of this song in the areas above on a scale of 1–5, 5 being the best.

Individual and Group Performance Evaluation

To further measure growth of musical skills presented in this lesson, direct students to complete the Evaluation section on page 249.

- After singing the Vocal examples with a partner, evaluate the performance by asking, "Were the altered pitches in tune?"
- After chanting or clapping the rhythms in measures 5–13 that contain dotted notes, rate the performance using the following scale: (1) all rhythms were correct, (2) most rhythms were correct, (3) only a few rhythms were correct.

TEACHING STRATEGY

Performing a Solo

To gain experience in performing a solo, direct students to memorize "The Star Spangled Banner." Have students identify the musical symbols and terms relating to tempo, dynamics and articulation found in the music. Then, have students take turns performing "The Star Spangled Banner" as a solo for the class. Assess how well the singer was able to interpret the musical symbols and terms for tempo, dynamics and articulation as they sang the solo.

Tunggare
OVERVIEW

Composer: Stephen Leek
Text: Aboriginal
Voicing: SATB
Key: F mixolydian
Meter: 4/4 and 5/4
Form: Through-composed
Style: Contemporary Australian Song
Accompaniment: A cappella
Programming: Festival, Contest, Concert

Vocal Ranges:

Soprano

Alto

Tenor

Bass

OBJECTIVES

After completing this lesson, students will be able to:

- Demonstrate accurate intonation while performing moderately difficult literature.
- Define concepts of rhythm/meter using standard terminology.
- Perform expressively from notation a varied repertoire of music representing styles from diverse cultures.

VOCABULARY

Have students review vocabulary in student lesson. Introduce terms found in the music. A complete glossary of terms is found on page 260 of the student book.

Tunggare

Composer: Stephen Leek
Text: Aboriginal
Voicing: SATB

VOCABULARY

ostinato
intervals
mixed meter

SKILL BUILDERS

To learn more about mixed meter, see Proficient Sight-Singing, *pages 107 and 128.*

Focus

- Sing intervals with good intonation.
- Identify and perform an ostinato pattern in music written in mixed meter.
- Sing with artistic expression appropriate for the style and structure.

Getting Started

What do you know about the music of Australia? Have you ever experienced the vocal and instrumental sounds of the Aboriginal people of this particular country? The Aboriginal people are said to represent society at its most primitive form. At one time they were nomads, moving from place to place, with no permanent home. Their religion centered on a great respect for land and nature. As you learn to sing "Tunggare," you will explore a vocal style that features interesting harmonies and fascinating rhythmic energy.

◆ History and Culture

"Tunggare" is an Australian aboriginal word meaning "voice" or "to sing." When pronounced, it should rhyme with "fun-far-mah." This choral fanfare is the opening movement of a larger choral work entitled *Man to Tree,* written by Australian composer Stephen Leek. It was commissioned by the Australian Society for Music Education for the 1997 National ASME Conference. As with many of his choral compositions, Mr. Leek attempts to capture the sound and spirit of the Australian Aboriginal people.

This highly rhythmic and energetic piece is written in regular four-bar phrases consisting of three measures of $\frac{4}{4}$ meter followed by one measure of $\frac{5}{4}$ meter. "Tunggare" opens with a syncopated **ostinato** *(a repeated musical figure, rhythmic pattern or phrase)* in the Bass part. The other vocal parts are added one at a time as the piece progresses. Enjoy learning music from the country "down under"—Australia.

RESOURCES

Proficient Sight-Singing

Reading Rhythms in 4/4 Meter, pages 2, 6, 27

Read Rhythms in Mixed Meter, pages 107, 128–129, 132–133 166–167

Reading Modes and Modal Scales, pages 157–159

Teacher Resource Binder

Teaching Master 31, *Pronunciation Guide for "Tunggare"*

Evaluation Master 15, *Diction Check-up*

Skill Builder 20, *Naming Intervals*

Skill Builder 27, *Rhythm Challenge in Mixed Meter*

For additional resources, see TRB Table of Contents.

Links to Learning

◆ **Vocal**

To become more familiar with the **intervals** (*the distance between two notes*) that you will encounter in the piece, perform the following example on the neutral syllable "loo." Sing in your appropriate range.

◆ **Theory**

Clap through the following rhythmic pattern that represents a four-bar phrase. Be sure to observe the **mixed meter** (*a technique in which the time signature or meter changes frequently within a piece of music*).

To perform the ostinato patterns, divide the syncopated patterns in the $\frac{4}{4}$ measures into eight-note groupings like this: **1**-2-3 **1**-2-3 **1**-2. Place an accent on the bolded numbers.

Evaluation

Demonstrate how well you have learned the skills and concepts featured in the lesson "Tunggare" by completing the following:

• To demonstrate your ability to sing intervals with good intonation, sing your part from measures 17–28 on neutral syllables. Evaluate how well you did.

• Create a two-part, four-bar rhythmic pattern phrase. Write one part as an ostinato. Use measures 5–8 in the music as a guide. Check your work for correct notation and rhythms.

• Circle all the dynamic and articulation markings in the score, then perform the piece in a manner that shows you know how to interpret them correctly. Check your work with a classmate.

Choral Library *Tunggare* **253**

LINKS TO LEARNING

Vocal

The Vocal section is designed to prepare students to sing intervals that will be encountered in the piece.

Have students:

• Sing the exercises using solfège syllables in F Mixolydian.

• Sing the exercises on the neutral syllable "loo."

Theory

The Theory section is designed to prepare students to read and perform rhythm patterns in 4/4 and 5/4 meters.

Have students:

• Read the exercises using the preferred counting system.

• Clap the exercises.

• Add accents to the notes in exercise 2.

Tunggare

For SATB, a cappella

STEPHEN LEEK

254 Proficient Mixed

LESSON PLAN

Suggested Teaching Sequence and Performance Tips

1. Introduce

- Read and discuss the information found in the Getting Started section on page 252.
- Practice singing the intervals as shown in the Vocal section on page 253. Relate to intervals used in the piece.
- Practice reading rhythms in 4/4 and 5/4 meters as shown in the Theory section on page 253. Find these time signatures in the composition. *(For example, measures 1 and 4)*

Progress Checkpoints

Observe students' progress in:

✓ Their ability to sing intervals accurately using solfège syllables.

✓ Their ability to perform rhythms in mixed meter.

2. Rehearse

Direct students to:

- Review the rhythms found in sections A through D.
- Sight-sing the Bass and Tenor parts sections A through D. Notice that the phrases repeat every four measures. When pitches are secure, add the text.
- At letter B, the Altos should sight-sing their part. When pitches are secure, repeat sections A through D.

TEACHER2TEACHER

Like many of his compositions, Stephen Leek's "Tunggare" seeks to capture the essence of aboriginal Australian culture in his choral writing. His composition often sets a small number of aboriginal words in ostinato patterns that gradually build in texture, dynamics and harmonic complexity. "Tunggare" will challenge the students to develop rhythmic independence as well as sharpen their skills in ear training.

- Go to rehearsal letter D. Sopranos should sight-sing their part. Notice the repetition that occurs after four measures. When pitches are secure, add the Alto part. Rehearse the two parts until harmonies are secure, especially the A♮ and B♭ dissonance that occurs in measures 18 and 22. Add text in both parts.

- Rehearse all parts together at a slow tempo from the beginning through section D.

- Sight-sing the Tenor and Bass parts at section E. Then slowly rehearse the Soprano part at section E, paying close attention to the syncopated hand claps. When pitches are secure, add text.

- Discover that sections F and G are the same as previous material.

- Go to rehearsal letter H. Notice that this section is a slight rhythmic variation of rehearsal letter D. Sopranos should sight-sing their part. When pitches are secure, add the Alto part. Rehearse the two parts until harmonies are secure, especially the A♮ and B♭ dissonance that occurs. Add text in both parts, then add the Tenor and Bass parts.

- At letter I, allow Tenor and Bass parts to experiment with and practice their part. Next, allow Sopranos and Altos to sight-sing their parts. Put all parts together and rehearse.

Progress Checkpoints

Observe students' progress in:

✓ Their ability to sing intervals with accuracy.

✓ Their ability to sight-sing in 4/4 and 5/4 meters.

MORE ABOUT...

Composer Stephen Leek

Stephen Leek (born in Sydney, Australia, 1959) has established a reputation for his unique work in the Australian community as a composer who takes music out of the concert hall and to the people. He has received the highest accolades for his work, especially for his choral compositions which are "fresh and imaginative, whilst easy on the ear." His compositional output ranges from simple songs for the youngest singer to masterworks of the choral repertoire for more mature voices. His "Once On A Mountain" received the Sounds Australian Award for the Best Choral Composition by an Australian Composer in 1991.

3. Refine

Direct students to:

- On the board or on a sheet of paper, map out the overall dynamic scheme of the piece. Notice that the piece begins very soft and gradually moves section by section to a *forte* dynamic and then gradually moves to a very soft dynamic again. Discuss this design with the class and how it will affect the overall performance.

- Perform the piece, paying strict attention to all dynamic and articulation markings.

Progress Checkpoints

Observe students' progress in:

✓ Their ability to understand the overall dynamic scheme of the piece.

✓ Their ability to observe and perform all dynamic and articulation markings in the score.

ASSESSMENT

Informal Assessment

In this lesson, students showed the ability to:

- Sing with good intonation in four-measure phrases.
- Sing expressively, performing all the dynamic and articulation markings in the score.
- Understand the meaning and historical context of the text and the style of the piece.

EXTENSION

Research

Have students initiate a research project on Australian aboriginal music. Learn more about the sound of this music, including what instruments are used and how the music functions in society. Sample questions could include: What is a songman? What are corroborees? What is a didgeridoo and how does it function? Can a boomerang be played as a musical instrument? If possible, locate and listen to some traditional aboriginal music. Share the data and discuss how this information can enhance the performance of "Tunggare."

Choral Library *Tunggare* **257**

Additional National Standards

The following National Standards are addressed through the Assessment, Extension, Enrichment and bottom-page activities:

4. Composing and arranging music within specific guidelines. **(a)**

5. Reading and notating music. **(a, b)**

7. Evaluating music and music performances. **(a)**

9. Understanding music in relation to history and culture. **(a)**

Student Self-Assessment

Have students evaluate their individual performances based on the following:

- Phrasing
- Foreign Language
- Expressive Singing
- Accurate Pitches
- Accurate Rhythms

Have each student rate his/her performance of this song in the areas above on a scale of 1–5, 5 being the best.

Individual and Group Performance Evaluation

To further measure growth of musical skills presented in this lesson, direct students to complete the Evaluation section on page 253.

- After singing measures 17–28 as quartets with one on a part, evaluate each performance by asking, "How accurate were the intervals? How in tune were the parts?"

- After writing a two-part, four-bar rhythmic pattern, compare your composition with a friend's. Check each other's work for accurate rhythms and perform the compositions for each other.

- After circling the dynamic and articulation markings in the score, sing your part in a quartet with one on a part. Evaluate the performance by asking, "Did each member of the quartet observe his/her dynamic and articulation markings and sing their parts accordingly?"

MELISMAS

Objectives

- Perform melismas with accurate intonation and rhythm.

Suggested Teaching Sequence

Direct students to:

- Read the Spotlight On Melismas on student page 258 and discuss the definitions of *syllabic* and *melisma*.

- Sing "My Country 'tis of Thee" to demonstrate an example of syllabic text setting.

- Identify melismas by finding examples in "Cantate Domino" beginning on student page 42. *(measures 8–12, 29, 31, 37, 43–44)*

- Practice the example found on page 258 by first slowly singing the pitches on solfège syllables.

- Count-sing the rhythm of the melisma.

- Sing the melisma on a neutral syllable such as *doo*. Begin slowly and then gradually increase the tempo.

- Sing the melisma with the text.

Progress Checkpoints

Observe students' progress in:

- ✓ Their ability to recognize the difference between syllabic text setting and melismas.

- ✓ Their ability to sing an example of a syllabic text setting.

- ✓ Their ability to properly sing a melisma.

 SPOTLIGHT

Melismas

Sing the first phrase of "My Country 'Tis of Thee" as shown below. Notice that every syllable of the text receives exactly one note.

My coun-try 'tis of thee, sweet land of li-ber-ty of thee I sing.

This style of text setting is known as **syllabic** (*one syllable for every note*). Can you think of other songs with syllabic text settings?

When one syllable is given many pitches, this is referred to as melismatic singing. A **melisma** is *a group of notes sung to a single syllable*. Melismatic singing became popular in the Middle Ages (c. 400–1450), when as many as several dozen notes would have been sung on the final syllable of a Gregorian chant. The example below shows a melisma on the word "alleluia" similar to those found in Mozart's "Alleluia".

Al - le - lu - ia.

When learning to sing a melisma, the key is to begin slowly. First, learn the pitches on syllables or numbers, and then, count-sing the rhythm of the melisma. Once your pitches and rhythms are secure, sing the melisma on a neutral syllable, such as "doo." Start at a slow tempo, gradually increasing your speed over several weeks. With each repetition, make sure every note is distinct, yet smoothly connected to one another. When you are able to sing the melisma clearly on "doo," switch to the syllable "ah." Once again, begin slowly, then gradually increase your speed to the performance tempo.

Singing a melisma is a vocal skill that may take time to master. With diligent practice, you will soon sing them musically and beautifully!

RESOURCES

Teacher Resource Binder

Vocal Development 11, *Flexibility and Range*
Reference 7, *Building a Musical Vocabulary*

National Standards

1. Singing, alone and with others. **(b)**

Glossary

2/2 meter A time signature in which there are two beats per measure and the half note receives the beat.

2/4 meter A time signature in which there are two beats per measure and the quarter note receives the beat.

3/2 meter A time signature in which there are three beats per measure and the half note receives the beat.

3/4 meter A time signature in which there are three beats per measure and the quarter note receives the beat.

3/8 meter A time signature in which there is one group of three eighth notes per measure and the dotted quarter note receives the beat. When the tempo is very slow, this meter can be counted as having three beats per measure, with the eighth note receiving the beat.

4/4 meter A time signature in which there are four beats per measure and the quarter note receives the beat.

5/8 meter A time signature in which there are five beats per measure and the eighth note receives the beat.

6/4 meter A time signature in which there are two groups of three quarter notes per measure and the dotted half note receives the beat. When the tempo is very slow, this meter can be counted as having six beats per measure, with the quarter note receiving the beat.

6/8 meter A time signature in which there are two groups of three eighth notes per measure and the dotted quarter note receives the beat. When the tempo is very slow, this meter can be counted as having six beats per measure, with the eighth note receiving the beat.

9/8 meter A time signature in which there are three groups of three eighth notes per measure and the dotted quarter note receives the beat. When the tempo is very slow, this meter can be counted as having nine beats per measure, with the eighth note receiving the beat.

12/8 meter A time signature in which there are four groups of three eighth notes per measure and the dotted quarter note receives the beat.

A

a cappella *(ah-kah-PEH-lah)* [It.] A style of singing without instrumental accompaniment.

a tempo *(ah TEM-poh)* [It.] A tempo marking that indicates to return to the original tempo of a piece or section of music.

ABA form A form in which an opening section (A) is followed by a contrasting section (B), which leads to the repetition of the opening section (A).

accelerando *(accel.) (ah-chel-leh-RAHN-doh)* [It.] A tempo marking that indicates to gradually get faster.

accent A symbol placed above or below a given note to indicate that the note should receive extra emphasis or stress. ($\overset{>}{\bullet}$)

accidental Any sharp, flat or natural that is not included in the key signature of a piece of music.

adagio *(ah-DAH-jee-oh)* [It.] Slow tempo, but not as slow as *largo*.

ad libitum *(ad. lib.)* [Lt.] An indication that the performer may vary the tempo or add or delete a vocal or instrumental part.

Aeolian scale *(ay-OH-lee-an)* [Gk.] A modal scale that starts and ends on *la*. It is made up of the same arrangement of whole and half steps as a natural minor scale.

al fine *(ahl FEE-neh)* [It.] To the end.

aleatory music *(AY-lee-uh-toh-ree)* A type of music in which certain aspects are performed randomly. Also known as *chance music*.

alla breve Indicates cut time; a duple meter in which there are two beats per measure, and half note receives the beat. *See* cut time.

allargando (*allarg.*) (*ahl-ahr-GAHN-doh*) [It.] To broaden, become slower.

allegro (*ah-LEH-groh*) [It.] Brisk tempo; faster than *moderato*, slower than *vivace*.

allegro non troppo (*ah-LEH-groh nohn TROH-poh*) [It.] A tempo marking that indicates not too fast. Not as fast as *allegro*.

altered pitch Another name for an accidental.

alto (*AL-toh*) The lowest-sounding female voice.

andante (*ahn-DAHN- teh*) [It.] Moderately slow; a walking tempo.

andante con moto (*ahn-DAHN- teh kohn MOH-toh*) [It.] A slightly faster tempo, "with motion."

andantino (*ahn-dahn-TEE-noh*) [It.] A tempo marking that means "little walking," a little faster than *andante*.

animato Quickly, lively; "animated."

anthem A choral composition in English using a sacred text.

answer In a fugue, the entry of the theme at a different pitch, usually the interval of a fourth or fifth away, than that of the original subject.

antiphon In the Roman Catholic liturgy, a chant with a prose text connected with the psalm, sung by two choirs in alternation. The *antiphon* is usually a refrain for the psalm or canticle verses. Its melodies are often simple, with only one note per syllable.

arpeggio (*ahr-PEH-jee-oh*) [It.] A chord in which the pitches are sounded successively, usually from lowest to highest; in broken style.

arrangement A piece of music in which a composer takes an existing melody and adds extra features or changes the melody in some way.

arranger A composer who takes an original or existing melody and adds extra features or changes the melody in some way.

art songs Musical settings of poetry. Songs about life, love and human relationships that are written by a professional composer and have a serious artistic purpose, as opposed to a popular song or folk song.

articulation The amount of separation or connection between notes.

articulators The lips, teeth, tongue and other parts of the mouth and throat that are used to produce vocal sound.

avant-garde A term used in the arts to denote those who make a radical departure from tradition.

avocational Not related to a job or career.

B

ballad A strophic folk song with a distinctly narrative element. Ballads tell stories.

barbershop A style of *a cappella* singing in which three parts harmonize with the melody. The lead sings the melody while the tenor harmonizes above and the baritone and bass harmonize below.

barcarole A Venetian boat song.

baritone The male voice between tenor and bass.

barline A vertical line placed on the musical staff that groups notes and rests together.

Baroque period (*bah-ROHK*) [Fr.] The historical period in Western civilization from 1600 to 1750.

bass The lowest-sounding male voice.

bass clef A clef that generally indicates notes that sound lower than middle C.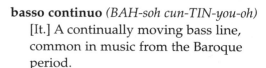

basso continuo (*BAH-soh cun-TIN-you-oh*) [It.] A continually moving bass line, common in music from the Baroque period.

beat The steady pulse of music.

bebop style Popular in jazz, music that features notes that are light, lively and played quickly. Often the melodic lines are complex and follow unpredictable patterns.

blues scale An altered major scale that uses flatted or lowered third, fifth and seventh notes: *ma* (lowered from *mi*), *se* (lowered from *sol*) and *te* (lowered from *ti*).

blues style An original African American art form that developed in the early twentieth century in the Mississippi Delta region of the South. The lyrics often express feelings of frustration, hardship or longing. It often contains elements such as call and response, the blues scale and swing.

breath mark A symbol in vocal music used to indicate where a singer should take a breath. (ˌ)

breath support A constant airflow necessary to produce sound for singing.

C

cadence A melodic or harmonic structure that marks the end of a phrase or the completion of a song.

call and response A derivative of the field hollers used by slaves as they worked. A leader or group sings a phrase (call) followed by a response of the same phrase by another group.

calypso A style of music that originated in the West Indies and which features syncopated rhythms and comical lyrics.

canon A musical form in which one part sings a melody, and the other parts sing the same melody, but enter at different times. Canons are sometimes called *rounds*.

cantabile *(con-TAH-bee-leh)* [It.] In a lyrical, singing style.

cantata *(con-TAH-tah)* [It.] A large-scale musical piece made up of several movements for singers and instrumentalists. Johann Sebastian Bach was a prominent composer of cantatas.

cantor *(CAN-tor)* A person who sings and/or teaches music in a temple or synagogue.

canzona [It.] A rhythmic instrumental composition that is light and fast-moving.

carol A strophic song of the Middle Ages, sung in English or Latin, beginning with a refrain which is then repeated after each verse. In recent times, the word *carol* refers to a strophic song about Christmas or the Virgin Mary.

chamber music Music performed by a small instrumental ensemble, generally with one instrument per part. The string quartet is a popular form of chamber music, consisting of two violins, a viola and a cello. Chamber music was popular during the Classical period.

chanson *(shaw[n]-SOH[N])* [Fr.] Literally "song" in French, a *chanson* is a vocal composition to French words. The rich history of the *chanson* dates back to the late Middle Ages and continues to the present day, incorporating many styles and composers.

chantey *See* sea chantey.

chanteyman A soloist who improvised and led the singing of sea chanteys.

chest voice The lower part of the singer's vocal range.

chorale *(kuh-RAL)* [Gr.] Congregational song or hymn of the German Protestant Church.

chord The combination of three or more notes played or sung together at the same time.

chromatic Moving by half-steps. Also, notes foreign to a scale.

chromatic scale *(kroh-MAT-tick)* [Gk.] A scale that consists of all half steps and uses all twelve pitches in an octave.

Classical period The historical period in Western civilization from 1750 to 1820.

clef   The symbol at the beginning of a staff that indicates which lines and spaces represent which notes.

close harmony   Harmony in which notes of the chord are kept as close together as possible, often within an octave.

coda   A special ending to a song. A concluding section of a composition. (⊕)

Collegium musicum (*col-LAY-gee-oom MOO-zee-koom*)   [Lat.] A musical group, usually at a university, that presents period-style performances of Renaissance and Baroque music.

commission   A musical work created by the composer for a specific event or purpose. The composer is approached by the commissioning organization (orchestra, chorus, academic institution, church) or individual, and an acceptable fee is agreed upon.

common time   Another name for 4/4 meter. Also known as common meter. (**C**)

composer   A person who takes a musical thought and writes it out in musical notation to share it with others.

compound meter   Any meter in which the dotted quarter note receives the beat, and the division of the beat is based on three eighth notes. 6/8, 9/8 and 12/8 are examples of compound meter.

con moto (*kohn MOH-toh*)   [It.] With motion.

concert etiquette   A term used to describe what is appropriate behavior in formal or informal musical performances.

concerto (*cun-CHAIR-toh*)   [Fr., It.] A composition for a solo instrument and orchestra.

concerto grosso (*cun-CHAIR-toh GROH-soh*)   [Fr., It.] A multi-movement Baroque piece for a group of soloists and an orchestra.

conductor   A person who uses hand and arm gestures to interpret the expressive elements of music for singers and instrumentalists.

conductus   A thirteenth-century song for two, three or four voices.

consonance   Harmonies in chords or music that are pleasing to the ear.

Contemporary period   The historical period from 1900 to the present.

countermelody   A separate melodic line that supports and/or contrasts the melody of a piece of music.

counterpoint   The combination of two or more melodic lines. The parts move independently while harmony is created. Johann Sebastian Bach is considered by many to be one of the greatest composers of contrapuntal music.

contrary motion   A technique in which two melodic lines move in opposite directions.

crescendo (*creh-SHEN-doh*)   [It.] A dynamic marking that indicates to gradually sing or play louder. ◁

cumulative song   A song form in which more words are added each time a verse is sung.

cut time   Another name for *2/2 meter*. (¢)

D

da capo (*D.C.*) (*dah KAH-poh*)   [It.] Go back to the beginning and repeat; *see also* dal segno *and* al fine.

dal segno (*D.S.*) (*dahl SAYN-yah*)   [It.] Go back to the sign and repeat.

D. C. al Fine (*FEE-nay*)   [It.] A term that indicates to go back to the beginning and repeat. The term *al fine* indicates to sing to the end, or *fine*.

decrescendo (*DAY-creh-shen-doh*)   [It.] A dynamic marking that indicates to gradually sing or play softer. ▷

descant   A special part in a piece of music that is usually sung higher than the melody or other parts of the song.

diatonic interval   The distance between two notes which are indigenous to a major or minor scale.

diatonic scale (*die-uh-TAH-nick*)   A scale that uses no altered pitches or accidentals. Both the major scale and the natural minor scale are examples of a diatonic scale.

diction   The pronunciation of words while singing.

diminished chord   A minor chord in which the top note is lowered one half step from *mi* to *me*.

diminuendo (*dim.*) (*duh-min-yoo-WEN-doh*) [It.] Gradually getting softer; *see also* decrescendo.

diphthong   A combination of two vowel sounds.

dissonance   A combination of pitches or tones that clash.

dolce (*DOHL-chay*)   [It.] Sweetly.

dominant chord   A chord built on the fifth note of a scale. In a major scale, this chord uses the notes *sol, ti* and *re*, and it may be called the **V** ("five") chord. In a minor scale, this chord uses the notes *mi, sol* and *ti* (or *mi, si* and *ti*), and it may be called the **v** or **V** ("five") chord.

Dorian scale (*DOOR-ee-an*)   [Gk.] A modal scale that starts and ends on *re*.

dot   A symbol that increases the length of a given note by half its value. It is placed to the right of the note.

dotted half note   A note that represents three beats of sound when the quarter note receives the beat. ♩.

dotted rhythms   A dot after a note lengthens the note by one-half its original value. When notes are paired, the first note is often three times longer than the note that follows (e.g., dotted half note followed by quarter note, dotted quarter note followed by eighth note, dotted eighth note followed by sixteenth note).

double barline   A set of two barlines that indicate the end of a piece or section of music.

D. S. al coda (*dahl SAYN-yoh ahl KOH-dah*) [It.] Repeat from the symbol (𝄋) and skip to the coda when you see the sign. (⊕)

duet   A group of two singers or instrumentalists.

duple   Notes in equal groups of two.

dynamics   Symbols in music that indicate how loud or soft to sing or play.

eighth note   A note that represents one-half beat of sound when the quarter note receives the beat. Two eighth notes equal one beat of sound when the quarter note receives the beat. ♪ ♫

eighth rest   A rest that represents one-half beat of silence when the quarter note receives the beat. Two eighth rests equal one beat of silence when the quarter note receives the beat.   ♮

expressionism   Music of the early twentieth century usually associated with Germany that was written in a deeply subjective and introspective style.

expressive singing   To sing with feeling.

fanfare   A brief celebratory piece, usually performed by brass instruments and percussion, at the beginning of an event.

falsetto   [It.] The register in the male voice that extends far above the natural voice. The light upper range.

fermata (*fur-MAH-tah*)   [It.] A symbol that indicates to hold a note or rest for longer than its given value. (⌢)

fine (*fee-NAY*)   [It.] A term used to indicate the end of a piece of music.

fixed do (*doh*)   A system of syllables in which the note C is always *do*. *See also* movable do.

flat   A symbol that lowers the pitch of a given note by one half step. (♭)

folk music   Music that passed down from generation to generation through oral tradition. Traditional music that reflects a place, event or a national feeling.

folk song   A song passed down from generation to generation through oral tradition. A song that reflects a place, event or a national feeling.

form   The structure or design of a musical composition.

forte *(FOR-tay)* [It.] A dynamic that indicates to sing or play loud. (*f*)

fortissimo *(for-TEE-see-moh)* [It.] A dynamic that indicates to sing or play very loud. (*ff*)

fugue *(FYOOG)* A musical form in which the same melody is performed by different instruments or voices entering at different times, thus adding layers of sound.

fusion Music that is developed by the act of combining various types and cultural influences of music into a new style.

G

glee A homophonic, unaccompanied English song, usually in three or four vocal parts. The texts of early glees, from the seventeenth century, were usually about eating and drinking, but also about patriotism, hunting and love.

glissando *(glees-SAHN-doh)* An effect produced by sliding from one note to another. The word, pseudo-Italian, comes from the French word *glisser*, "to slide."

gospel music Religious music that originated in the African American churches of the South. This music can be characterized by improvisation, syncopation and repetition.

gradual In the Roman Catholic liturgy, a chant that follows the reading of the Epistle. The texts are usually from the Psalms. The melodies often contain several notes per syllable. The term *gradual* (from the Latin *gradus*, "a step") is so called because it was sung while the deacon was ascending the steps to sing the Gospel.

grand opera A large-scale opera that is sung throughout, with no spoken dialogue. *See* Singspiel.

grand staff A staff that is created when two staves are joined together.

grandioso [It.] Stately, majestic.

grave *(GRAH-veh)* [It.] Slow, solemn.

grazioso *(grah-tsee-OH-soh)* [It.] Graceful.

Gregorian chant A single, unaccompanied melodic line sung by male voices. Featuring a sacred text and used in the church, this style of music was developed in the medieval period.

guiro *(GWEE-roh)* A Latin American percussion instrument made from an elongated gourd, with notches cut into it, over which a stick is scraped to produce a rasping sound.

H

half note A note that represents two beats of sound when the quarter note receives the beat.

half rest A rest that represents two beats of silence when the quarter note receives the beat. ■

half step The smallest distance (interval) between two notes on a keyboard; the chromatic scale is composed entirely of half steps.

harmonic intervals Two or more notes which are sung or played simultaneously.

harmonic minor scale A minor scale that uses a raised seventh note, *si* (raised from *sol*).

harmonics Small whistle-like tones, or overtones, that are sometimes produced over a sustained pitch.

harmony A musical sound that is formed when two or more different pitches are played or sung at the same time.

head voice The higher part of the singer's vocal range.

hemiola In early music theory, *hemiola* denotes the ratio 3:2. In the modern metrical system, it refers to the articulation of two bars in triple meter as if they were three bars in duple meter.

High Renaissance The latter part of the Renaissance period, c. 1430-1600.

homophonic *(hah-muh-FAH-nik)* [Gk.] A texture where all parts sing similar rhythm in unison or harmony.

homophony *(haw-MAW-faw-nee)* [Gk.] A type of music in which there are two or more parts with similar or identical rhythms being sung or played at the same time. Also, music in which melodic interest is concentrated in one voice part and may have subordinate accompaniment.

hymn A song or poem that offers praise to God.

I

imitation The act of one part copying what another part has already played or sung.

improvisation The art of singing or playing music, making it up as you go, or composing and performing a melody at the same time.

interlocking Short melodic or rhythmic patterns performed simultaneously that fit together to create a continuous musical texture.

interlude A short piece of music that is used to bridge the acts of a play or the verses of a song or hymn.

International Phonetic Alphabet (IPA) A phonetic alphabet that provides a notational standard for all languages. Developed in Paris, France, in 1886.

interval The distance between two notes.

intonation The accuracy of pitch, in-tune singing.

Ionian scale *(eye-OWN-ee-an)* [Gk.] A modal scale that starts and ends on *do*. It is made up of the same arrangement of whole and half steps as a major scale.

J

jazz An original American style of music that features swing rhythms, syncopation and improvisation.

K

key Determined by a song's or scale's home tone, or keynote.

key signature A symbol or set of symbols that determines the key of a piece of music.

Eb major
C minor

L

Ländler *(LEND-ler)* [Ger.] A slow Austrian dance, performed in 3/4 meter, similar to a waltz.

largo [It.] A tempo marking that indicates broad, slow, dignified in style.

ledger lines Short lines that appear above, between treble and bass clefs, or below the bass clef, used to expand the notation.

legato *(leh-GAH-toh)* [It.] A connected and sustained style of singing and playing.

lento *(LEN-toh)* [It.] Slow; a little faster than *largo*, a little slower than *adagio*.

lied *(leet)* [Ger.] A song in the German language, generally with a secular text.

lieder *(LEE-der)* [Ger.] Plural of *lied*. Songs in the German language, especially art songs of the Romantic period. These songs usually have a secular text.

liturgical text A text that has been written for the purpose of worship in a church setting.

lute An early form of the guitar.

Lydian scale *(LIH-dee-an)* [Gk.] A modal scale that starts and ends on *fa*.

lyricist The writer of the words (lyrics) to a song.

lyrics The words of a song.

M

madrigal A poem that has been set to music in the language of the composer. Featuring several imitative parts, it usually has a secular text and is generally sung *a cappella*.

maestoso (*mah-eh-STOH-soh*) [It.] Perform majestically.

major chord A chord that can be based on the *do, mi,* and *sol* of a major scale.

major scale A scale that has *do* as its home tone, or keynote. It is made up of a specific arrangement of whole steps and half steps in the following order: W + W + H + W + W + W + H.

major second Two notes a whole step apart.

major tonality A song that is based on a major scale with *do* as its keynote, or home tone.

manniboula A rustic pizzicato bass instrument consisting of a wooden resonance box with a rose window on its front panel where there are three metallic blades that sound when manipulated by the fingers of the player sitting on it. Also called a *manniba*.

marcato (*mar-CAH-toh*) [It.] A stressed and accented style of singing and playing.

Mass A religious service of prayers and ceremonies originating in the Roman Catholic Church consisting of spoken and sung sections. It consists of several sections divided into two groups: proper (text changes for every day) and ordinary (text stays the same in every Mass). Between the years 1400 and 1600, the mass assumed its present form consisting of the Kyrie, Gloria, Credo, Sanctus and Agnus Dei. It may include chants, hymns and Psalms as well. The Mass also developed into large musical works for chorus, soloists and even orchestra.

measure The space between two barlines.

Medieval period The historical period in Western civilization also known as the Middle Ages (400–1430).

medley A collection of songs musically linked together.

melisma (*muh-LIZ-mah*) [Gk.] A group of notes sung to a single syllable or word.

melismatic singing (*muh-liz-MAT-ik*) [Gk.] A style of text setting in which one syllable is sung over many notes.

melodic contour The overall shape of the melody.

melodic minor scale A minor scale that uses raised sixth and seventh notes: *fi* (raised from *fa*) and *si* (raised from *sol*). Often, these notes are raised in ascending patterns, but not in descending patterns.

melody A logical succession of musical tones.

meno mosso (*MEH-noh MOHS-soh*) [It.] A tempo marking that indicates "less motion," or slower.

merengue (*meh-REN-geh*) [Sp.] A Latin American ballroom dance in moderate duple meter with the basic rhythm pattern:

It is the national dance of the Dominican Republic.

messa di voce (*MES-sah dee VOH-cheh*) [It.] A technique of singing a crescendo and decrescendo on a held note. The term literally means "placing of the voice."

meter A way of organizing rhythm.

meter signature *See* time signature.

metronome marking A sign that appears over the top line of the staff at the beginning of a piece or section of music that indicates the tempo. It shows the kind of note that will receive the beat and the number of beats per minute as measured by a metronome.

mezzo forte (*MEH-tsoh FOR tay*) [It.] A dynamic that indicates to sing or play medium loud. (*mf*)

mezzo piano (*MEH-tsoh pee-AH-noh*) [It.] A dynamic that indicates to sing or play medium soft. (*mp*)

mezzo voce (*MEH-tsoh VOH-cheh*) [It.] With half voice; reduced volume and tone.

minor chord A chord that can be based on the *la, do,* and *mi* of a minor scale.

minor scale A scale that has *la* as its home tone, or keynote. It is made up of a specific arrangement of whole steps and half steps in the following order: W + H +W + W + H + W + W.

minor tonality A song that is based on a minor scale with *la* as its keynote, or home tone.

minstrel The term *minstrel* originally referred to a wandering musician from the Middle Ages. In the late nineteenth century, the word was applied to black-face entertainers who presented a variety show consisting of comic songs, sentimental ballads, soft-shoe dancing, clogging, instrumental playing, comedy skits, sight gags and jokes.

missa brevis (*MEES-sah BREH-vees*) [Lat.] Literally, a "brief mass." The term refers to a short setting of the Mass Ordinary.

mixed meter A technique in which the time signature or meter changes frequently within a piece of music.

Mixolydian scale (*mix-oh-LIH-dee-an*) [Gr.] A modal scale that starts and ends on *sol*.

modal scale A scale based on a mode. Like major and minor scales, each modal scale is made up of a specific arrangement of whole steps and half steps, with the half steps occurring between *mi* and *fa*, and *ti* and *do*.

mode An early system of pitch organization that was used before major and minor scales and keys were developed.

modulation A change in the key or tonal center of a piece of music within the same song.

molto [It.] Very or much; for example, *molto rit.* means "much slower."

monophony (*mon-AH-foh-nee*) Music with only a single melody line (e.g., Gregorian chant).

motet (*moh-teht*) Originating as a medieval and Renaissance polyphonic song, this choral form of composition became an unaccompanied work, often in contrapuntal style. Also, a short, sacred choral piece with a Latin text that is used in religious services but is not a part of the regular Mass.

motive A shortened expression, sometimes contained within a phrase.

moveable do (*doh*) A system of syllables in which the first note of each diatonic scale is *do*. *See also* fixed do.

music critic A writer who gives an evaluation of a musical performance.

music notation Any means of writing down music, including the use of notes, rests and symbols.

musical A play or film whose action and dialogue are combined with singing and dancing.

musical theater An art form that combines acting, singing, and dancing to tell a story. It often includes staging, costumes, lighting and scenery.

mysterioso [It.] Perform in a mysterious or haunting way; to create a haunting mood.

N

narrative song A song that tells a story.

national anthem A patriotic song adopted by nations through tradition or decree.

nationalism Patriotism; pride of country. This feeling influenced many Romantic composers such as Wagner, Tchaikovsky, Dvořák, Chopin and Brahms.

natural A symbol that cancels a previous sharp or flat, or a sharp or flat in a key signature. (♮)

natural minor scale A minor scale that uses no altered pitches or accidentals.

neo-classicism Music of the early twentieth century characterized by the inclusion of contemporary styles of features derived from the music of the seventeenth and eighteenth centuries.

New Romanticism   A genuine tonal melody composed with exotic textures and timbres.

no breath mark   A direction not to take a breath at a specific place in the composition. (N.B.)

non troppo *(nahn TROH-poh)*   [It.] Not too much; for example, *allegro non troppo*, "not too fast."

notation   Written notes, symbols and directions used to represent music within a composition.

nuance   Subtle variations in tempo, phrasing, articulation, dynamics and intonation that are used to enhance a musical performance.

O

octave   An interval of two pitches that are eight notes apart on a staff.

ode   A poem written in honor of a special person or occasion. These poems were generally dedicated to a member of a royal family. In music, an ode usually includes several sections for choir, soloists and orchestra.

opera   A combination of singing, instrumental music, dancing and drama that tells a story.

operetta *(oh-peh-RET-tah)*   [It.] A light opera, often with spoken dialogue and dancing.

optional divisi *(opt.div.)*   Indicating a split in the music into optional harmony, shown by a smaller cued note.

oral tradition   Music that is learned through rote or by ear and is interpreted by its performer(s).

oratorio *(or-uh-TOR-ee-oh)*   [It.] A dramatic work for solo voices, chorus and orchestra presented without theatrical action. Usually, oratorios are based on a literary or religious theme.

ostinato *(ahs-tuh-NAH-toh)*   [It.] A rhythmic or melodic passage that is repeated continuously.

overture   A piece for orchestra that serves as an introduction to an opera or other dramatic work.

P

palate   The roof of the mouth; the hard palate is at the front, the soft palate is at the back.

pambiche *(pahm-BEE-cheh)*   [Sp.] A dance that is a slower version of the merengue.

parallel keys   Major and minor keys having the same keynote, or home tone (tonic).

parallel minor scale   A minor scale that shares the same starting pitch as its corresponding major scale.

parallel motion   A technique in which two or more melodic lines move in the same direction.

parallel sixths   A group of intervals that are a sixth apart and which move at the same time and in the same direction.

parallel thirds   A group of intervals that are a third apart and which move at the same time and in the same direction.

part-singing   Two or more parts singing an independent melodic line at the same time.

pentatonic scale   A five-tone scale using the pitches *do, re, mi, sol* and *la.*

perfect fifth   An interval of two pitches that are five notes apart on a staff.

perfect fourth   An interval of two pitches that are four notes apart on a staff.

phrase   A musical idea with a beginning and an end.

phrasing   A method of punctuating a musical idea, comparable to a line or sentence in poetry.

Phrygian scale *(FRIH-gee-an)*   [Gk.] A modal scale that starts and ends on *mi.*

pianissimo *(pee-ah-NEE-see-moh)*   [It.] A dynamic that indicates to sing or play very soft. (*pp*)

piano *(pee-AH-noh)*   [It.] A dynamic that indicates to sing or play soft. (*p*)

Picardy third   An interval of a major third used in the final, tonic chord of a piece written in a minor key.

pitch Sound, the result of vibration; the highness or lowness of a tone, determined by the number of vibrations per second.

pitch matching In a choral ensemble, the ability to sing the same notes as those around you.

più *(pyoo)* [It.] More; for example, *più forte* means "more loudly."

più mosso *(pyoo MOHS-soh)* [It.] A tempo marking that indicates "more motion," or faster.

poco *(POH-koh)* [It.] Little; for example *poco dim.* means "a little softer."

poco a poco *(POH-koh ah POH-koh)* [It.] Little by little; for example, *poco a poco cresc.* means "little by little increase in volume."

polyphony *(pah-LIH-fun-nee)* [Gk.] Literally, "many sounding." A type of music in which there are two or more different melodic lines being sung or played at the same time. Polyphony was refined during the Renaissance, and this period is sometimes called "golden age of polyphony."

polyrhythms A technique in which several different rhythms are performed at the same time.

portamento A smooth and rapid glide from one note to another, executed continuously.

psalm A sacred song or hymn. Specifically, one of the 150 Psalms in the Bible.

presto *(PREH-stoh)* [It.] Very fast.

program music A descriptive style of music composed to relate or illustrate a specific incident, situation or drama; the form of the piece is often dictated or influenced by the nonmusical program. This style commonly occurs in music composed during the Romantic period.

Q

quarter note A note that represents one beat of sound when the quarter note receives the beat.

quarter note triplet Three equal divisions of a half note.

quarter rest A rest that represents one beat of silence when the quarter note receives the beat.

quartet A group of four singers or instrumentalists.

R

rallentando *(rall.)* *(rahl-en-TAHN-doh)* [It.] Meaning to "perform more and more slowly." *See also* ritard.

refrain A repeated section at the end of each phrase or verse in a song. Also known as a *chorus*.

register, vocal A term used for different parts of the singer's range, such as head register, or head voice (high notes); and chest register, or chest voice (low notes).

relative minor scale A minor scale that shares the same key signature as its corresponding major scale. Both scales share the same half steps, between *mi* and *fa*, and *ti* and *do*.

Renaissance period The historical period in Western civilization from 1430 to 1600.

repeat sign A symbol that indicates that a section of music should be repeated.

repetition The restatement of a musical idea; repeated pitches; repeated "A" section in ABA form.

requiem *(REK-wee-ehm)* [Lt.] Literally, "rest." A mass written and performed to honor the dead and comfort the living.

resolution The progression of chords or notes from the dissonant to the consonant, or point of rest.

resonance Reinforcement and intensification of sound by vibration.

rest A symbol used in music notation to indicate silence.

rhythm The combination of long and short notes and rests in music. These may move with the beat, faster than the beat or slower than the beat.

ritard *(rit.) (ree-TAHRD)* [It.] A tempo marking that indicates to gradually get slower.

Romantic period The historical period in Western civilization from c. 1820 to 1900.

Romantic style In music history, the Romantic period dates from ca. 1820–1900, following the Classical period. The word *romantic* (in music, as in art and literature) has to do with romance, imagination, strangeness and fantasy. Music composed in the *Romantic style*, when compared with the balance and restraint of the *Classical style*, is freer and more subjective, with increasing use of chromaticism.

rondo form A form in which a repeated section is separated by several contrasting sections.

rote The act of learning a song by hearing it over and over again.

round *See* canon.

rubato *(roo-BAH-toh)* [It.] The freedom to slow down and/or speed up the tempo without changing the overall pulse of a piece of music.

S

sacred music Music associated with religious services or themes.

scale A group of pitches that are sung or played in succession and are based on a particular home tone, or keynote.

scat singing An improvisational style of singing that uses nonsense syllables instead of words. It was made popular by jazz trumpeter Louis Armstrong.

Schubertiad Gatherings held in the homes of Viennese middle-class families; they featured amateur performances of songs and instrumental works by Franz Schubert (1797–1828).

score A notation showing all parts of a musical ensemble, with the parts stacked vertically and rhythmically aligned.

sea chantey A song sung by sailors, usually in rhythm with their work.

second The interval between two consecutive degrees of the diatonic scale.

secular music Music not associated with religious services or themes.

sempre *(SEHM-preh)* [It.] Always, continually.

sempre accelerando *(sempre accel.)* *(SEHM-preh ahk-chel)* [It.] A term that indicates to gradually increase the tempo of a piece or section of music.

sequence A successive musical pattern that begins on a higher or lower pitch each time it is repeated.

serenata [It.] A large-scale musical work written in honor of a special occasion. Generally performed in the evening or outside, it is often based on a mythological theme.

seventh The interval between the first and seventh degrees of the diatonic scale.

sforzando *(sfohr-TSAHN-doh)* [It.] A sudden strong accent on a note or chord. (*sfz*)

sharp A symbol that raises the pitch of a given note one half step. (♯)

sight-sing Reading and singing music at first sight.

simile *(sim.) (SIM-ee-leh)* [It.] To continue the same way.

simple meter Any meter in which the quarter note receives the beat, and the division of the beat is based on two eighth notes. 2/4, 3/4 and 4/4 are examples of simple meter.

singing posture The way one sits or stands while singing.

Singspiel *(ZEENG-shpeel)* [Ger.] A light German opera with spoken dialogue, e.g., Mozart's *The Magic Flute*.

sixteenth note A note that represents one quarter beat of sound when the quarter note receives the beat. Four sixteenth notes equal one beat of sound when the quarter note receives the beat.

sixteenth rest A rest that represents one quarter beat of silence when the quarter note receives the beat. Four sixteenth rests equal one beat of silence when the quarter note receives the beat.

skipwise motion The movement from a given note to another note that is two or more notes above or below it on the staff.

slur A curved line placed over or under a group of notes to indicate that they are to be performed without a break.

solfège syllables Pitch names using *do, re, mi, fa, sol, la, ti, do,* etc.

solo One person singing or playing an instrument alone.

sonata-allegro form A large ABA form consisting of three sections: exposition, development and recapitulation. This form was made popular during the Classical period.

soprano The highest-sounding female voice.

sostenuto *(SAHS-tuh-noot-oh)* [It.] The sustaining of a tone or the slackening of tempo.

sotto voce In a quiet, subdued manner; "under" the voice.

spirito *(SPEE-ree-toh)* [It.] Spirited; for example, *con spirito* ("with spirit").

spiritual Songs that were first sung by African American slaves, usually based on biblical themes or stories.

staccato *(stah-KAH-toh)* [It.] A short and detached style of singing or playing.

staff A series of five horizontal lines and four spaces on which notes are written. A staff is like a ladder. Notes placed higher on the staff sound higher than notes placed lower on the staff.

stage presence A performer's overall appearance on stage, including enthusiasm, facial expression and posture.

staggered breathing In ensemble singing, the practice of planning breaths so that no two singers take a breath at the same time, thus creating the overall effect of continuous singing.

staggered entrances A technique in which different parts and voices enter at different times.

stanza A section in a song in which the words change on each repeat. Also known as a *verse.*

stepwise motion The movement from a given note to another note that is directly above or below it on the staff.

straight tone A singing technique that uses minimal vocal vibrato.

strophe A verse or stanza in a song.

strophic A form in which the melody repeats while the words change from verse to verse.

style The particular character of a musical work, often indicated by words at the beginning of a composition, telling the performer the general manner in which the piece is to be performed.

subdominant chord A chord built on the fourth note of a scale. In a major scale, this chord uses the notes *fa, la* and *do,* and it may be called the **IV** ("four") chord, since it is based on the fourth note of the major scale, or *fa.* In a minor scale, this chord uses the notes *re, fa* and *la,* and it may be called the **iv** ("four") chord, since it is based on the fourth note of the minor scale, or *re.*

subito (sub.) *(SOO-bee-toh)* [It.] Suddenly.

subject The main musical idea in a fugue.

suspension The holding over of one or more musical tones in a chord into the following chord, producing a momentary discord.

swell A somewhat breathy, sudden crescendo. It is often used in gospel music.

swing rhythms Rhythms in which the second eighth note of each beat is played or sung like the last third of triplet, creating an uneven, "swing" feel. A style often found in jazz and blues. Swing rhythms are usually indicated at the beginning of a song or section.

syllabic *See* syllabic singing.

syllabic singing A style of text setting in which one syllable is sung on each note.

syllabic stress The stressing of one syllable over another.

symphonic poem A single-movement work for orchestra, inspired by a painting, play or other literary or visual work. Franz Liszt was a prominent composer of symphonic poems. Also known as a *tone poem.*

symphony A large-scale work for orchestra.

syncopation The placement of accents on a weak beat or a weak portion of the beat, or on a note or notes that normally do not receive extra emphasis.

synthesizer A musical instrument that produces sounds electronically, rather than by the physical vibrations of an acoustic instrument.

T

tag The ending of a barbershop song, usually the last four to eight bars, often considered the best chords in the song.

tamburo *(tahm-BOO-roh)* [It.] A two-headed drum played horizontally on the player's lap.

tempo Terms in music that indicate how fast or slow to sing or play.

tempo I or tempo primo *See* a tempo.

tenor The highest-sounding male voice.

tenuto *(teh-NOO-toh)* [It.] A symbol placed above or below a given note indicating that the note should receive stress and/or that its value should be slightly extended.

terraced dynamics Sudden and abrupt dynamic changes between loud and soft.

tessitura *(tehs-see-TOO-rah)* [It.] The average highness or lowness in pitch of a vocal piece.

text Words, usually set in a poetic style, that express a central thought, idea or narrative.

texture The thickness of the different layers of horizontal and vertical sounds.

theme A musical idea, usually a melody.

theme and variation form A musical form in which variations of the basic theme make up the composition.

third An interval of two pitches that are three notes apart on a staff.

tie A curved line used to connect two or more notes of the same pitch together in order to make one longer note.

tied notes Two or more notes of the same pitch connected together with a tie in order to make one longer note.

timbre The tone quality of a person's voice or musical instrument.

time signature The set of numbers at the beginning of a piece of music. The top number indicates the number of beats per measure. The bottom number indicates the kind of note that receives the beat. Time signature is sometimes called *meter signature.*

to coda Skip to (⊕) or CODA.

tonality The relationship of a piece of music to its *keynote* (tonic).

tone color That which distinguishes the voice or tone of one singer or instrument from another; for example, a soprano from an alto, or a flute from a clarinet. *See also* timbre.

tonic chord A chord built on the home tone, or keynote of a scale. In a major scale, this chord uses the notes *do, mi* and *sol,* and it may be called the **I** ("one") chord, since it is based on the first note of the major scale, or *do.* In a minor scale, this chord uses the notes *la, do* and *mi,* and it may be called the **i** ("one") chord, since it is based on the first note of the minor scale, or *la.*

treble clef A clef that generally indicates notes that sound higher than middle C.

trio A group of three singers or instrumentalists with usually one on a part.

triple A grouping of notes in equal sets of three.

triplet A group of notes in which three notes of equal duration are sung in the time normally given to two notes of equal duration.

troppo (*TROHP-oh*) [It.] Too much; for example, *allegro non troppo* ("not too fast").

tutti (*TOO-tee*) [It.] Meaning "all" or "together."

twelve-tone music A type of music that uses all twelve tones of the scale equally. Developed in the early twentieth century, Arnold Schoenberg is considered to be the pioneer of this style of music.

two-part music A type of music in which two different parts are sung or played.

U

unison All parts singing or playing the same notes at the same time.

upbeat One or more notes of a melody that occur before the first barline or which fall on a weak beat that leans toward the strong beat.

V

vaccin An instrument consisting of one or two sections of bamboo, blown with the lips like one would play the mouthpiece of a brass instrument. Also called a *bambou.*

vibrato (*vee-BRAH-toh*) [It.] A fluctuation of pitch on a single note, especially by singer and string players.

variation A modification of a musical idea, usually after its initial appearance in a piece.

villancico (*bee-ahn-SEE-koh*) [Sp.] A Spanish musical and poetic form consisting of several verses linked by a refrain. In modern day Spain and Latin America, the term *villancico* usually means simply "Christmas carol."

vivace (*vee-VAH-chay*) [It.] Very fast; lively.

vocal jazz A popular style of music characterized by strong prominent meter, improvisation and dotted or syncopated patterns. Sometimes sung *a cappella.*

W

whole note A note that represents four beats of sound when the quarter note receives the beat. o

whole rest A rest that represents four beats of silence when the quarter note receives the beat. ▬

whole step The combination of two successive half steps.

word painting A technique in which the music reflects the meaning of the words.

word stress The act of singing important parts of the text in a more accented style than the other parts.

Classified Index

Instruments

Music & History

Poetry

Seasonal, Patriotic

Vocal Jazz

Listening Selections

Index of Songs and Spotlights

Spotlights

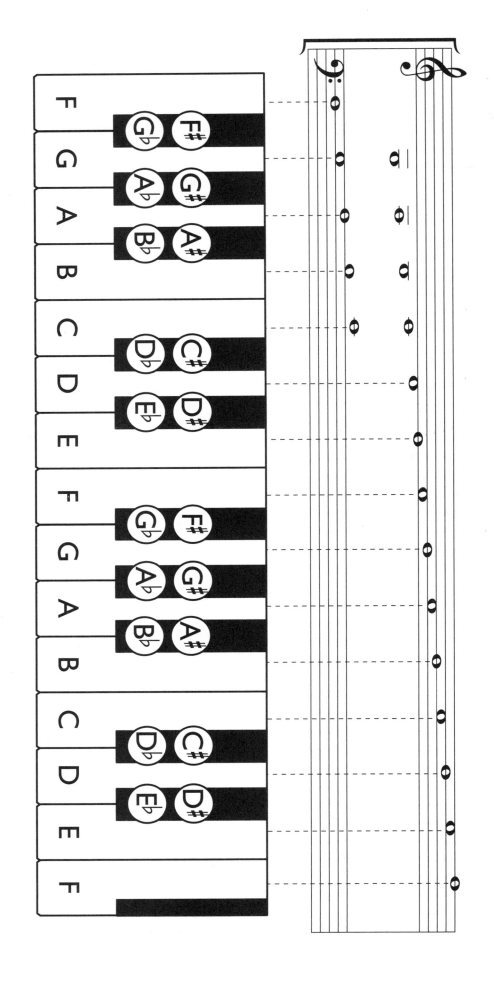